Catalog + Web
GRAPHICS

P·I·E BOOKS

Copyright © 2000 by P·I·E BOOKS
All rights reserved. No part of this publication may be reproduced in any form or by any means, graphic, electronic or mechanical, including photocopying and recording by an information storage and retrieval system, without permission in writing from the publisher.

P·I·E BOOKS
Villa Phoenix Suite 301, 4-14-6,
Komagome, Toshima-ku, Tokyo 170-0003 Japan
Tel: 03-3940-8302 Fax: 03-3576-7361
E-mail:editor@piebooks.com   sales@piebooks.com
http://www.piebooks.com

ISBN4-89444-144-6 C3070   Printed in Japan

Catalog+Web
GRAPHICS

Editorial Notes
＜CREDIT FORMAT＞

カタログ紹介ページ　Catalog Page

- ブランド名もしくは、会社名　"Company Name" or "Company"
- カタログ形態　"Catalog Format"
- カタログサイズ　"Catalog Size"
- カタログ紹介文もしくは、会社紹介文　"Catalog Information" or "Company Information"
- クライアント業種　"Type of Business"
- 作品制作年　"Year Designed"

CL: Client　　　　　　I: Illustrator
CD: Creative director　CW: Copywriter
AD: Art director　　　DF: Design firm
D: Designer　　　　　SB: Submittor
P: Photographer

ホームページ紹介ページ　Web Site Page

- ブランド名もしくは、会社名　"Company Name" or "Company"
- ホームページアドレス　"Web Site Address"
- チャート図　"Site Map"
- ホームページ紹介文　"Web Site Information"
- クライアント業種　"Type of Business"
- 作品制作年　"Year Designed"

CL: Client　　　　　　CW: Copywriter
CD: Creative director　CG: CG creator
AD: Art director　　　M: Movie creator
D: Designer　　　　　PR: Programmer
P: Photographer　　　DF: Design firm
I: Illustrator　　　　　SB: Submittor

※ 上記以外の制作者呼称は、省略せずに記載しています。
　Full names of all others involved in the creation/production of the work.

※ 各企業名に付随する "株式会社、㈱" 及び "有限会社、㈲" は、省略して記載しています。
　The 株式会社 (kabushiki - gaisha, literally, "incorporated") and
　有限会社 (yugen - gaisha, literally, "limited") portion of company names will
　printed in their standard abbreviated forms, as ㈱ [kabu] and ㈲ [yu] respectively.

はじめに

今まで、商品カタログを手に入れる場合、店先でもらう、請求して送ってもらうのが、おもな手段でした。しかし最近では全く異なった媒体であるホームページ上で手軽に見られるようになり、その種類は驚くほど豊富です。近年のインターネット人気で、ホームページの商品カタログを利用する人も増え、それに伴いホームページを制作する仕事も増えています。

そこで、印刷カタログに限らずホームページの制作に携わる方々に向けて「衣・食・住の商品カタログとそのホームページ・デザイン」を特集しました。デザインや制作コンセプトの違い、共通点を比較・一覧できるように、連続したレイアウトで見やすく紹介しています。掲載している厳選した約70作品の中には、印刷メディア・デジタルメディアの特徴を最大限に生かした優れた作品が満載です。

例えばカタログの表紙を両面表紙にして、片側からはイメージをふくらませる写真集的構成、逆側からは商品情報をきっちり説明する構成にした作品。また触感効果を狙って紙質を厳選し、中ページのデザインとの融合をはかった作品などがあります。

ホームページでは java などによる画面の動きや、サウンド効果を取り入れた作品。早いページ展開をさせるために重い写真データを使用せず、軽いイラストデータを効率よく配置した作品があります。関連性やシリーズ性を出すために印刷カタログとホームページの写真を共通にしている作品もあります。

本書が、デジタル媒体の出現によるデザインの多様化が進む中、印刷メディアとデジタルメディアの橋渡しとしてクリエイターの方々に役立つバイブルになることを願っています。

ピエ・ブックス　編集部

atalo
+ V
G

alog
+Web

GRAPHIC

INTRODUCTION

Traditional ways of acquiring product catalogs have included picking them up at stores, receiving them in the mail, or buying them at a bookstore. These days, however, you can find catalogs online, as a completely different type of media, in an amazing multitude of forms. Thanks to the recent popularization of the Internet, people are increasingly using product catalogs that are included within Web sites; this has in turn led to an increase in the number of people working to design Web sites. With this trend in mind, we have published "Catalog and Web Graphics" for those designers who are engaged in creating Web sites as well as printed catalogs.

The book's layout makes it easy for the reader to easily compare the differences and similarities of production concept and design of the two media. Each of the more than 70 works included in this book showcases the prominent quality for which the characteristics of the respective printed or digital medium has been given the highest consideration. One printed catalog, for example, has two front covers; one opens to a collection of photography, aimed at enhancing the reader's image of the product; the other cover leads to a product information catalog filled with product performance statistics and other data. Another example shows the effect of texture, by strictly selecting paper in coordination with inside page design.

On various Web sites, there are Java-run animations and effectively used sound files, and pages designed with small illustrations as opposed to heavy photographic data, to better ensure quick appearance. Some catalogs create links with to their corresponding Web site by shared use of the same photos. The emergence of digital media has brought more diversification to design, and we hope that this book will help to bridge the two worlds of printed and digital media.

P·I·E BOOKS

CONTENTS

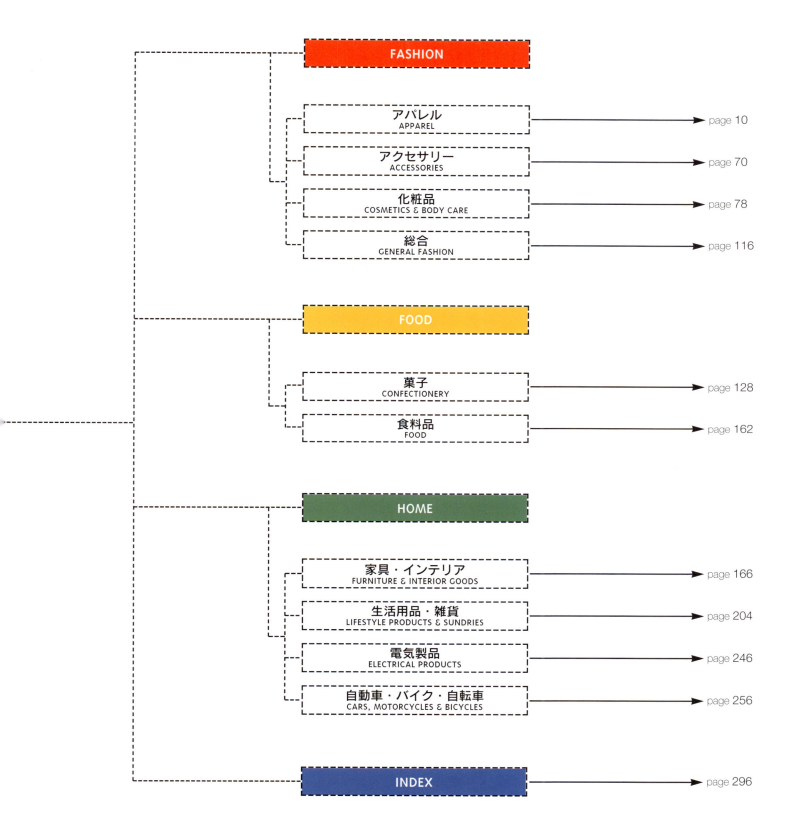

Catalog+Web

BAYCREW*S

中綴 Stapled in the center／152×257mm

page 5, 6

page 11, 12

page 29, 30

ブランドのシーズンテーマ、"SHOWER OF FLOWER & COLOR"をふまえた上でデザインしてもらいました。テーマカラーを使用し、色と柄との組み合わせの楽しさを表現しています。綴じ紐はカラーゴムを使用し、ピンクとイエローの2バージョンを製作しました。

The catalog was designed with the brand's seasonal theme, "Shower of Flower & Color;" the use of theme colors expresses the fun of combining colors and patterns. Two kinds of color rubber bands, pink and yellow, were used to make two styles of binding.

アパレル　APPAREL 2000

CL, SB: ベイクルーズ
BAYCREW*S Co., Ltd.
AD, D: 岩淵 まどか　Madoka Iwabuchi
P: 藤巻 斉　Hitoshi Fujimaki (Still photograph)
／北島 明　Akira Kitajima (Model photograph)
STYLIST: 酒井 美方子　Mihoko Sakai

FASHION: アパレル APPAREL

1. page 5, 6

2-A. page 19, 20

2-B. page 5, 6

1. アパレル APAREL 2000

CL: ベイクルーズ BAYCREW'S Co., Ltd.
AD: フジモト ヤスシ + キャップ Yasushi Fujimoto+Cap
D: オザワ ナゴミ Nagomi Ozawa
P: Andrewolff (Model photograph)
　フジマキ ヒトシ Hitoshi Fujimaki (Still photograph)
SB: ドゥーズィエムクラス DEUXIÈME CLASSE

2-A, B. アパレル APAREL 2000

CL: ベイクルーズ BAYCREW'S Co., Ltd.
CD, SB: ジャーナル スタンダード JOURNAL STANDARD
AD, D: 下田法晴 Michiharu Shimoda
P: Angela Hill (Model)
　内田将二 Shoji Uchida (Still)

1. カタログキット（カバー・中綴・カード）
　Catalog kit (Cover・Stapled in the center・Card)
　カバー Cover／219×219mm
　中綴＆カード Stapled in the center & Card／200×200mm

このシーズンのテーマ "静かなカントリーサイド" をイメージしています。ニューヨーカーやヨーロピアンが休暇を過ごしに来る ノスタルジックな雰囲気を残した小さな島（ナンタケット島・ジャージィー島など）の静かなビーチスタイルをヴィジュアルで表現したいと思い、制作しました。ポストカード形式のヴィジュアル7カット＆商品物撮りのブックで構成しています。

The catalog was produced with the seasonal theme of "The Quiet Countryside." We wanted to express visually the nostalgic atmosphere of quiet beaches found on the type of small island, such as Nantucket and Jersey, that are often frequented by New Yorkers and Europeans on vacation. The catalog consists of 7 postcard-like images, and product photographs.

2-A, B. カタログキット（ビニールカバー・中綴×2）
　Catalog kit (Vnyl cover・Stapled in the center ×2)
　ビニールカバー Vnyl Cover／317×157mm
　中綴 Stapled in the center／150×151mm

毎シーズン、各ショップに設置している販促用のカタログです。毎回、制作スタッフは変わりますが、ジャーナル スタンダード（JOURNAL STANDARD）と、デザイナーなど制作スタッフとのコラボレーションによるものです。無料配布ですが、一部の書店では購買も可能です。

A new promotional catalog, produced each season for distribution at retail shops. Each catalog is created by a different design team, but is always a collaborative effort between Journal Standard and designers and other design staff. Distributed free of charge, the catalog is also sold at some stores.

Catalog + Web

BAYCREW*S

中綴 Stapled in the center／210×275mm

IÉNAはフレンチシックな日常着を今日的で心地よい空間とともに提案するショップです。自分の生き方にきちんとポリシーを持つ、知的で都会的な女性達が、肩の力をぬいた自己表現として選ぶ服。IÉNAの商品はその背景にパリに住むひとりの女性の日常をイメージしています。上質でベーシック、トレンドはあくまでもスパイスとして取り入れ、アートや自然を感じさせるものを愛する今日的で心地よい空間とともに提案しています。

IÉNA is a shop that offers chic French daily wear in a modern and comfortable atmosphere. Intellectual and urban women, with their own lifestyle policies, would choose this clothing for a means of self-expression while relaxing. As a background to IÉNA's products, an image is presented of a woman who lives in Paris. IÉNA offers basic items of good quality, with some trendiness as a bit of spice, a love of art, and goods in which you can feel nature.

アパレル　APPAREL 2000

CL: ベイクルーズ　BAYCREW*S Co., Ltd.
CD, AD: 稲葉純一　Jun-ichi Inaba
D: 築野和久　Kazuhisa Tsukuno
P: 高橋ヨーコ　Yoko Takahashi
SB: ベイクルーズ　IÉNA事業部　BAYCREW*S Co., Ltd. IÉNA div

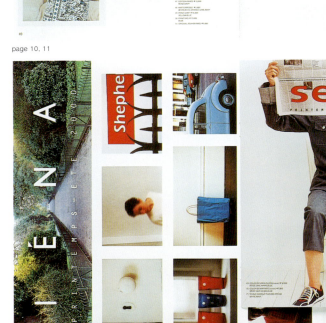

page 10, 11

page 18, 19 (差し込みページ　Insert Page 1)

page 18, 19 (差し込みページ　Insert Page 6, 9)

FASHION: アパレル APPAREL

page 6, 7

page 6, 7

page 18, 19

平綴：両面表紙 Bound :
Double cover／106×176mm

商品販売目的のカタログの側面を極力排し、よりその空気感に溶け込ませ、リアリティのあるモノとし、ÉDIFICEの持つ世界感を表現する事に終始しました。フランス各界の才人（カトリーヌ、J・P トゥーサン）をモデルとして起用しながら、スタイリングの全てを独自で行い、有名カメラマンに頼らず、新進気鋭の人物を登用するなどして、非商業的に仕上げた点はÉDIFICE独特のスノビズムであり、非文化的商業用カタログへのアンチテーゼである。

By removing the sales aspect as much as possible, the catalog can focus on expressing the ÉDIFICE world, with atmosphere and reality. Using the talented French models Catherine and J.P. Toussaint, styling was done entirely in-house, with an up-and-coming photographer, not a famous one, behind the camera. These non commercial-oriented points are typical of ÉDIFICE's unique snobbism. We think that this is the antithesis of a non-cultural, commercial catalog.

アパレル　APPAREL 2000

CL, SB: ベイクルーズ BAYCREW*S Co., Ltd.
CD: 松浦 弥太郎　Yataro Matsuura
AD: 梶野 彰一　Shoichi Kajino
D: 宇賀田 直人　Naoto Ugata
P: 伊藤まゆみ　Mayumi Ito

Catalog + Web

BAYCREW*S

www.baycrews.co.jp

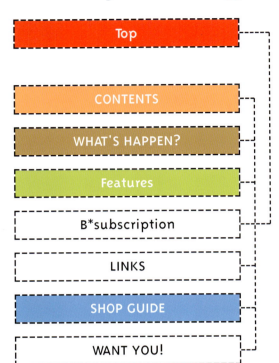

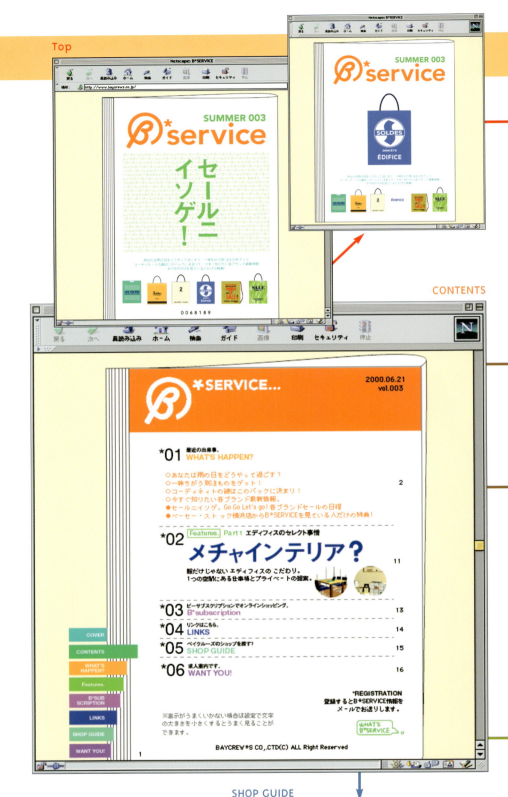

ベイクルーズのホームページ "B* Service"。ウェブマガジンとして創刊されました。シーズンごとの特集、各ブランドのHOTなニュース、ショップの情報、そして期間限定の "B* Subscription" というオンラインショッピングのページもあり、楽しめるページが満載です。

The Web site of BAYCREW*S' "B*service" was initiated as a Web magazine. It consists of special features that change seasonally; hot news from each of the featured brands; shop information; and "B* subscription," an online shop. Full of interesting pages.

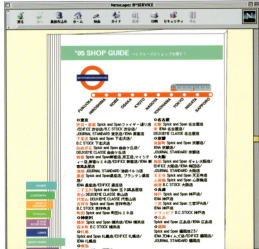

アパレル　APAREL 2000

CL, SB: ベイクルーズ　BAYCREW*S Co., Ltd.
CD, AD, D, P, PR: 渡辺えり子　Eriko Watanabe
AD, CW, P: 小柳洋子　Yoko Koyanagi
D, P, PR: 黒田裕紀　Yuki Kuroda
CG, CAD DESIGN: 高梨美帆　Miho Takanashi - Features page
※2000年7月11日現在のデータを使用　As of July 11, 2000

FASHION: アパレル APPAREL

Catalog + Web

TRANS CONTINENTS

www.trans813.com/

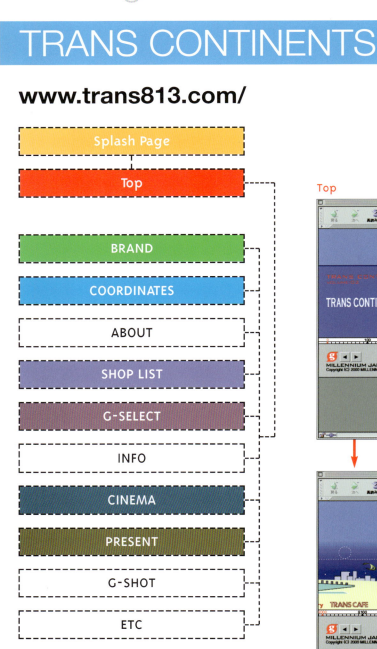

サイト名の「GALVANIZE」とは「電気的な刺激を与える」などの意味。「ユーザーをガルバナイズ」というコンセプトで制作しました。

One of the meanings of "GALVANIZE," the name of this site, is "to stimulatein an almost electric manner." With this in mind, the site was designed togalvanize the viewer.

アパレル　APPAREL 1999

CL: ミレニアム・ジャパン　MILLENNIUM JAPAN LTD.
CD: 小林貴禎　Takayoshi Kobayashi
AD, D: 岩崎智則　Tomonori Iwasaki
I: 荒木由聖　Yoshikiyo Araki
CW: 嶋 えみ　Emi Shima
HTM RECORDING: 種子田 隆之　Takayuki Taneda
池和田 有輔　Yusuke Ikewada／香月 聡　Satoshi Kagetsu
板東丈寛　Takehiro Bando
PR: 橘 浩史　Koji Tachibana
SB: コンテンツ　Contents Co., Ltd.
※2000年7月11日現在のデータを使用　As of July 11, 2000

FASHION: アパレル APPAREL

BRAND

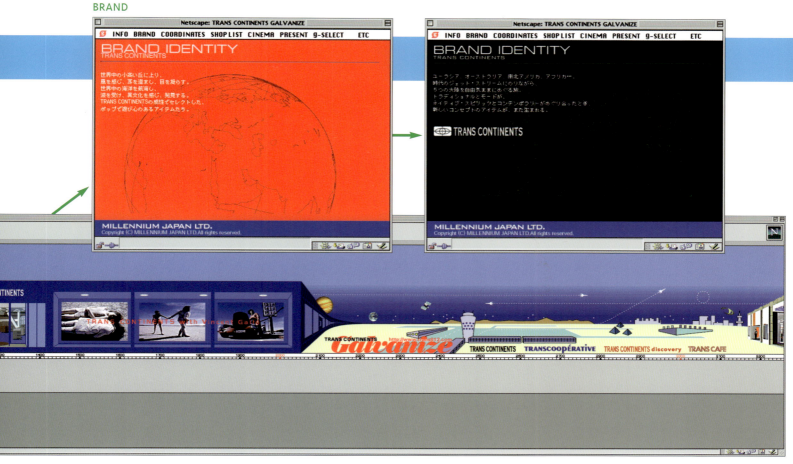

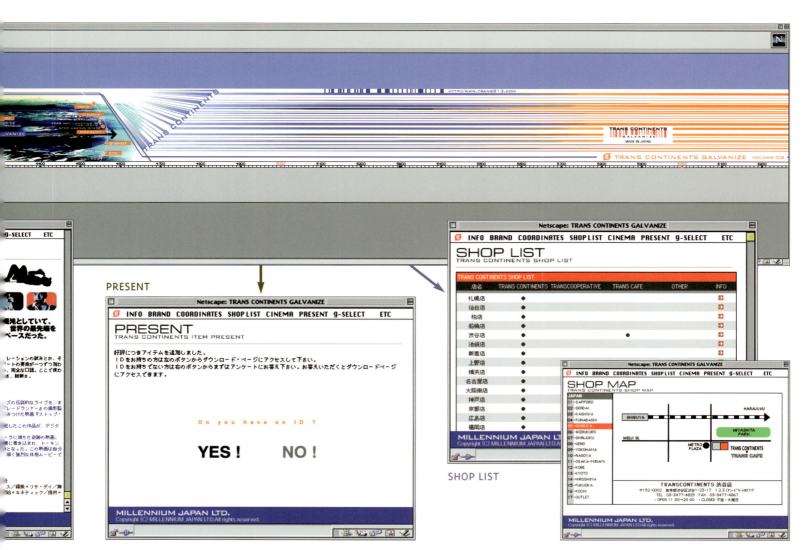

PRESENT

SHOP LIST

Catalog + Web

TRANS CONTINENTS

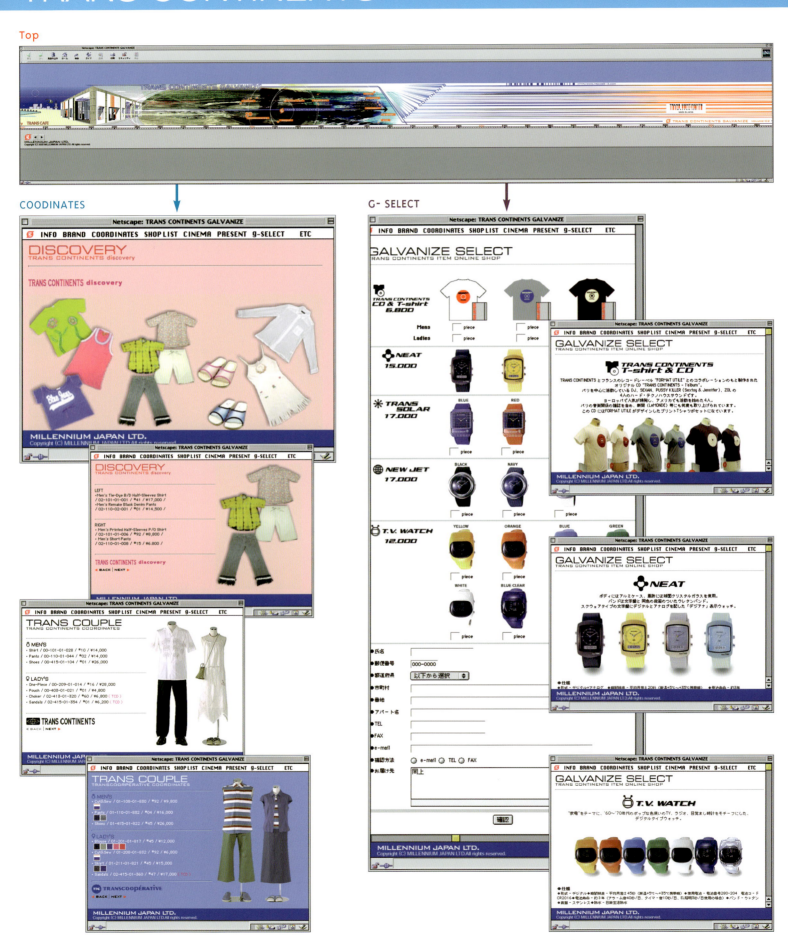

FASHION: アパレル APPAREL

アパレル　APPAREL 1999
CL: ミレニアム・ジャパン　MILLENNIUM JAPAN LTD.
CD: 小林貴禎　Takayoshi Kobayashi
AD, D: 岩崎智則　Tomonori Iwasaki
I: 荒木由聖　Yoshikiyo Araki
CW: 嶋 えみ　Emi Shima
HTM RECORDING: 種子田 隆之　Takayuki Taneda
　池和田 有輔　Yusuke Ikewada／香月 聡　Satoshi Kagetsu
　板東丈寛　Takehiro Bando
PR: 橘 浩史　Koji Tachibana
SB: コンテンツ　Contents Co., Ltd.

※1999年9月現在のデータを使用　As of September, 1999

Catalog + Web
Collaboration

カタログキット（ビニールパック・8ツ折・シート）
Catalog kit (Vinyl bag・Eightfold・Sheet)

ビニールパック Vinyl bag／218×319mm
8ツ折 Eightfold／257×182mm
（開いた状態 When fully unfolded：514×728mm）
シート Sheet／200×297mm

FAX、メールオーダーの通信販売カタログです。ただの通販カタログというより、ポスターとして使えるカタログにしたいと考え、製作しました。内容的には、わかりやすく、見栄えのいいカタログをテーマに製作しました。

Mail and fax order sales catalog. It was designed to be more than just a catalog: it can also be used as a poster. During production, priorities were placed on making the catalog easy to understand as well as attractive.

front

アパレル　APPAREL 1999

CL, SB: コラボレーション　Collaboration Co., Ltd.
AD: ノーザングラフィック　Northern Graphics
P: 高梨光司　Koji Takanashi

FASHION: アパレル APPAREL

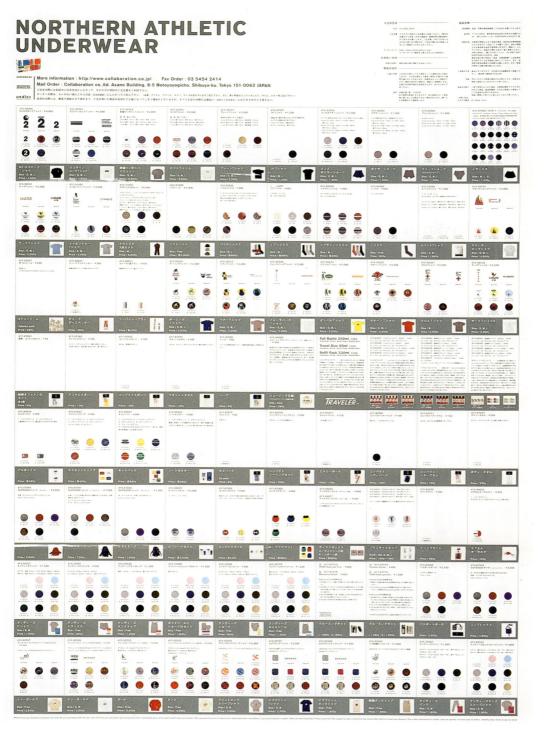

back

Catalog + Web

Collaboration

www.collaboration.co.jp

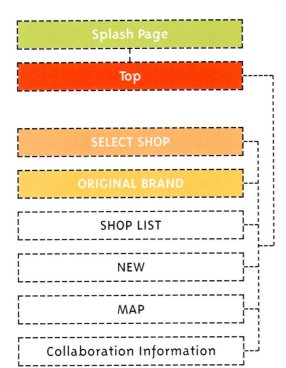

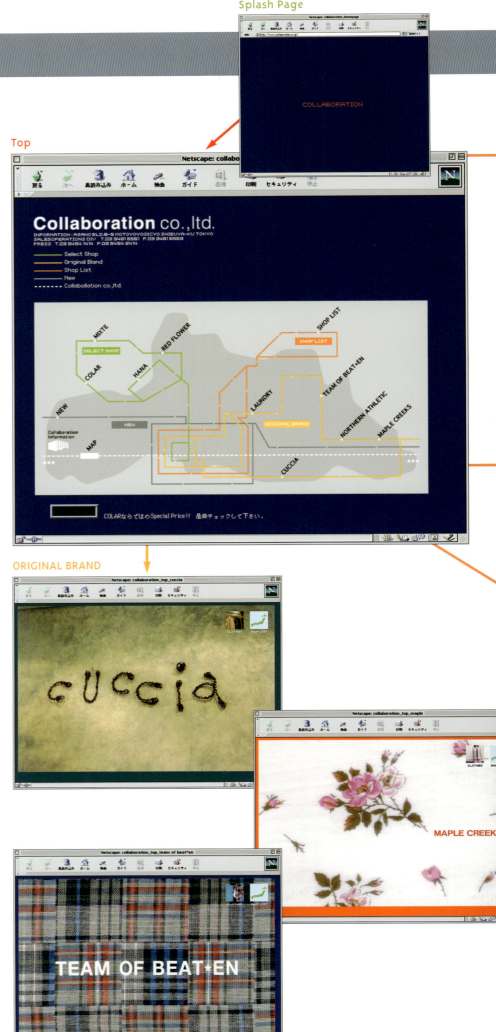

コラボレーションブランド／ショップ展開がわかりやすいようなホームページ制作を考えました。このページを見た人に、ショップへ足を運んでもらえることを目的として制作しました。ブランドを知ってもらい、ショップの内容を理解して頂けたら幸いです。ブランド／ショップの数が多いので、画面での個々のイメージづくりが大変でした。今後は、ページごとに見せ方を変えていき、見る人を楽しませるホームページにしていけたらと思っています。生の声を取り入れて、ホームページならではの作り方を考えていきたいと思います。

The site is designed to make people understand easily the structure of the development of the Collaboration brand and shops, aiming at people who actually visit the stores. It is our hope that people can become familiar with both the brand and shop contents. Because of the number of brands and shops, it was a challenge for us to include each image on the screen. In the future, we are planning to make the site more entertaining for the visitors, with a different look for each page. We would also like to incorporate a special way of including visitor comments, which is a feature ideally suited to Web sites.

アパレル　APPAREL 2000

CL, SB: コラボレーション　Collaboration Co., Ltd.
D: ノーザングラフィック　Northern Graphics
CG: 山本真至　Masashi Yamamoto
Rana -Page of Laundry
※2000年7月11日現在のデータを使用　As of July 11, 2000

FASHION: アパレル APPAREL

SELECT SHOP

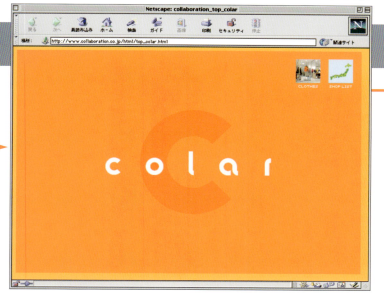

SELECT SHOP

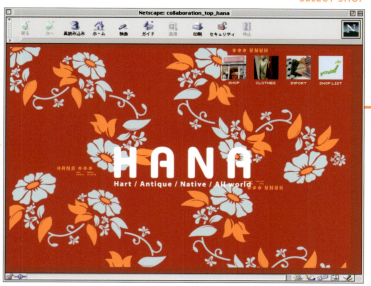

SELECT SHOP

Catalog + Web

A.P.C.

中綴 Stapled in the center／150×210mm

1994年春夏よりカタログ通信販売を開始。通常カタログというとアメリカ的に定番的な商品を大量に提案する形態を目にするが、このカタログはマスへの大量販売への欲求から作られたものではありません。これは多店舗によりデザイナーの目の行き届かない店舗を全国に持つよりも、このカタログ販売がA.P.C.の服をより求め易く、より身近に共感できる媒体となることを信じ作られています。デザイナーにとって愛着のある服、小物を各シーズンのコレクションからセレクトし、ゲストデザイナーを迎え、カタログの為に服をデザインしてもらう構成となっています。

A.P.C. began to offer catalog shopping in the 1994 spring/summer season. As in the U.S., catalogs in Japan typically offer a large selection of products year-round. However, this catalog is not intended for a mass market, but to make it easy to get A.P.C. clothing by catalog on a closer and more personal level, rather than at shops around the country that are beyond the reach of the designers. Designers select their favorite clothing and accessories from each season's collection, and guest designers are invited to design clothes exclusively for the catalog.

衣料雑貨輸入・販売
CLOTHING IMPORT & SALES 2000

CL, SB: イースト バイ ウエスト　EAST by WEST Co., Ltd.

Catalog + Web

A.P.C.

www.apc.fr

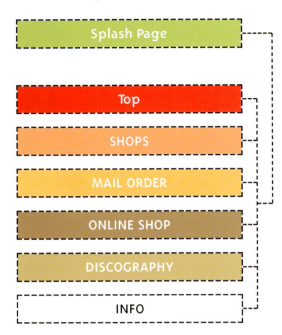

フランスのレディス、メンズのプレタポルテメゾンA.P.C.のウェブサイトです。限定されてはいるが、広範囲に至る全世界のショップアドレスを始め、洋服作りと同じプロセスで制作されるA.P.C.レーベルのCDも紹介しています。CDは試聴も可能です。セキュリティシステムにより保障されたオンラインショップは、ペーパーカタログと同様のレイアウトにて、各シーズンA.P.C.のコレクションよりセレクトした商品を展開。2000年8月下旬より新しいインターフェイスにて展開しています。

The Web site of A.P.C., the French ladies' and men's pret-a-porter house. The site includes the addresses of selected A.P.C. shops in a wide range of cities around the world, and introduces CDs from the A.P.C. label, which are produced with the same philosophy as their clothes. It is possible to listen to the CDs online. The online shop, which showcases selected items from each season's collection with the same layout as the printed catalogs, is fully secure. There are plans to renovate the site in late August 2000, with a re-designed interface.

衣料雑貨輸入・販売
CLOTHING IMPORT & SALES 2000

CL, SB: イースト バイ ウエスト EAST by WEST Co., Ltd.

※2000年7月5日現在のデータを使用 As of July 5, 2000

FASHION: アパレル APPAREL

ONLINE SHOP

SHOPS

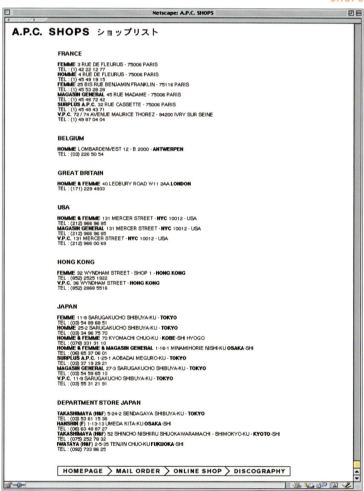

MAIL ORDER

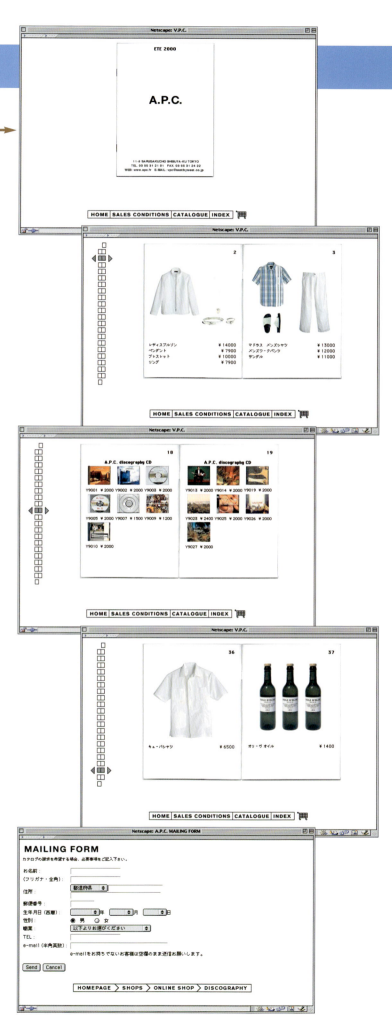

27

Catalog + Web

SHIPS

www.shipsltd.co.jp

- Top
- SHIPS最新情報 What's up?
- 最新カタログ紹介 Catalog
- SHIPSお薦め情報 More Ships
- NAVEL SHIPS情報 Navel
- 店舗マップ Piers Map
- 掲示板 Lounge
- 会社概要等 About Us

セレクトショップ「SHIPS」のウェブサイト。シーズンのテーマに合わせ、毎年2度のデザインリニューアルを行っています。企業サイトとしては希な、公開式の掲示板があり、どなたでも自由にSHIPSのスタッフと掲示板を通したコミュニケーションが行えます。

The Web site of SHIPS, a fashion brand shop. The site is given a complete design renewal twice each year with seasonal themes. Unusual for a corporate site, there is an open bulletin board where anyone can freely communicate with SHIPS staff members.

アパレル　APPAREL 1998
CL: シップス　SHIPS, LTD.
CD: 中澤芳之　Yoshiyuki Nakazawa
AD, D: 小林シンヤ　Shinya Kobayashi
PR: 鈴木利宏　Toshihiro Suzuki
SB: コロン　:Colon inc.
※2000年7月4日現在のデータを使用　As of July 4, 2000

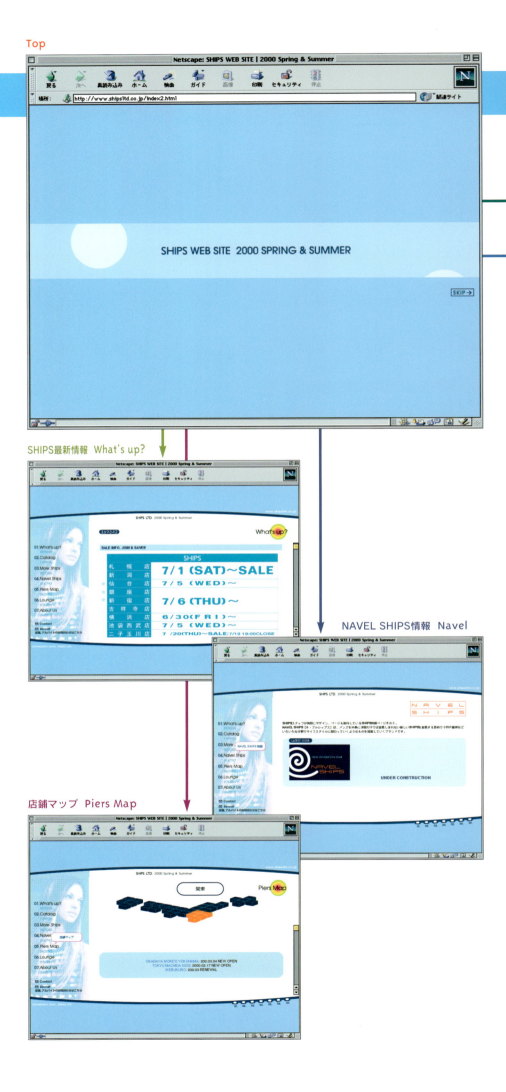

FASHION: アパレル APPAREL

最新カタログ紹介 Catalog

SHIPS お薦め情報 More Ships

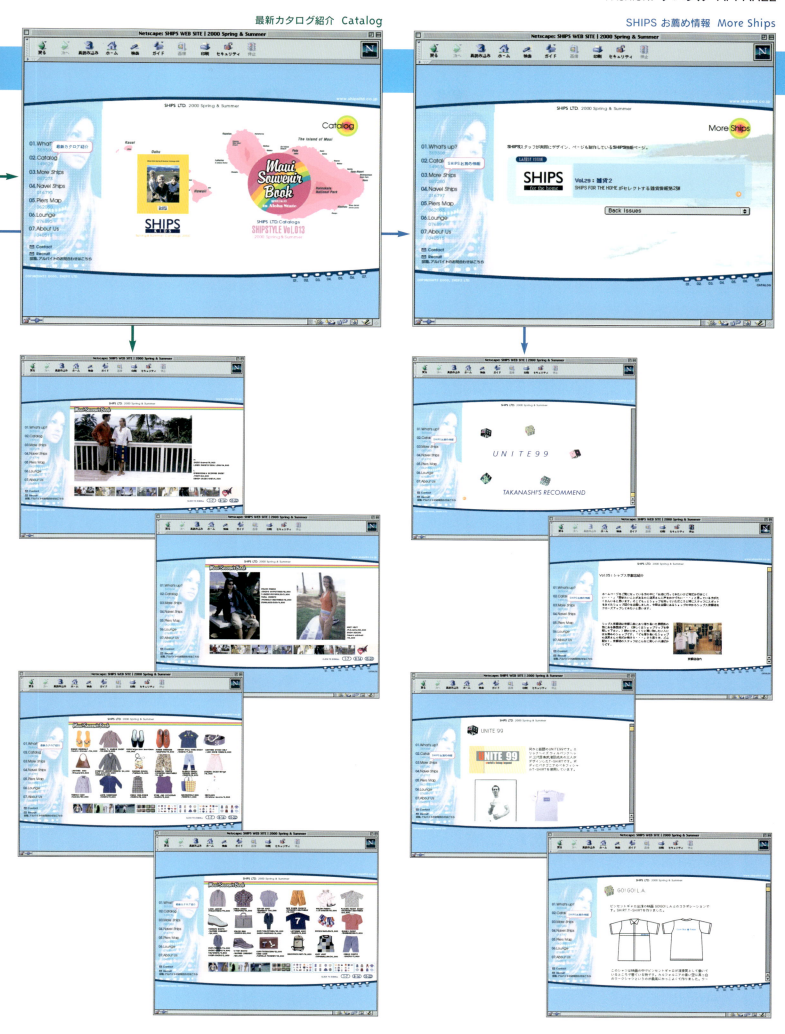

Catalog + Web

ONWARD

www.onward.co.jp/

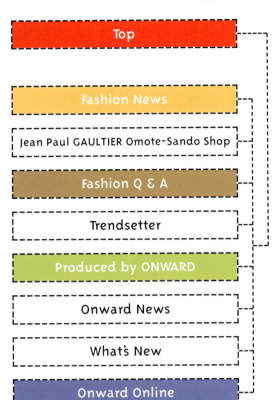

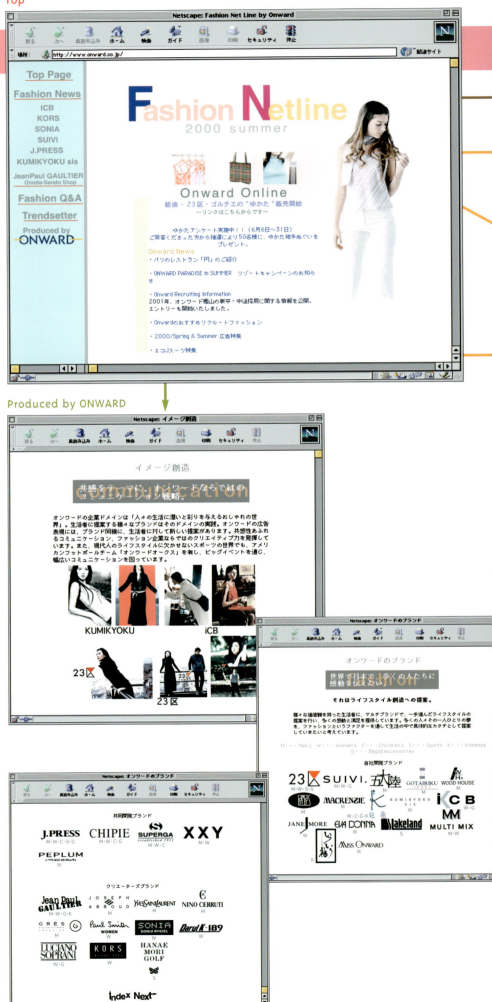

「ファッションネットライン」は、オンワードグループの活動から生まれる情報を、より多くの生活者に発信したいというコンセプトにより、1996年3月にスタートしました。内容はアパレルの流行にとどまらず、より広いライフスタイル情報を基本としております。このサイトを運営していくにあたり、一番心掛けている点は、ユーザーにとってメリットのあるサイトかどうか、ということです。この考えに基づき、2000年3月に「オンワードオンライン」という、販売サイトを制作しました。これからも、一人でも多くの方々に利用していただきたいと思います。

"Fashion Net Line" was launched in March 1996. It was conceived to send out information, generated by activities of the Onward Group, to a large number of people. This information is not limited to fashion in the apparel world, but also as relates to a wide range of lifestyles. The main point that I consider regarding operation of this Web site is whether or not the site provides content that is worthwhile to viewers. With this in mind, we created a shop site called "Onward Online" in March 2000. I hope that more and more people will make use of it.

アパレル　APPAREL 1996

CL, SB: オンワード樫山　Onward Kashiyama Co., Ltd.
CD: 高木 直　Nao Takagi
※2000年7月11日現在のデータを使用　As of July 11, 2000

FASHION: アパレル APPAREL

Fashion News

Fashion Q&A

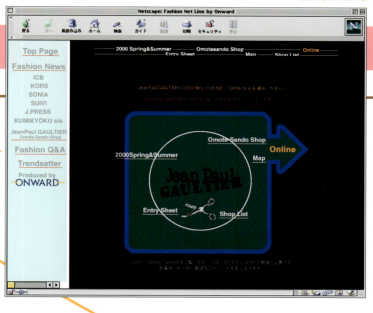

Fashion News

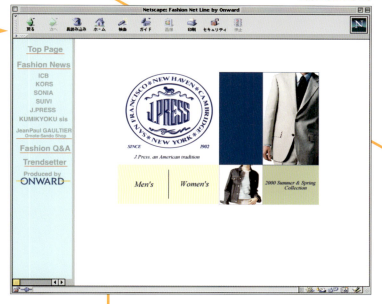

Fashion News

Catalog + Web

ONWARD

Top

Fashion News

Fashion News

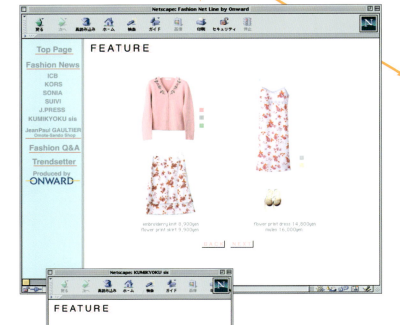

Fashion News

※2000年7月11日現在のデータを使用 As of July 11, 2000

FASHION: アパレル APPAREL

Fashion News

Onward Online

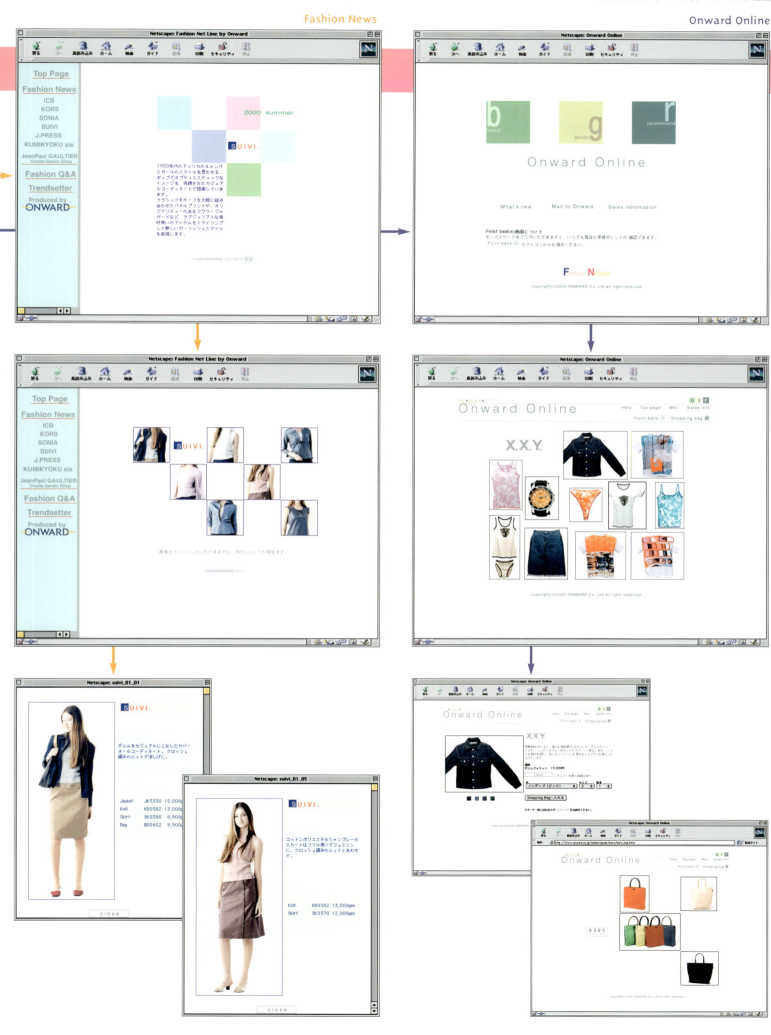

Catalog +Web
PERSON'S

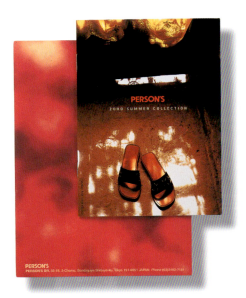

カタログキット（封筒・中綴）
Catalog kit (Envelope・Stapled in the center)

封筒 Envelope／130×180mm
中綴 Stapled in the center／106×150mm

1976年、パーソンズは小さな小さな存在でした。自分たちが着たい服や靴を作ろう。原宿に自分たちの店を持とう。まずは自分たちが気持ち良く生活できる環境づくり。そんな小さな発想から生まれたパーソンズも、現在では日本全国から世界各国にまで多くのファンを持つ組織に発展しました。私達パーソンズは、つねに自分たちの手の中から新しい世界を創造していきたい。新しい時代を創造していきたいのです。これから21世紀に向かっても、ブランディングを基本とした、より大きなパーソンズワールドを創造していきます。

In 1976, Persons was very, very tiny. "Let's create clothes and shoes that WE want to wear. Let's open a shop in Harajuku." First, we had to prepare an environment that we could live in comfortably ourselves. Persons was born from such a small idea. Now it has grown to be a company with fans both nationwide and all around the world. We at Persons would like to create a new world and new era with our own hands. Heading into the 21st Century, we will use branding to create an even bigger Persons world.

アパレル **APPAREL 2000**

CL, SB: フーセンウサギ　FUSEN-USAGI Corporation
AD, I: 飯田 淳　Jun Iida
D: 芳川昌幸　Masayuki Yoshikawa
P: 斉藤 亢　Koo Saito

page 1, 2

page 3, 4

FASHION: アパレル APPAREL

page 7, 8

page 11, 12

PERSON'S
FUSEN-USAGI Corporation

page 13, 14

Catalog + Web

PERSON'S

www.persons.com

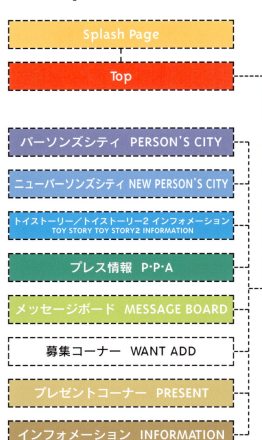

幼児から成人まで、幅広いユーザーをターゲットとする為、操作面、デザイン面、双方において、シンプルで判り易いページ制作を目指しました。また、数多くのライセンスブランドを抱えている為、"個々のブランド・キャラクターを主張し、尚且つ、全体としての統一感を持たせる"事も課題となりました。メインページをMAPにする事により、街を散歩している様な感覚で、個々のブランド情報を手に入れる事が出来ます。街を出たり、入ったりという段階を利用した変化、統一された架空の世界観を楽しんでほしいと考えています。

Because Persons targets a wide range of consumers, from infants to grown-ups, we wanted both operational and design aspects of the site to be simple and easy to navigate. Because of the company's many licensed brands, it was important to stress the characteristics of each brand individually, and at the same time create a united feeling overall. The main page was designed in the form of a map, where people can get brand information as if they are walking on the street. We hope that people will enjoy the changes as they wander around the town, and the feeling of a united virtual world.

アパレル **APPAREL 2000**

CL, SB: パーソンズ PERSON'S CO., LTD
CD, D: 山澤 紳一郎 Shinichiro Yamazawa
I: 飯田 淳 Jun Iida

※2000年7月5日現在のデータを使用 As of July 5, 2000

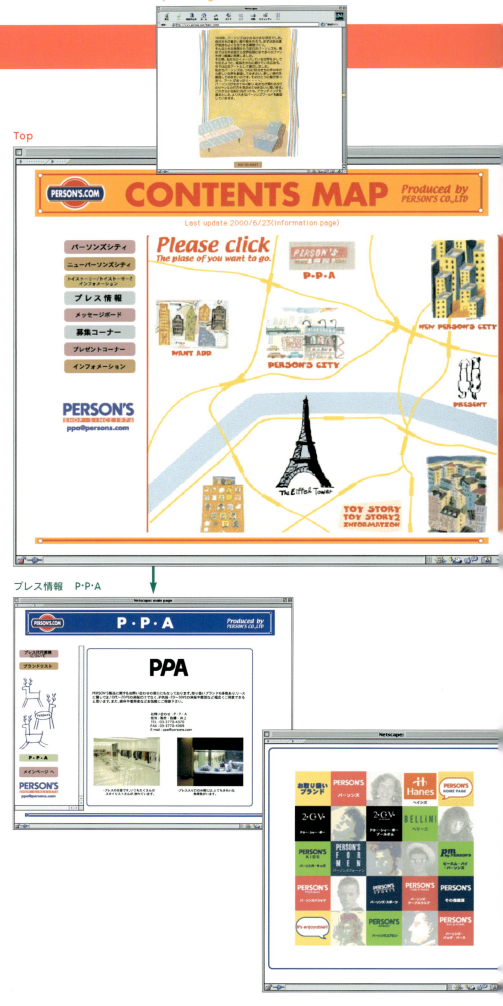

FASHION: アパレル APPAREL

ニューパーソンズシティ NEW PERSON'S CITY

Catalog + Web

PERSON'S

Top

プレゼントコーナー PRESENT

パーソンズシティ PERSON'S CITY

トイストーリー／トイストーリー2 インフォメーション
TOY STORY TOY STORY2 INFORMATION

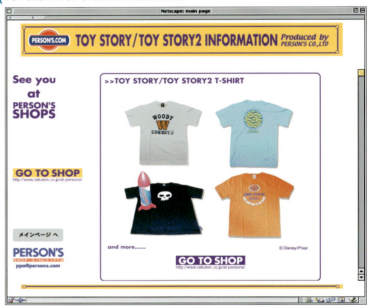

インフォメーション INFORMATION

メッセージボード MESSAGE BOARD

※2000年7月5日現在のデータを使用 As of July 5, 2000

FASHION: アパレル APPAREL

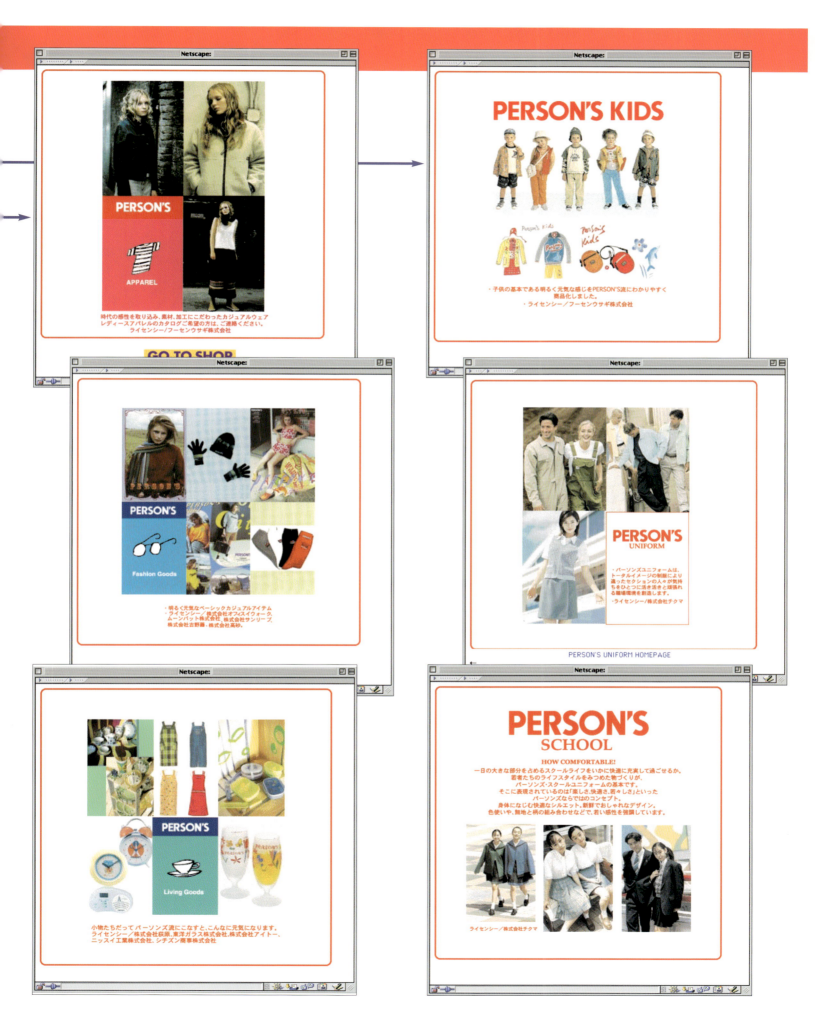

Catalog+Web

ROPÉ

カタログキット（紙ケース・カード）
Catalog kit (Paper case・Card)

紙ケース Paper case／265×191mm
カード Card／256×182mm

シーズンテーマの「Light & Pleasure」のイメージを表現しています。光を感じる明るく新鮮なカラーと、輝きが楽しいクリーンなスタイルの魅力を引き出すため、抜けるような青空と白い建物をバックに選びました。また、形態もポストカードとしてご使用いただける仕様のリーフレットを制作し、大変ご好評を頂きました。

The catalog introduces images of "Light and Pleasure," the brand's seasonal theme. A clear blue sky and white buildings were chosen for the background, to bring out the beauty of the light-like bright and fresh colors, with a shining, clean fashion style. The leaflet's postcard shape was popular among customers.

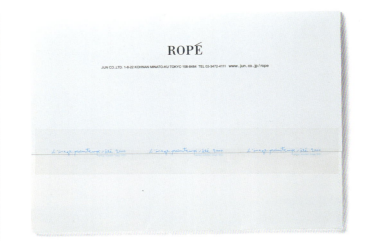

アパレル APPAREL 2000

CL: ジュン ロペ Jun Co., Ltd. ROPÉ
AD, D: 渡辺陽子 Yoko Watanabe
P: 中村和孝 Kazutaka Nakamura
DF: ロペ事業部文化部 ROPÉ Division Bunka-bu
STYLING: 清水恵子 Keiko Shimizu
SB: ジュン Jun Co., Ltd.

FASHION: アパレル APPAREL

Catalog + Web

ROPÉ

jun.co.jp/rope

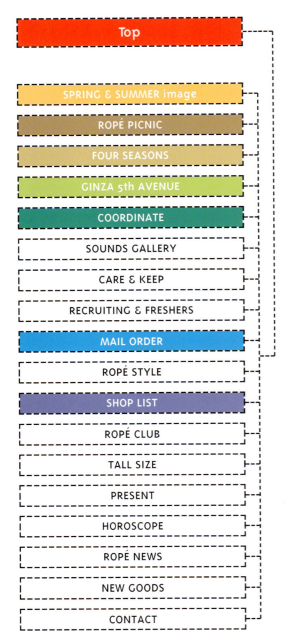

ロペのブランドイメージが伝わりやすいように、全体にフレンチテイストで上品な仕上がりを目標に制作。雑誌風にコンテンツを作り、そこから自由に見たいページに入れるように工夫しました。1ヶ月毎に更新するページを設け、ロペの新しい商品とコーディネート、銀座本店からのお知らせ等をオンタイムでスピーディにご紹介。オンラインショッピングは、シーズンを通してショッピングできる商品群に加えて、1ヶ月毎に新しい商品が増え、よりタイムリーにショッピングできるように工夫しています。

In order to easily convey Rope's brand image, we wanted this site to have an overall feeling of French taste and elegance. Like a magazine, we included a table of contents page, where people can select the pages they want to visit. Some pages are updated monthly, presenting new products and coordination ideas as well as timely information from the main Ginza store. On the online shopping pages, there are a group of products that are available for the entire season, and new products are introduced monthly. The site is designed for timely shopping.

※2000年7月11日現在のデータを使用 As of July 11, 2000

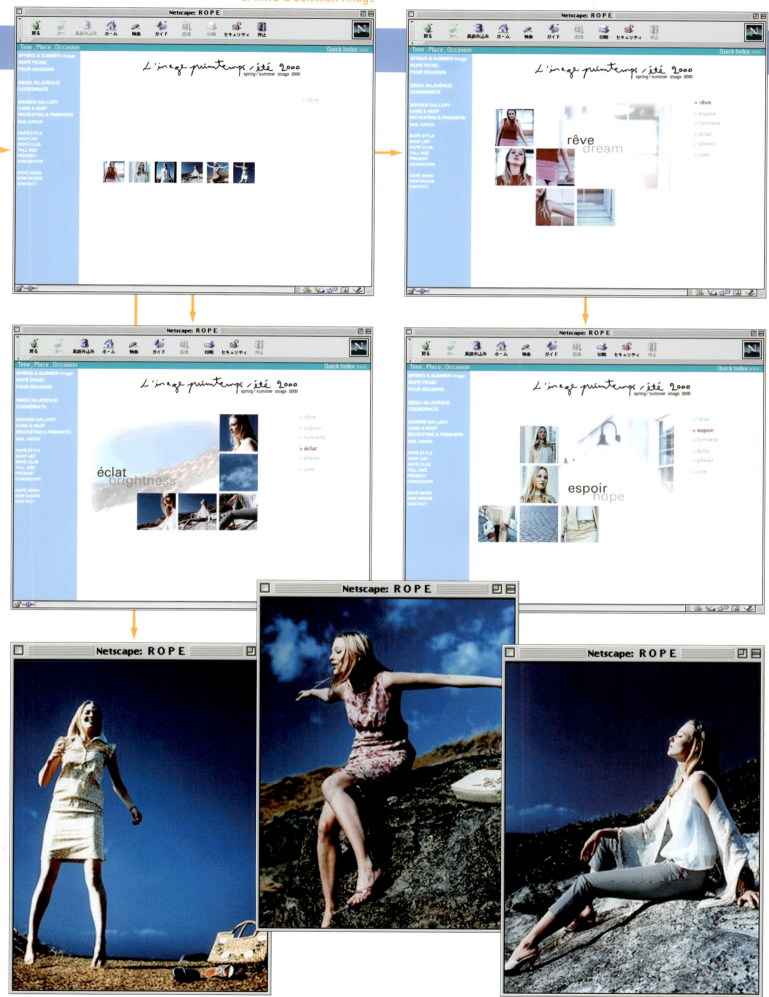

SPRING & SUMMER image

FASHION: アパレル APPAREL

Catalog + Web

ROPÉ

Top

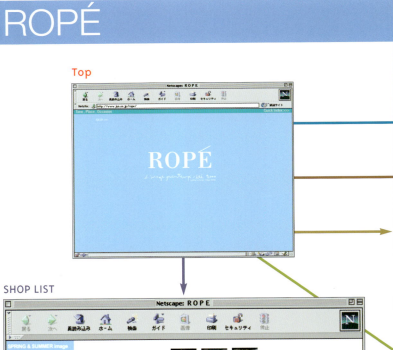

FOUR SEASONS

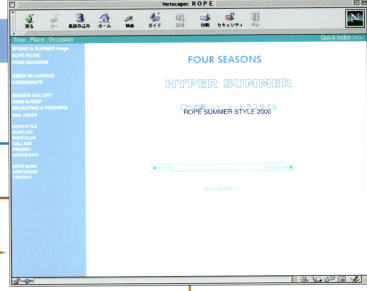

SHOP LIST

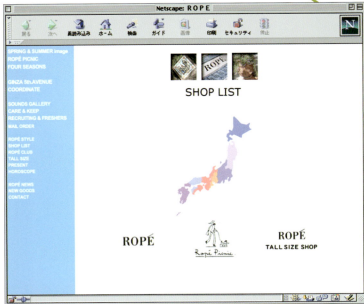

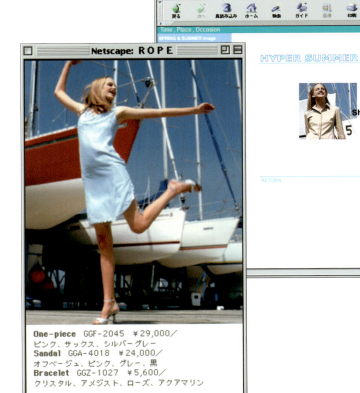

アパレル　APPAREL 2000

CL: ジュン ロペ　Jun Co., Ltd. ROPÉ
AD, D: 渡辺陽子　Yoko Watanabe
P: 中村和孝　Kazutaka Nakamura
M: コスモ・インタラクティブ　Cosmo Interactive Inc.
DF: ロペ事業部文化部　ROPÉ Division Bunka-bu
SB: ジュン　Jun Co., Ltd.

※2000年7月11日現在のデータを使用　As of July 11, 2000

FASHION: アパレル APPAREL

ROPÉ PICNIC

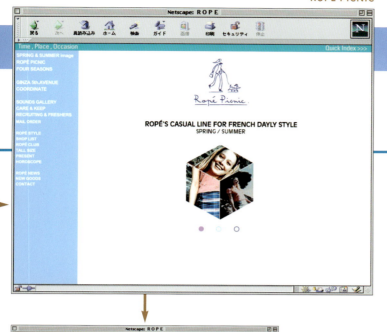

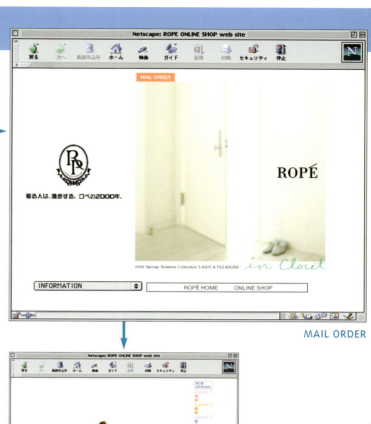

MAIL ORDER

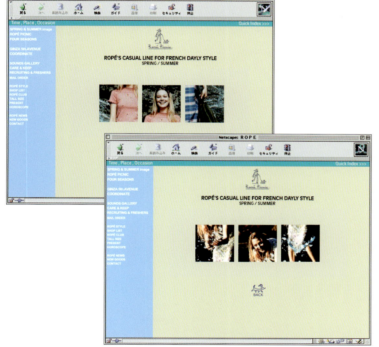

GINZA 5th AVENUE

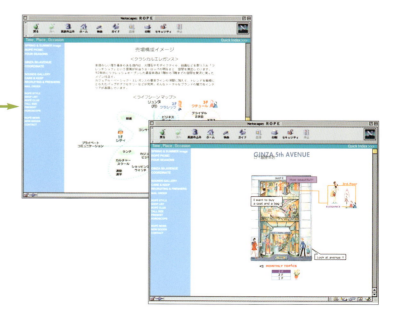

Catalog + Web

BEAMS

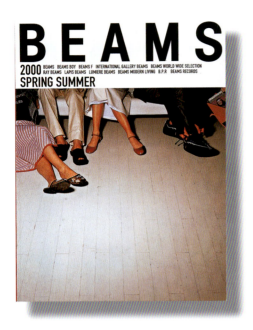

平綴 Bound／129×180mm

page 1, 2

page 5, 6

アパレル　APPAREL 2000

CL: ビームス　BEAMS Co., Ltd.
CD, SB: ビームスクリエイティブ　BEAMS CREATIVE INC.
AD, D: 山口アツシ　Atsushi Yamaguchi
P: 北島 明　Akira Kitajima／青野 正　Tadashi Aono
清水哲治　Tetsu Shimizu／高瀬 博　Hiroshi Takase
WRITER: 小林あつこ　Atsuko Kobayashi

FASHION: アパレル APPAREL

BRAND NEWS

RUFFO RESEARCH (ルッフォ リサーチ)

ALAIN MIKLI (アラン ミクリ)

NORMAL (ノーマル)
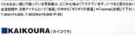

KAIKOURA (カイコウラ)

BRAND NEWS

S.WAUCHOB (シャロン ウォコブ)

琉球絣 (リュウキュウカスリ)

AKABA (アカバ)

BRUNO MATHSSON (ブルーノ マットソン)

page 55, 56

BEAMS RECORDS

NEW RELEASE Mondo Erotica!/JUN MIYAKE
1.Switch 2.Flesh for Eve 3.Sus-pecte 4.La Cle' 5.Jewel
6.Jelly 7.Elfin 8.Cream 9.Endure 10.Ave Maria
CD/BEX-6002 ¥3,000(税別)

NOW ON SALE Glam Exotica!/JUN MIYAKE
1.Rain Forest 2.Lotus Isle 3.River of Gold
4.Mosquito Path 5.Gnossienne#1 6.Pico Birds 7.Lost Honeymoon
8.Brazil 9.Stones bearing Flowers 10.Lokasa 11.Raft of Love 12. Postcard !
CD/BEX-6001 ¥3,000(税別)

三宅 純

page 107, 108

INFORMATION

● ビームス プラスが3月18日、原宿にオープン

● ビームス ボーイが3月4日、長崎にオープン

INFORMATION

● ARTCODIF

● MIKLI par MIKLI ミクリ パー ミクリのサングラスが登場

● LUMIERE BEAMS オリジナル

page 111, 112

47

Catalog + Web

BEAMS

www.beams.co.jp

- Top
- From BEAMS
- Internet Gallery BEAMS
- BEAMS STYLE
- The BRAINS
- Uniform Circus
- What's New!?
- What's BE@MS!?
- BEAMS CO. LTD.
- CONTENTS
- Information

セレクトショップ「BEAMS」のホームページ。商品・ショップの情報はもちろん、バイヤーの生の声などをお伝えします。深くて新鮮な情報です。

The Web site of Beams, a retail fashion shop, presenting product and shop information, as well as suggestions from their buyers. Filled with the latest, complete information.

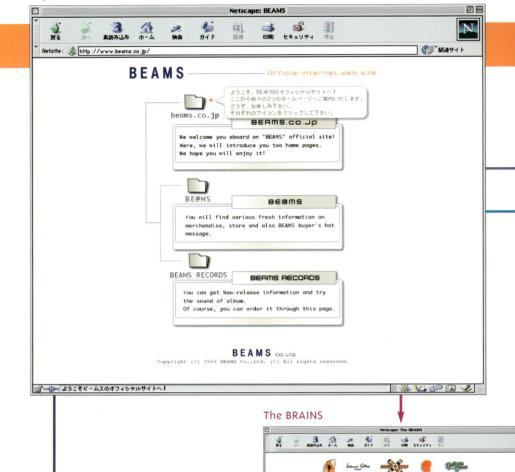

アパレル　APPAREL 1998

CL: ビームス　BEAMS Co., Ltd.
D: モンキー王国　MONKEY KINGDOM Inc.
SB: ビームスクリエイティブ　BEAMS CREATIVE INC.
※2000年7月11日現在のデータを使用　As of July 11, 2000

FASHION: アパレル APPAREL

Internet Gallery BEAMS

From BEAMS

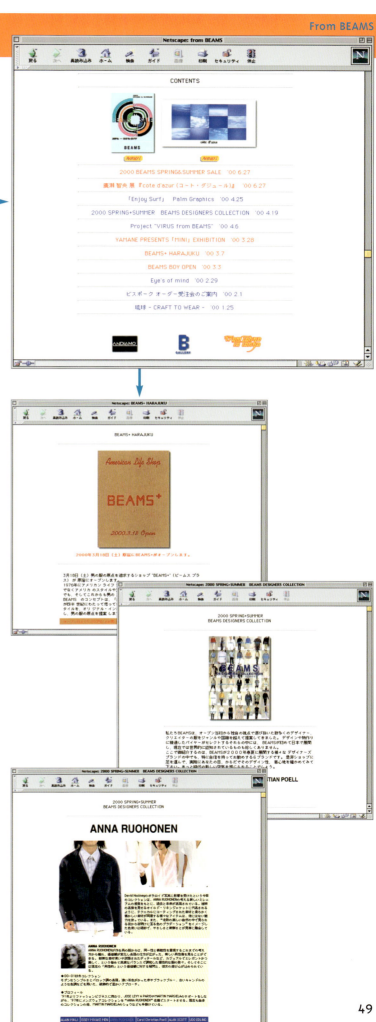

Catalog + Web

BEAMS RECORDS

www.beams.co.jp

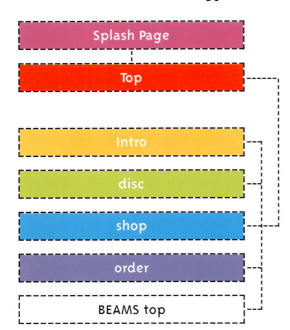

ビームス・レコードのホームページです。新着情報はもちろん、視聴ができて、CDもご購入いただけます。

The Web site of Beams Records. The site presents the latest news, as well as the opportunity to listen to music files and order CDs online.

Splash Page

Top

order

shop

アパレル　APPAREL 1998

CL: ビームスレコード　BEAMS RECORDS
D: スズキ スムース (スピードグラフィックス)
SUZUKI SUMUSU (Speed Graphics)
SB: ビームスクリエイティブ　BEAMS CREATIVE INC.

※2000年7月11日現在のデータを使用　As of July 11, 2000

FASHION: アパレル APPAREL

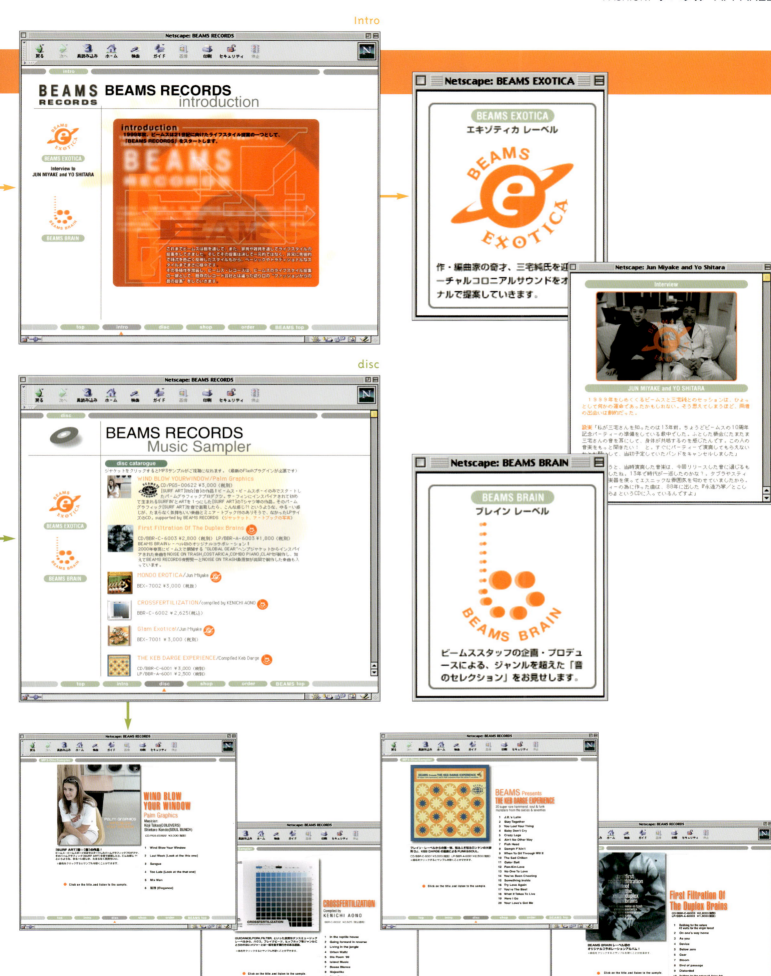

Catalog+Web
beauty:beast

シート Sheet／270×341mm

生誕10周年を向かえたbeauty:beastとしてのファイナルコレクションとなる、『children of the DAMNED』collection。太陽も街もない 公園もなく 日の光りもない 灯された光は ただ心の光だけ 見失った理由でもなく ただ未完のまま 最も新しい そして 最後の提案 それは死 それは失うこと そして心の安らぎ 己を信じる本来の光りはそこに見失った理由ではない これは最後の提案

On the occasion of its 10th anniversary, beauty:beast introduced their final collection, "Children of the DAMNED." After much consideration, it was decided that the beauty:beast brand would be retired. The concept behind "Children of the DAMNED" is visually expressed in the catalog.

アパレル　APPAREL 2000
CL, SB: ビューティ ビースト　beauty:beast LTD
CD, AD: 山下隆生　Takao Yamashita
P: Kazutaka Nakamura
HAIR & MAKE-UP: iNOMATA (as:coeur)
©バウハウス2000『スリル』

FASHION: アパレル APPAREL

Catalog + Web

beauty:beast

www.beautybeast.co.jp

- Splash Page
- Top
  - 9re clearance
  - UFO CATCHER collection
  - b:b 10th記念企画再発決定！ 10th Anniversary's Project
  - 00/01 A/W fainal collection
  - Bad News RECORDS
  - VIRTUA DRIVE SHOP
  - www. vsonline. net
- history
- bbs
- Dark Knight 2000
- shop
- 9re
- clas : six

Splash Page

00/01 A/W fainal collection

Top

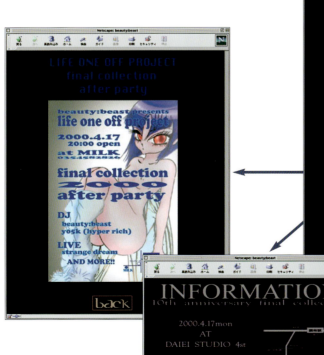

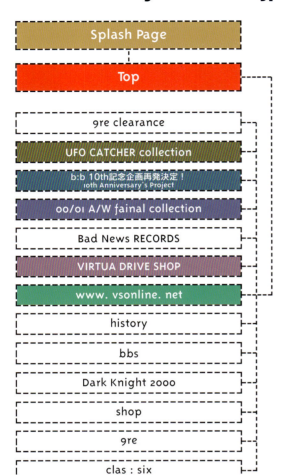

FASHION: アパレル APPAREL

b:b 10th記念企画再発決定！
10th Anniversary's Project

www.vsonline.net

UFO CATCHER collection

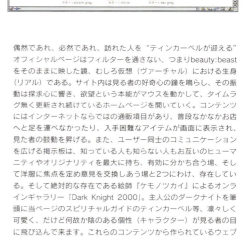

VIRTUA DRIVE SHOP

偶然であれ、必然であれ、訪れた人を"ティンカーベルが迎える"オフィシャルページはフィルターを通さない、つまりbeauty:beastをそのままに映した鏡、むしろ仮想（ヴァーチャル）における生身（リアル）である。サイト内は見る者の好奇心の鐘を鳴らし、その振動は探求心に響き、欲望という本能がマウスを動かして、タイムラグ無く更新され続けているホームページを開いていく。コンテンツにはインターネットならではの通販項目があり、普段なかなかお店へと足を運べなかったり、入手困難なアイテムが画面に表示され、見た者の鼓動を昇げる。また、ユーザー同士のコミュニケーションを広げる掲示板は、知っている人も知らない人もお互いのヒューマニティやオリジナリティを最大に持ち、有効に分かち合う場、そして洋服に焦点を定め意見を交換しあう場と2つにわけ、存在している。そして絶対的な存在である絵師『ケモノツカイ』によるオンラインギャラリー「Dark Knight 2000」。主人公のダークナイトを筆頭に当ページのスピリチャルガイドのティンカーベル等、凛々しく可愛く、だけど何故か陰のある個性（キャラクター）が見る者の目に飛び込んで来ます。これらのコンテンツから作られているウェブサイト＝仮想空間は、見た者への正しい情報そしてbeauty:beastの精神をリアルに発信し続けています。

This site consists of eight categories of information, including NEWS, in the menu. Each keyword representing the content will pique the viewer's curiosity, inducing them to "turn" one page after another. An on-line shopping corner offers many hard-to-find items to people who are not able to visit shops. It increases the viewer's desire to purchase. A bulletin board helps to develop communication between users, and is made up of two sections: one is for people to share their personality and originality fully, with other people both known or unknown; the other is for the exchange of opinions regarding clothing. There is also an on-line gallery called Dark Knight 2000, led by artist Kemono-tsukai. The gallery's many characters, with their strong originality will attract viewers eyes instantly. The Web site (= a virtual space) created by these contents continues to deliver information and the spirit of beauty:beast to customers.

アパレル   APPAREL 1999

CL, SB: ビューティ ビースト beauty:beast LTD

CD, AD, D, CG, PR: y 05k

CD, AD, D, CW, CG, PR, DF: lou

I: 獣使い kemonotukai

※2000年7月13日現在のデータを使用 As of July 13, 2000

55

Catalog + Web

APPLE HOUSE

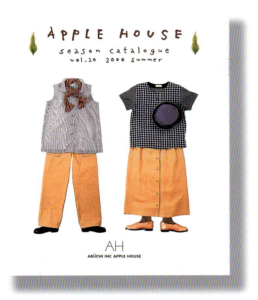

中綴 Stapled in the center／182×220mm

アップルハウスは「やさしさ」にこだわったシンプルな洋服と雑貨のブランドです。綿・麻などの天然素材を自然の色に染めあげた、独自のカラー展開が人気を集めています。アップルハウスのシーズンカラーカタログは、春・夏・盛夏・秋・冬の年5回の発行です。B5変形サイズのかわいいカタログです。「やさしい」イメージを大切にし、素朴で柔かい色使いと見やすさを心がけています。また、エッセイや読者参加のページを設け、読み物としても楽しめる作りになっています。

Apple House is an unpretentious fashion and goods brand whose theme is "gentleness." Natural materials such as cotton and linen are dyed with natural colors, and the original color variations are quite popular. Apple House's Seasonal Colors catalog is published five times a year: spring, summer, mid-summer, fall and winter. It is an attractive catalog in an irregular B5 size. Emphasizing the brand's "gentle" image, the catalogs are visually appealing, and are designed using soft, simple colors. Also, with pages devoted to essays and readers' participation, the catalog is also interesting as reading matter.

婦人服製造・販売
WOMEN'S CLOTHING MANUFACTURE & SALES 2000

CL, SB: あぶち・アップルハウス　ABUCHI INC APPLE HOUSE

page 1, 2

page 5, 6

page 11, 12

Catalog+Web

FASHION: アパレル APPAREL

www.applehouse.com

- Top
- お店のご紹介 Shop Information
- 商品のご紹介 Products Information
- 林檎會のご案内 Member's Information
- Shop Info & コラム Column
- トピックス Topics
- 小売店バイヤーの方への営業ご案内 Business Information for Retail Buyer's

アップルハウスは、自然の素材と優しい色合いが特徴の婦人服メーカーです。コンセプトである「自然」と「優しさ」をそのまま生かした、シンプルで見やすいホームページ制作をしています。ホームページの内容は、全国のお店の情報、商品の紹介、コラムなど。ホームページを初めて見る方にもわかりやすく、興味を持っていただけるような構成となっています。

Apple House is an apparel maker whose clothes for women feature natural fabrics and soft colors. Embodying the concepts of "Nature" and "Softness," their Web site is simple and pleasing to the eye, and includes information about shops in Japan, introductions of products, and articles. It is designed to interest even those people who are visiting the site for the first time.

婦人服製造・販売
WOMEN'S CLOTHING MANUFACTURE & SALES 2000

CL, SB: あぶち・アップルハウス ABUCHI INC APPLE HOUSE
CD: 神崎愛子 Aiko Kanzaki

※2000年7月13日現在のデータを使用 As of July 13, 2000

Catalog+Web

NIKE JAPAN

カタログキット（ビニールポシェット・カード）
Catalog kit (Vinyl pouch・Card)

ビニールポシェット Vinyl pouch／183×127mm
カード Card／148×100mm

1999年10月より開始した「ナイキ ウィメンズキャンペーン」において、広告と連動して制作した小売店頭用ツールです。女性をターゲットにしているので、パッケージに入れることで興味を喚起できるよう考慮しました。

This was designed to be a retail sales tool to accompany the "Nike Women's Campaign" advertising campaign that began in October 1999. This product catalog, placed into a translucent package with a plastic zipper, created a fashionable look. It was designed to interest women, the target buyers.

スポーツ用品販売　SPORTING GOODS SALES　1999

CL, SB: ナイキジャパン　NIKE JAPAN CORP.
CD, CW: 鶴田茂高　Shigetaka Tsuruta
AD, D: 木原雅也　Masaya Kihara
P: 田島 透　Toru Tajima

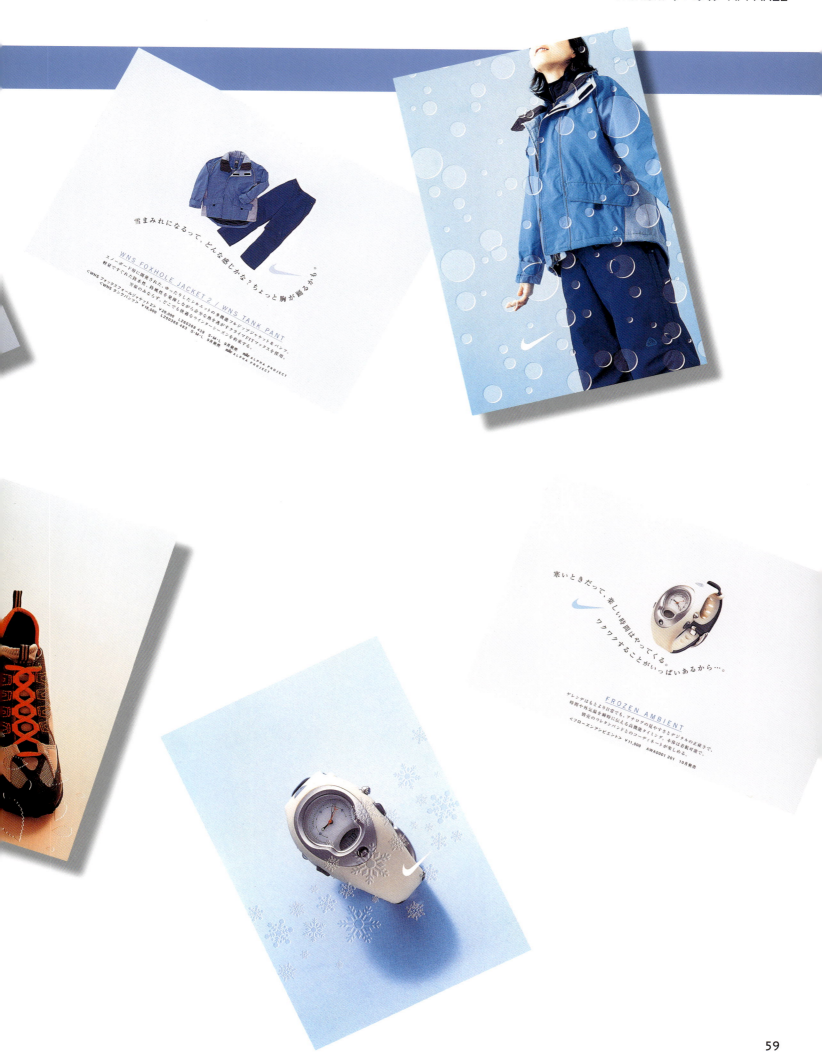

Catalog + Web

NIKE JAPAN

women.nikejapan.co.jp

- Top
- my nike STYLE
- fitness
- community
- product
- event
- Let's talk sports

「ちょっと運動してみたいけど、どうしたらいいんだろう？」そんな前向きな気持ちをもった女性たちに、気軽にカラダを動かすヒントとなる情報を紹介するサイト。またコミュニケーション・スペースもあり、ここではスポーツや健康に関するテーマについて意見交換をしながら、アクティブなライフスタイルへと誘うきっかけが生まれると思います。

"I'd like to get some exercise, but what should I do?" Nike's Web site suggests easy ways for positive-thinking women to become more active. There is also a communication space, where people can exchange their opinions on such themes as sports and health. The site offers possibilities for having a more active life style.

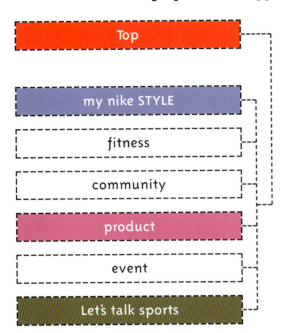
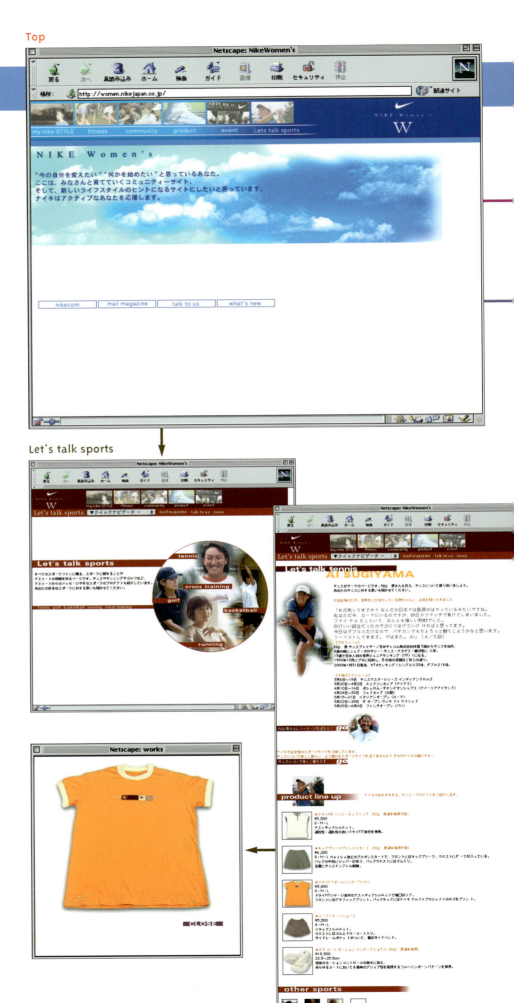

スポーツ用品販売　SPORTING GOODS SALES 1999

CL, SB: ナイキジャパン　NIKE JAPAN CORP.
D: 菅野 友　Tasuku Kanno
CW: 松本 キノコ　Kinoko Matsumoto
※2000年7月11日現在のデータを使用　As of July 11, 2000

FASHION: アパレル APPAREL

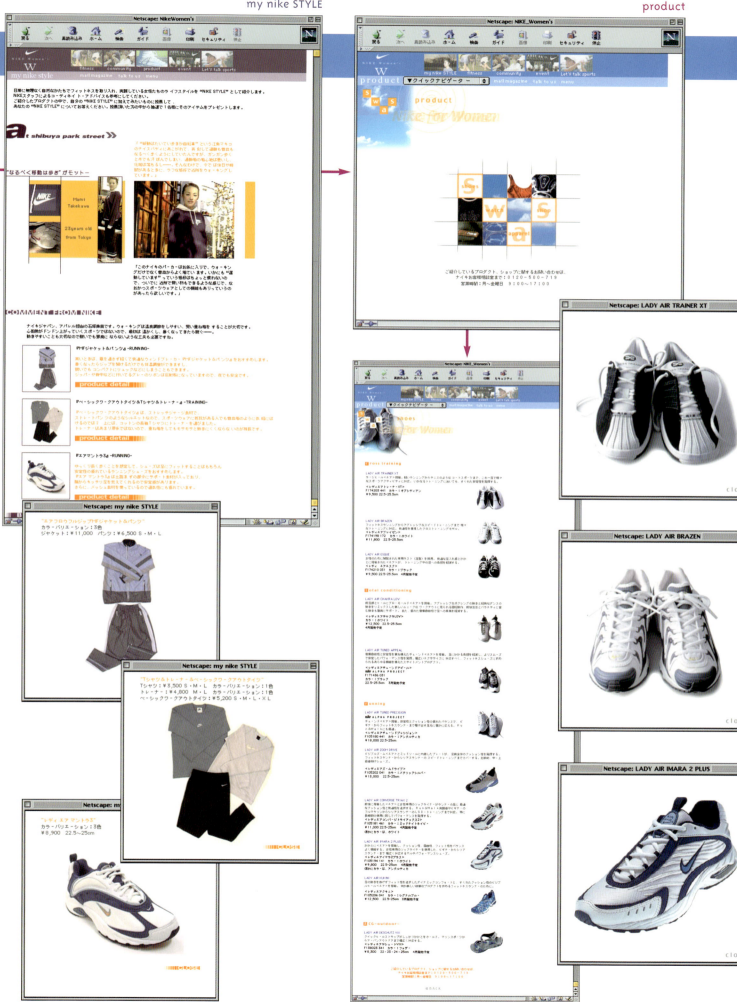

Catalog + Web

CHUMS

中綴 Stapled in the center／220×200mm

page 2, 3

page 4, 5

アメリカ・ユタ州の小さな町、ハリケーン市で生まれたアウトドアブランド・Chums（チャムス）の日本向けアクセサリーカタログ。（株）ランドウェル（Chumsアクセサリー輸入総代理店）の製作で、メガネリテイナー・バッジホルダー・キーホルダー・人気の携帯ストラップ等のアクセサリー全般を紹介。アメリカ本社のカタログをベースに翻訳し、日本向けアレンジしたもの。Simple・Wuality・Funというチャムスのコンセプトを基本に、非常に見やすく楽しいカタログです。

An accessory catalog especially targeted at Japan from Chums, an outdoor goods brand from the small USA town of Hurricane, Utah. Produced by Landwell Inc., the import agency for Chums accessories, the catalog introduces a wide range of accessories, from eyeglass holders and badge holders to popular cellular phone straps. Translated from the U.S. catalog, it was arranged for the Japanese market. Based on the concepts of simplicity, high quality, and fun, the catalog is interesting and enjoyable to look at.

アクセサリー，衣料輸入代理店
ACCESSARY·CLOTHING IMPORT & SALES 2000

CL, SB: ランドウェル LanDwell Inc.
TRANSLATION & ARRANGEMENTS:
バーンズ BARNS

FASHION: アパレル APPAREL

Catalog + Web

CHUMS

www.landwell.com/

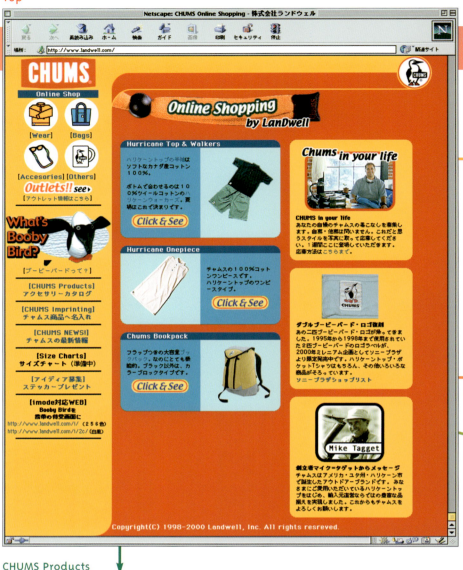

アメリカ・ユタ州の小さな町、ハリケーン市で生まれたアウトドアーブランド・chums（チャムス）の日本向けオンラインショップサイト。（株）ランドウェル（chumsアクセサリー輸入総代理店）の直営で、メガネリテイナー・人気の携帯ストラップ等のアクセサリー一類はもちろんのこと、ハリケーントップを代表とするウェアー類、色使いが特長のバック類まで、フルラインの商品が購入可能。Simple・Quality・Funというチャムスのコンセプトを基本に、非常に使いやすく楽しいウェブサイトです。

An online shopping site especially targeted at Japan from Chums, an outdoor goods brand from the small USA town of Hurricane, Utah. Managed by Landwell Inc., the import agency for Chums accessories, the site introduces a wide range of accessories, from eyeglass holders and popular cellular phone straps, to a line of clothing that includes the popular Hurricane Top, and a line of bags available in special colors. It is possible to purchase anything from the entire line of products. Based on the concepts of simplicity, high quality, and fun, the Web site is interesting and enjoyable to look at.

アクセサリー, 衣料輸入代理店
ACCESSORY·CLOTHING IMPORT & SALES 2000

CL, SB: ランドウェル LanDwell Inc.
DF: エヌエスビー NSB Corporation
※2000年7月10日現在のデータを使用 As of July 10, 2000

FASHION: アパレル APPAREL

Wear

Bags

Others

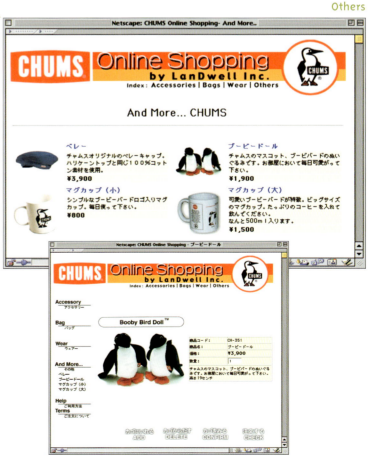

Catalog + Web

MIKI HOUSE

中綴 Stapled in the center／196×195mm

「子どもたちに本物の感動を与え、心の中に無形の財産を築いて欲しい。」1971年、このたった一つの想いから、ミキハウスは誕生しました。子どもたちの限りない夢への、真剣なまなざしと、その夢を実現しようとする、おさえきれない好奇心と、冒険心。その先にミキハウスのビッグドリームはあるのです。子どもと、子どもを取りまくすべてのことへ、新しい時代の、新しい文化を提案し続けるミキハウス。私たちのビッグドリームは、今、始まったばかりです。

Miki House was born in 1971 from just one hope: "We would like to give true impressions to children, so that they will have something valuable to store in their minds." The dreams of children are limitless; their curious and adventurous minds are free too try to make such dreams reality. And Miki House is there, ahead of them. Miki House will continue to propose new culture for a new era to children and everything around them. Our own big dream has just begun.

page 1

page 14, 15

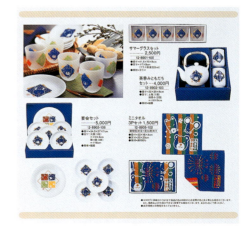

子供服製造・販売
CHILDREN'S CLOTHING MANUFACTURE & SALES 2000

CL, SB: 三起商行（ミキハウス）
MIKI SHOKO CO., LTD (MIKI HOUSE)
CD, CW: 篠原敦子　Atsuko Shinohara
AD, D: 大黒隆司　Takashi Daikoku
P: コオズハウス　CORD'S HOUSE
DF: ハンズ・プロジェクト　HAND'S PROJECT Inc.

FASHION: アパレル APPAREL

page 1, 2

page 3, 4

page 5, 6

page 7, 8

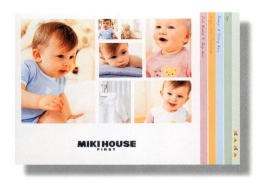

中綴 Stapled in the center／300×210mm

子供服製造・販売
CHILDREN'S CLOTHING MANUFACTURE & SALES 1999

CL, SB: 三起商行（ミキハウス）
MIKI SHOKO CO., LTD (MIKI HOUSE)
CD, CW: 篠原敦子 Atsuko Shinohara
AD, D: 大黒隆司 Takashi Daikoku
P: 広瀬唯二 Yuiji Hirose
I: 山村真代 Masayo Yamamura
DF: ハンズ・プロジェクト HAND'S PROJECT Inc.

Catalog + Web

MIKI HOUSE

www.mikihouse.co.jp/

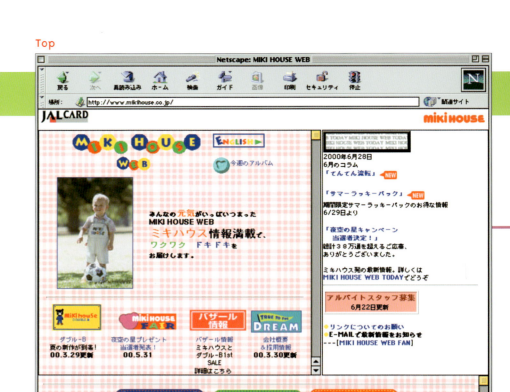

Top

Miki HOUSE FAIR

MIKI HOUSEへ遊びに行こう
Shop Information

バザール情報　Bazaar Information

ファッションを通して、明日の子供文化を創造するミキハウス。大人から子供まで楽しめる様にミキハウスらしいカラフルな色使いで、見た目にも楽しめる様に作りました。その内容も、より多くのお客様に何度でもアクセスしていただけるように、親子をテーマにしたコラムを月一回のペースで掲載したり、ミキハウスに所属しているスポーツ選手の活躍を紹介したりと多岐に渡っています。また、お客様同士で情報交換が出来るページを用意し、子育てに関する様々な情報を募集して、お客様との密なコミュニケーションをはかっています。

Miki House is creating a culture for tomorrow's children, by way of fashion. Typical of Miki House, the Web site is very colorful, so that it can be enjoyed by everyone from children to adults. A wide range of articles are included on the site, including a monthly column with the theme of "parents and children," and information about the performances of Miki House-supported athletes. Additionally, customers can exchange information amongst themselves on a page where we invite discussion of various topics concerning the rearing of children. This allows us to have better communication with our customers.

子供服製造・販売
CHILDREN'S CLOTHING MANUFACTURE & SALES　2000

CL, SB: 三起商行（ミキハウス）
MIKI SHOKO CO., LTD (MIKI HOUSE)
CD, AD: 斉藤修久　Nobuhisa Saito

※2000年7月11日現在のデータを使用　As of July 11, 2000

FASHION: アパレル APPAREL

Miki House DOUBLE-B

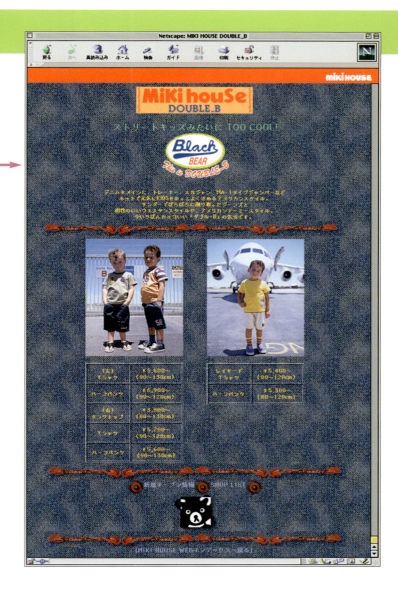

MIKI HOUSEオンラインショッピング　On-line Shopping

Catalog+Web

RUGIADA

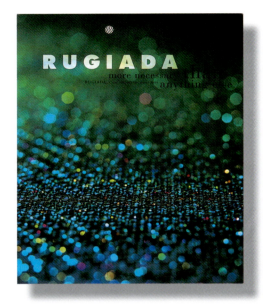

中綴 Stapled in the center／162×200mm

このカタログは、コンセプトブックとしての機能も持つイメージカタログとして構成されています。ルジアダの新しいイメージ展開を試みています。イメージカタログが女性の日常の中での輝きを写し出します。女性とジュエリーの関係の美しさを表現する事を考えて製作しました。

This catalog is designed as an image catalog that functions as a concept book. It is an attempt to develop Rugiada's new image. As a concept book, it tries to reflect shining moments from women's daily lives. The catalog was created to express the beauty of the relationship between women and jewelry.

ジュエリー，婦人服製造・販売／飲食店経営
JEWELRY · WOMEN'S CLOTHING MANUFACTURE & SALES/
RESTAURANT MANAGEMENT 2000

CL, SB: エフ・ディ・シィ・プロダクツ
F.D.C. PRODUCTS INC.
AD, D: 美澤 修 Osamu Misawa
D: 竹内 衛 Mamoru Takeuchi
P: 丹羽俊隆 Toshitaka Niwa
DF: 美澤修デザイン室 osamu misawa design room Co., Ltd.

page 1

page 2, 3

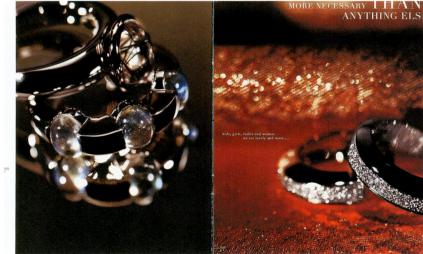

page 4, 5

FASHION: アクセサリー ACCESSORIES

page 1

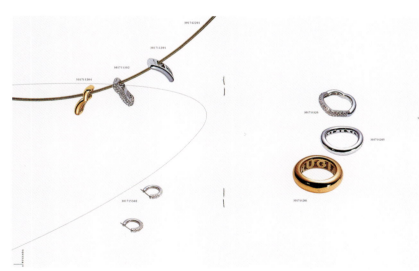

page 4.5

page 6.7

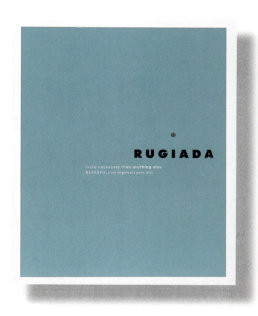

中綴 Stapled in the center／162×200mm

このカタログは、左ページ掲載のコンセプトブックと連動した商品カタログとして構成されています。商品をダイレクトに捉えながらも、シリーズによるイメージで各ページを表現しています。

This product catalog was designed to work together with the concept book shown on the left page. Each page contains a series of images, capturing product characteristics in a straightforward manner.

ジュエリー, 婦人服製造・販売／飲食店経営
JEWELRY・WOMEN'S CLOTHING MANUFACTURE & SALES／
RESTAURANT MANAGEMENT 2000

CL, SB: エフ・ディ・シィ・プロダクツ
F.D.C. PRODUCTS INC.
AD, D: 美澤 修 Osamu Misawa
D: 竹内 衛 Mamoru Takeuchi
P: 丹羽俊隆 Toshitaka Niwa
DF: 美澤修デザイン室 osamu misawa design room Co., Ltd.

Catalog + Web

RUGIADA

www.fdcp.co.jp

- Splash Page
- Top
- RUGIADA
- Spring & Summer Collection
- ショップリスト Shop Information

クライアントのカンパニーカラーと製品イメージを損なわないことを第一に、「Simple but Smart」をベースコンセプトに製作しました。同時に、ターゲットであるお客様のアクセス環境を考慮して、プラグインや最新技術の使用を控え、余計な情報をどの程度省けるか、製品とフォトデザインの魅力をどこまでアピールできるかに尽力しました。ジュエリーを手にした時のときめき－女性のハートの鼓動を表現するよう、現れては消える小さなロゴアニメーションを各ページの左肩に配置し、デザインコンセプト紹介ページへリンクさせています。

This site was designed with "Simple but Smart" as the basic concept, making sure to preserve the client's corporate colors and product image. Considering at the same time the target customer's accessing environment, plug-ins and the latest Web page technologies have been avoided. We focused on including only necessary information, how much products and photo design attraction can be appealed. A small animated logo, designed to mimic the throbbing of a woman's heart when she receives jewelry, fades in and out at the top left of each page, and is a link to a page introducing the company's design concepts.

ジュエリー, 婦人服製造・販売／飲食店経営
JEWELRY · WOMEN'S CLOTHING MANUFACTURE & SALES /
RESTAURANT MANAGEMENT 1999

CL: エフ・ディ・シィ・プロダクツ F.D.C. PRODUCTS INC.
SB: ミームデザイン Meme Design Ltd.

※2000年7月11日現在のデータを使用 As of July 11, 2000

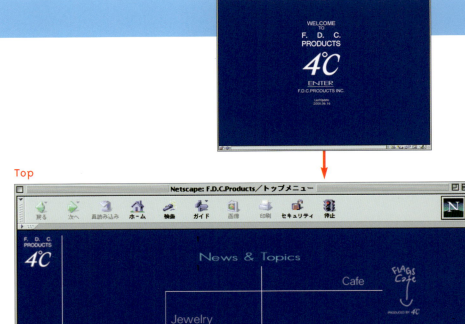

Splash Page

Top

ショップリスト
Shop Information

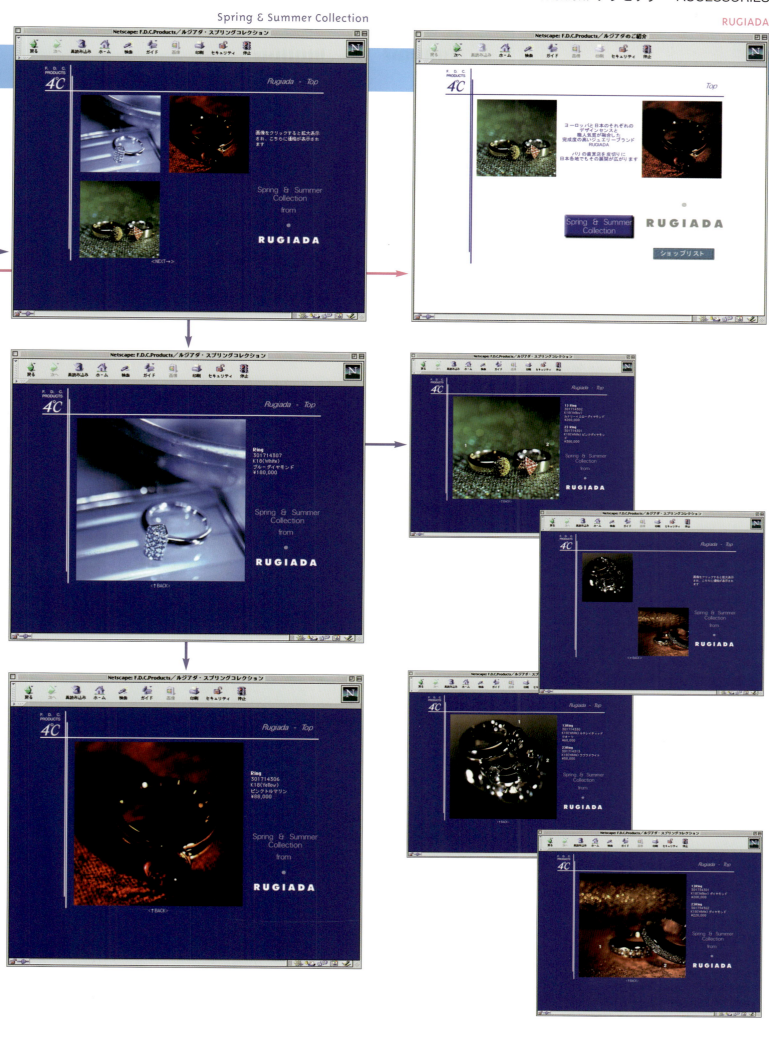

FASHION: アクセサリー ACCESSORIES
RUGIADA

Spring & Summer Collection

Catalog + Web

Fin

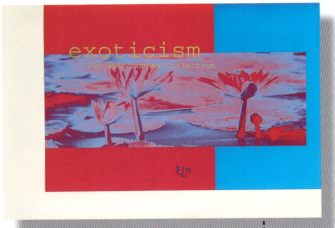

中綴 Stapled in the center／210×148mm

page 15, 16

page 19, 20

デザインテーマは〜exoticism〜異国趣味です。今回は、カタログを手にした方自身がリアルに異国を体感できる様に、あえてモデルを起用しておりません。また、「イメージページ」「商品紹介ページ」のそれぞれを、異素材の印刷紙を使用する事により、視覚だけでなく触覚からも素材感や独特の温もりを体感できる為の工夫をしています。そして撮影はタイで行い、日本では表現しきれないアジアが持つ独特の「光・影・空気感」を写真でも表現する事により、カタログ全般に〜exoticism〜というテーマ性を創り出しました。

This catalog was designed with "exoticism" as its theme. In order to give the reader a more authentic sensation of a foreign country, fashion models were not used in the catalog. The printing of Image Pages and Product Pages on different types of paper texturally accentuates the visual feeling of exoticism. The photographs were taken in Thailand, and capture the uniquely Asian "Light, Shadow, and Atmosphere" that cannot be adequately expressed in Japan, adding to the catalog's overall exotic theme.

婦人靴製造・販売
WOMEN'S SHOES MANUFACTURE & SALES 2000

CL, SB: フィン Fin inc.
CD: 塙 麻理子 Mariko Hanawa
CD, COVER DESIGN: 黒澤花子 Hanako Kurosawa
AD, D, P, CW: 遠藤宏樹 Hiroki Endo
DF: トップストーン TOP Stone

FASHION: アクセサリー ACCESSORIES

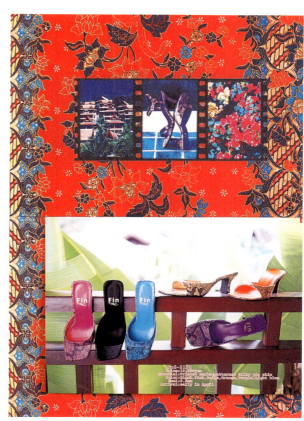

page 1, 2

page 3, 4

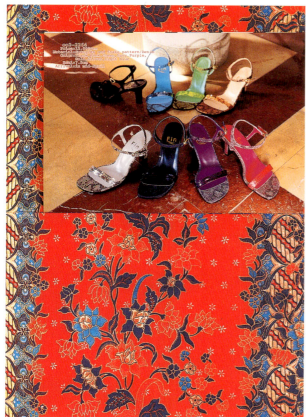

Client/
  Fin inc.
Creative Director/
  MARIKO HANAWA(Fin)
  HANAKO KUROSAWA(Fin)
Photograph/
  HIROKI ENDO
Cover Design/
  HANAKO KUROSAWA(Fin)
Design/
  HIROKI ENDO
Direction/
  HIROKI ENDO
Agency/
  C-EYES co.,ltd.
Staff
Coordinator/
  TOMMY K.TOMINAGA(Asia Coordination)
  SOMBOON KUNCHOKWANIT(Asia Coordination)
Special Thanks/
  THAVORN BEACH VILLAGE(PHUKET,THAILAND)

page 33, 34

page 7, 8

75

Catalog + Web

Fin

www.fin-inc.co.jp

- Splash Page
- Top
- Company Information
- Product Information
- Shop Information

Finと言う企業イメージと、製品イメージを毎シーズンオンタイムに表現できる様に工夫をしています。その為、社内デザイン／更新・管理を目標に、既に軌道に乗りつつあるカタログ製作での各アートディレクターとの協力で、Finのホームページはスタートしました。ウェブページの展開が重くなる要素を可能な限り減少させ、軽いページ展開で、可能な限りカタログ印刷のイメージに近づけ、なおかつウェブでの特性を活かした写真が盛り沢山のホームページを作っていきたいと、工夫を重ねています。

We try to express Fin's corporate image, and product image, seasonally and in a timely manner. For that reason, we wanted our Web site to be designed, updated, and managed in-house, with the cooperation of our art directors, who have been responsible for our well-received print catalogs. As many elements as possible that might slow down the site were eliminated, giving the Web site an appearance similar to that of a printed catalog, where the reader quickly and effortlessly turns the pages. At the same time, many photographs are used, to take advantage of the special potential of the Web.

Splash Page

Top

Company Information

Shop Information

婦人靴製造・販売
WOMEN'S SHOES MANUFACTURE & SALES 1999

CL, SB: フィン Fin inc.
CD, AD, D, CW, CG, PR: 坂本圭子 Keiko Sakamoto
P: 遠藤宏樹 Hiroki Endo
※2000年7月11日現在のデータを使用 As of July 11, 2000

FASHION: アクセサリー ACCESSORIES

Product Information

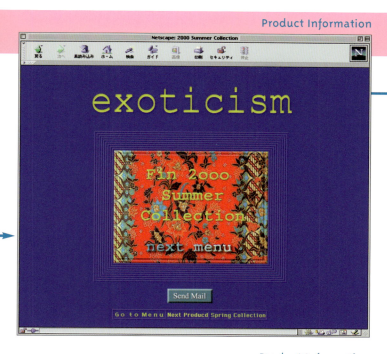

Product Information

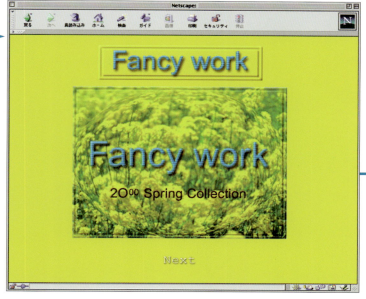

Product Information

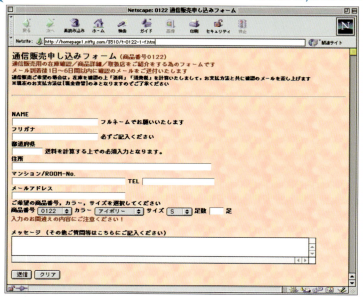

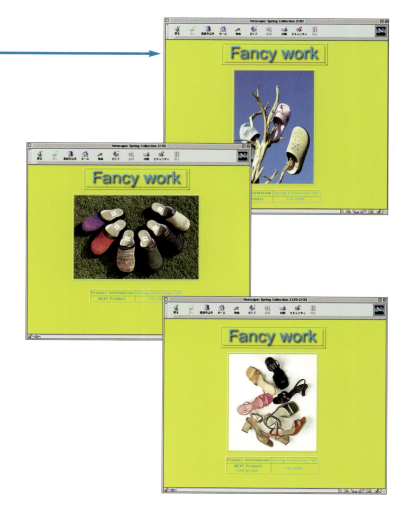

Catalog + Web

FSP

page 11, 12

page 17, 18

FSPのコンセプトは「天才的お化粧道具」。表現上のイメージは、FSPを携えて、いろんなことを攻略していく女の子、という感じです。そこでカタログ関係もすべて旅感のあるものにしています。ウェブとも密にリンクさせた内容で、ストーリーに広がりを持たせるようにしています。

FSP's concept is "Ingenious Cosmetics." The image character is a girl who, together with FSP, undertakes numerous challenges. For this reason, all of FSP's catalogs have a feeling of travel. Stories are extended, and closely linked to the contents of the Web site.

1. 中綴 Stapled in the center／88×124mm
2. カード Card／142×225mm
3. カバー付6ツ折 Sixfold with cover／113×180mm
   (開いた状態 When fully unfolded: 323×374mm)
4. カバー付8ツ折 Eightfold with cover／96×170mm
   (開いた状態 When fully unfolded: 365×321mm)
5. 中綴 Stapled in the center／105×180mm

FASHION: 化粧品 COSMETICS & BODY CARE

化粧品メーカー
COSMETICS MANUFACTURER 1999 - 2000

CL, SB: アクス AXE CO., LTD.
AD: 平林 奈緒美 Naomi Hirabayashi
D: 丸橋 桂 Katsura Marubashi
P: 金沢正人 Masato Kanazawa (1, 2, 4: Products)
古屋 徹 Toru Furuya (3, 5)／石田 東 Higashi Ishida (4: Jacket , 5)
I: ヒロ杉山 Hiro Sugiyama (2)
CW: 山本邦晶 Kuniaki Yamamoto
PLANNER: 吉田聖子 Shoko Yoshida

Catalog + Web

FSP

www.fsp.ne.jp

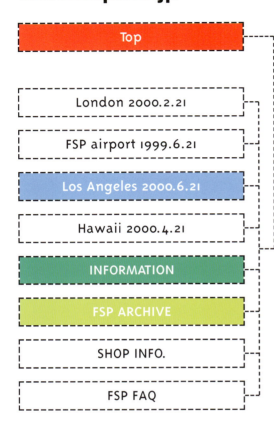

Top
London 2000.2.21
FSP airport 1999.6.21
Los Angeles 2000.6.21
Hawaii 2000.4.21
INFORMATION
FSP ARCHIVE
SHOP INFO.
FSP FAQ

1999年6月にデビューした化粧品FSPのサイトです。当初のコンセプトはエアポートで、2年目に入ってからは世界を飛びまわるイメージで展開しています。プロモーションと連動させながらも、読み物やゲーム的な要素も盛り込んだ楽しいページにしようと心がけています。

The Web site of FSP, a cosmetics brand that debuted in June 1999. The original concept used an airport theme, evolving in the second year to images of flying all over the world. Also tied in with the promotion are articles and game-like elements that help to make this an entertaining site.

化粧品メーカー　COSMETICS MANUFACTURER
1999
CL, SB: アクス　AXE CO., LTD.
AD: 平林 奈緒美　Naomi Hirabayashi
D: 足立裕司　Yuji Adachi
CW: Adriana Samaniego
PLANNER: 吉田聖子　Shoko Yoshida
山本邦晶　Kuniaki Yamamoto／丸橋 桂　Katsura Marubashi
※2000年7月5日現在のデータを使用　As of July 5, 2000

Top
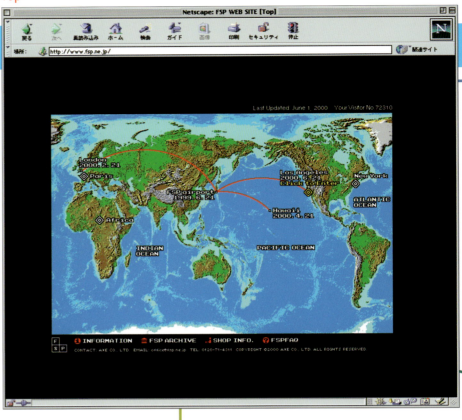

FSP ARCHIVE

FASHION: 化粧品 COSMETICS & BODY CARE

Los Angeles 2000.6.21

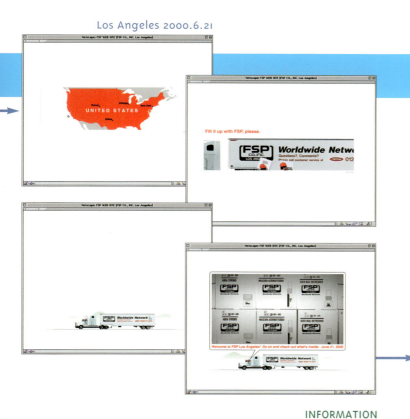

INFORMATION

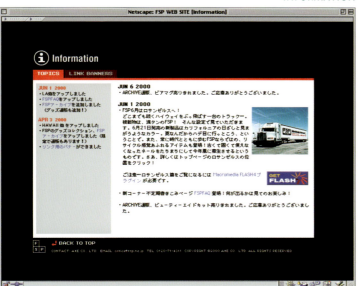

Catalog+Web

ETTUSAIS HOMME

中綴 Stapled in the center／90×256mm

若い男性にとっての化粧品の主な情報収集源は、雑誌のビューティーページや店頭のPOP情報、口コミであり、カタログはトイレタリー主流の現在、あまり存在していません。男性用化粧品のカタログで大切なことは、できる限りやさしく、どこに、何をしてくれるモノか？を明確に伝えることにあります。エテュセオムBOOKは「何に悩んでいるか？」を明確にしてあげながら、それに対して何をしてくれる商品か、をコピー、デザイン、アイコンできちんと伝え、それを店頭デザインとリンクさせることを主眼におきながらつくりあげました。

The main sources of cosmetic information for young men are the beauty pages of magazines, store displays, and word of mouth. There are few men's cosmetic catalogs because toiletries are still more widespread. It is important that men's cosmetic catalogs clearly, and as easily as possible, answer the questions, "What effects will this product have, and to which parts of my body?" By focusing on and clarifying "What are my skin problems?" and "How will this help my problems, if I use it?" the Ettusais Homme Book explains the products' effect on those problems by use of copy, design and icons. The catalog is also created to link to store design.

化粧品メーカー
COSMETICS MANUFACTURER 2000

CL, SB: エテュセ Ettusais Co., Ltd.
DF: ABCデザイン ABC DESIGN
PRODUCTION: 大日本印刷
DAI NIPPON PRINTING CO.,LTD.

page 1, 2

FASHION: 化粧品 COSMETICS & BODY CARE

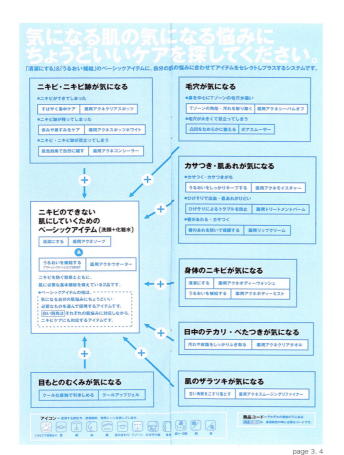

page 3, 4

page 5, 6

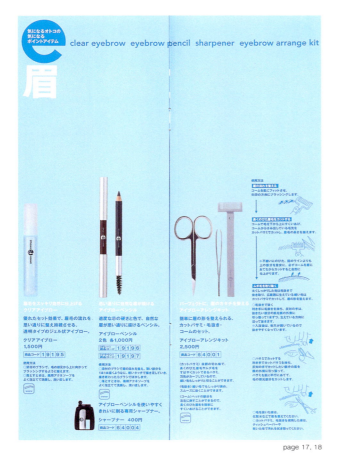

page 17, 18

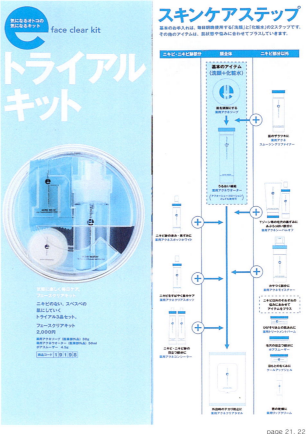

page 21, 22

Catalog + Web

ETTUSAIS HOMME

www.ettusaishomme.ne.jp

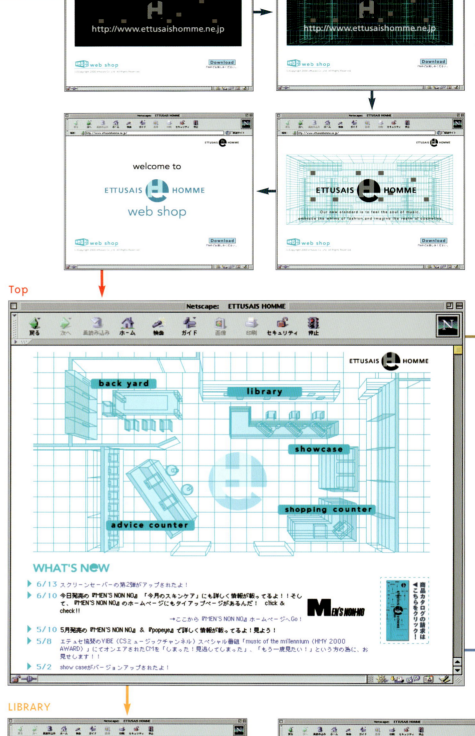

音楽やファッションのようには日常化していない男性の化粧行為。私たちは、そんな男性たちにも楽しく、カッコよく化粧品とつきあってもらいたいという想いで、このブランドを立ち上げました。「お店に行っても情報がない。」「かと言って、はずかしくて聞けない。」そんな彼らの欲求に応え、しかも24時間手軽に購入できるウェブサイトを目指しました。まだ完成したわけではなく、今後は、一人一人の肌カルテを作成し、その都度肌についてのアドバイスもできる環境づくりと、より見やすく、買いやすく、楽しく、カッコいいサイトづくりを目指していきます。

Unlike music or fashion, make-up is not a part of everyday life for most men. We created this brand for such men, so that they can enjoy a good relationship with cosmetics. On this Web site, we aim at easy, 24-hour shopping, responding to such comments as "I can't find information in stores," or "I'm too shy to ask about cosmetics." The site is not yet complete; we are planning to have a skin condition card for each customer, in order to give appropriate advice each time. We are also planning to make the Web site more attractive and entertaining, as well as making it even easier to shop.

化粧品メーカー　COSMETICS MANUFACTURER 2000
CL, SB: エテュセ　Ettusais Co., Ltd.
CL, AD: 川崎修二　Shuji Kawasaki
D: 中川直樹　Naoki Nakagawa
CW: 村山孝文　Takafumi Murayama
PR: ASATSU-DK
DF: ABCデザイン　ABC DESIGN
※2000年7月11日現在のデータを使用　As of July 11, 2000

FASHION: 化粧品 COSMETICS & BODY CARE

BACK YARD

カタログ請求 Printed Catalog Order

Catalog + Web

ETTUSAIS HOMME

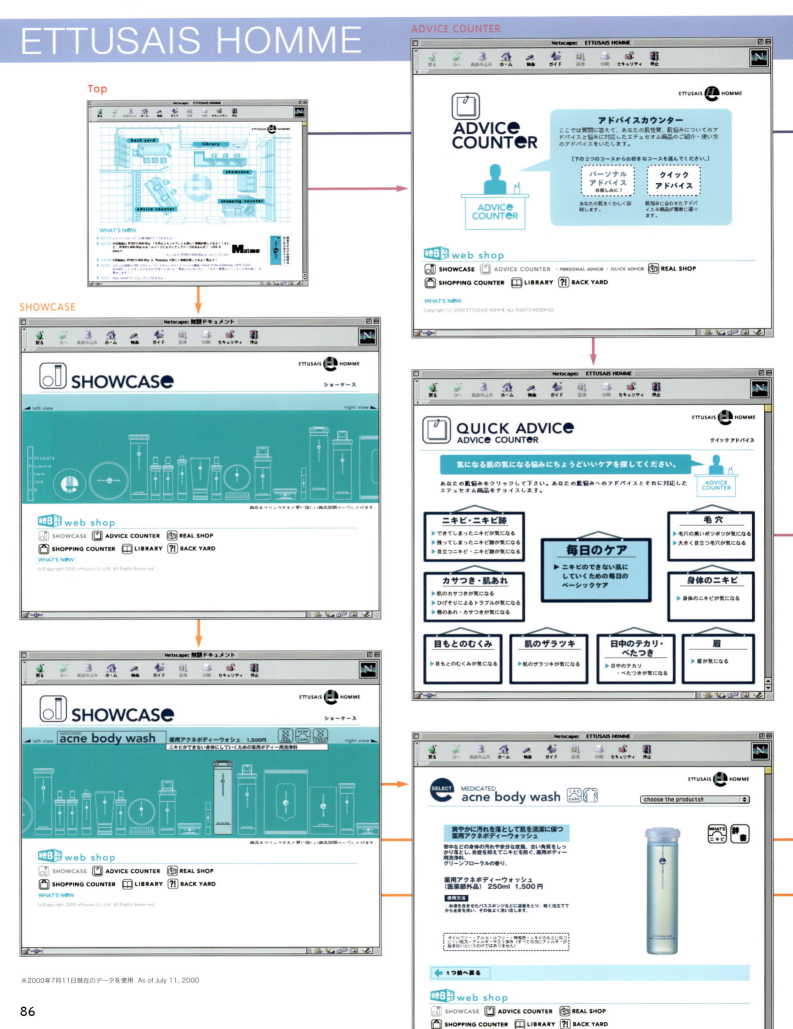

FASHION: 化粧品　COSMETICS & BODY CARE

SHOPPING COUNTER

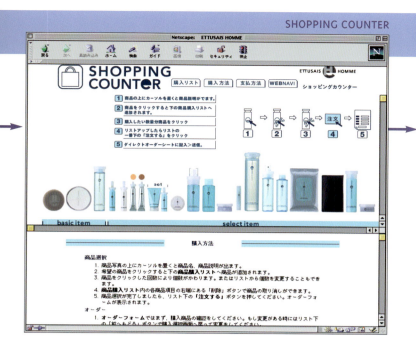

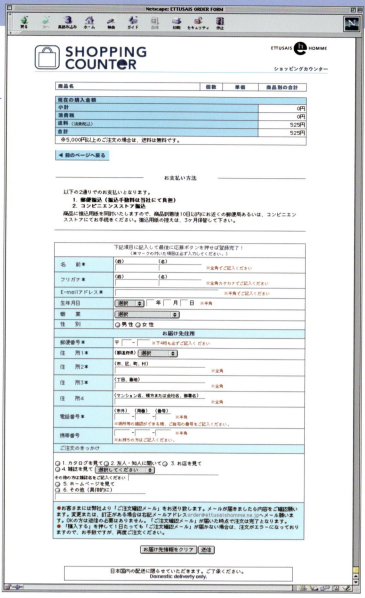

Catalog +Web

JOUR et NUIT

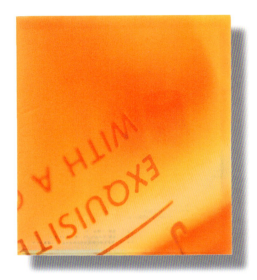

カタログキット：トレペ素材（カバー・シート）
Catalog kit (Cover・Sheet)

カバー Cover／149×171mm
シート Sheet／140×160mm

他にはないようなツールを目指しました。しかしながら、化粧品らしさは必要なことなので、紙のチョイスと写真の撮り方など工夫をしました。

We wanted to create a promotional tool unlike any other. The choice of paper and methods of taking photographs was an important part of the strategy to present the products in a manner befitting cosmetics.

家具, バッグ, アクセサリー, 雑貨等
輸入・製造販売／レストランビジネス
MERCHANDISE IMPORT & DISTRIBUTION +
RESTAURANT MANAGEMENT 2000

CL, SB: サザビー SAZABY Inc.
CD, AD: サザビー宣伝部 Design Advertising Team
D: 小林初子 Hatsuko Kobayashi／野元 陽 Yo Nomoto
P: 廣石尚子 Naoko Hiroishi／アマナ Amana

Catalog + Web

JOUR et NUIT

www.jour-et-nuit.gr.jp

化粧品ブランドのホームページです。ドメインもブランド名で独自に取得しました。単なる商品紹介に終わらない様、スキンケアに関する掲載をしています。内容に合わせて、アニメーションや2Dのイラストを、角質細胞などテクニカルな説明には3Dグラフィックなどを組み合わせて、説得力を持たせるよう留意しています。最近はブラウザーが急速にIE5に移行している様ですが、CSSレイヤは必ずテーブルに変換してからアップしています。ユーザー環境で見え方が変わる文字の大きさ、段落ごとの間隔等の設定に一番苦労します。

A cosmetics brand's Web site, which has a domain name separate from that of the company itself. The site includes not just product introductions, but articles about skin care as well. Animations and 2D illustrations provide additional explanations for the articles, and 3D graphics are used for technical information, such as explanation of keratin cells. Recently, Internet Explorer 5 is rapidly becoming the most popular browser, but we convert CSS files into tables before uploading. The most challenging aspect of designing this site was planning for the differences in font size and space between paragraphs that will differ depending on the browser settings of the user.

家具, バッグ, アクセサリー, 雑貨等
輸入・製造販売／レストランビジネス
MERCHANDISE IMPORT & DISTRIBUTION +
RESTAURANT MANAGEMENT 1999

CL, SB: サザビー SAZABY Inc.
AD, CG: サザビー宣伝部 Design Advertising Team
D: 金子秀俊 Hidetoshi Kaneko
CW: 笹木香代 Kayo Sasaki

※2000年7月11日現在のデータを使用 As of July 11, 2000

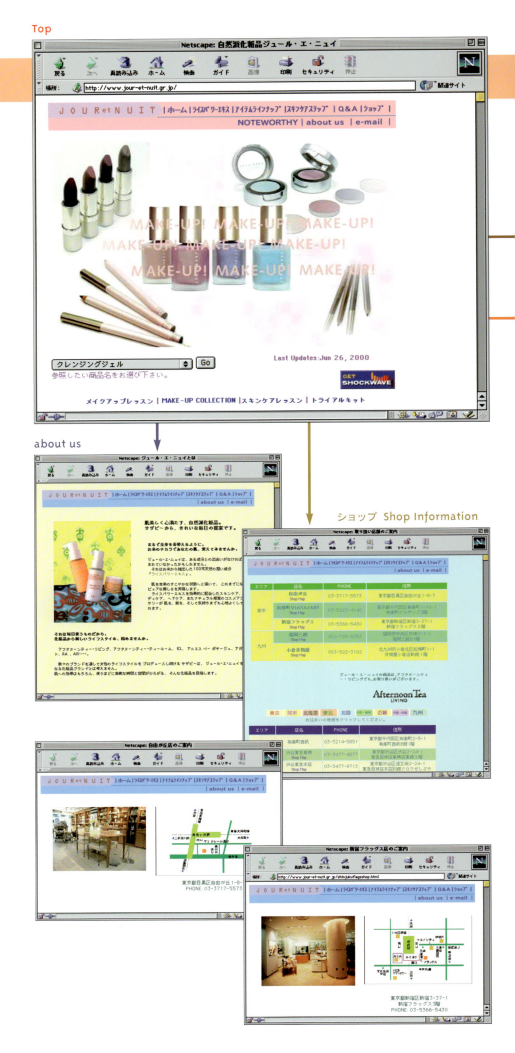

FASHION: 化粧品　COSMETICS & BODY CARE

アイテム ラインナップ　Products Information

ライスパワーエキス　Rice Power Extract

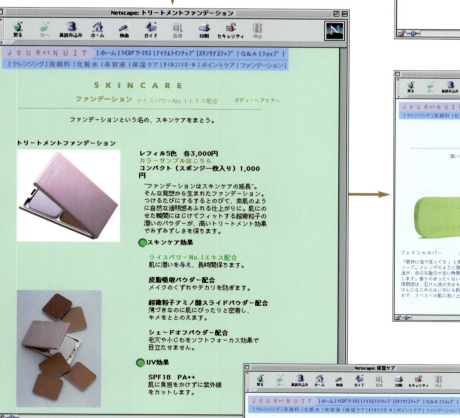
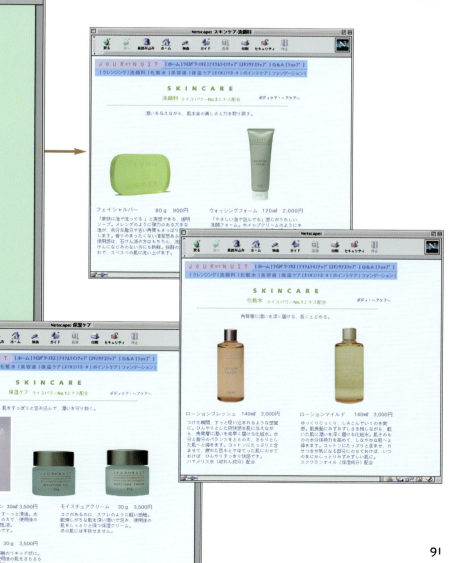

Catalog + Web

shu uemura

中綴 Stapled in the center／210×297mm

㈱シュウ ウエムラ化粧品のビューティブティック海外店舗で取り扱っている商品の総合カタログです。ただ単に同社の商品や色味の豊富さだけを強調するのではなく、関連商品を同一ページで紹介する構成とすることで、消費者に分かりやすく、かつ必要な商品を選びやすいものとしました。メールオーダーにも対応可能な内容とするため、同社のメイクアップ商品のカラーバリエーションの微妙な違いを再現するのに苦労しました。

A comprehensive catalog of products carried by the overseas branches of Shu Uemura Cosmetic's Beauty Boutique. By emphasizing the richness of products and number of colors, as well as introducing related products on the same page, we made the catalog more understandable and product selection easier. The most challenging point was accurately reproducing the delicate differences in color variation of the cosmetics.

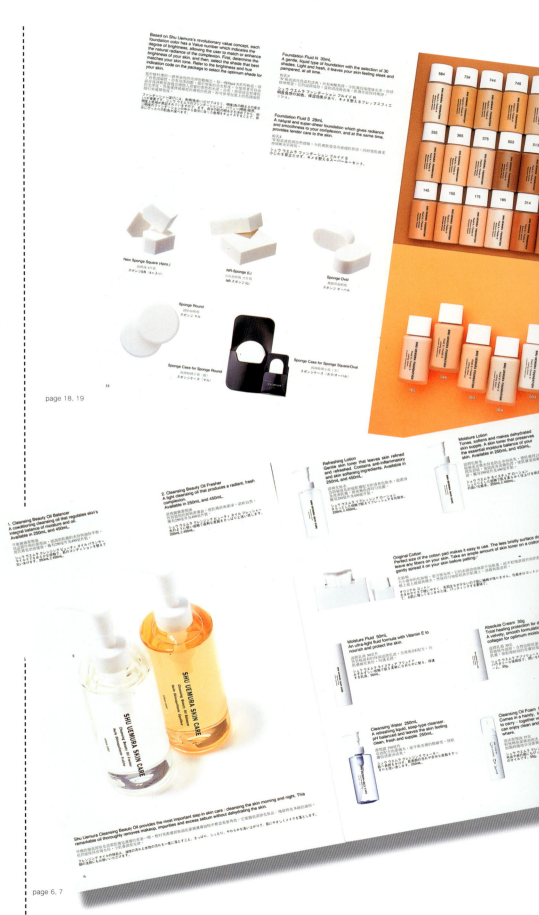

化粧品製造・販売
COSMETICS MANUFACTURE & SALES 1999

CL, SB: シュウ ウエムラ化粧品 Shu uemura cosmetics inc.
AD, CW: 堀内信治 Shinji Horiuchi
P: 小山 雄司郎 Yujiro Koyama
I: 向井佳子 Keiko Mukai
DF: 粋 Iki design office

FASHION: 化粧品 COSMETICS & BODY CARE

CONTENTS
Certain products may not be available in some markets.

Perfume
P4 – 5

Skin Care
P6 – 11

Depsea Water
P12 – 13

Body Care
P14 – 15

Makeup
P16 – 33

Nail Polish & Nail Care
P34 – 35

Bath Goods
P36 – 37

Brushes
P38 – 41

Accessories
P42 – 47

art direction : Shinji Horiuchi   photos : Yujiro Koyama   drawing : Keiko Mukai   design work : iki design office

page 2, 3

page 24, 25

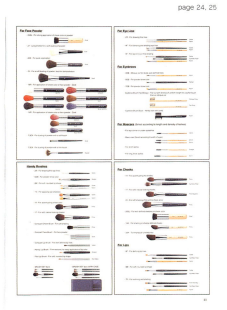

page 40, 41

Catalog + Web

shu uemura

www.shu-uemura.co.jp

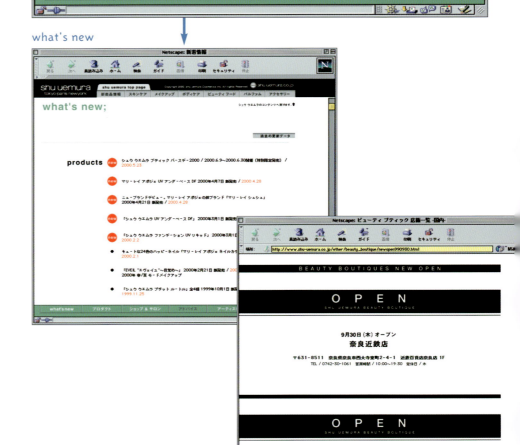

㈱シュウ　ウエムラ化粧品（以下同社）のウェブサイト。同社のブランドイメージの保守を第一にウェブの制限の中でいかにわかりやすく、美しいサイトを構築するかをコンセプトとし、そこが一番の苦労点でした。商品の美しさを活かすためにテキスト要素は画像を使用。重くなりすぎないように考慮しました。柔軟な情報更新のために情報枠を固定化し、カテゴリーも考慮しました。美しさ・インターフェース・訴求力・運用面を突き詰めたウェブサイトを目指しました。

The Web site of Shu Uemura Cosmetics. Maintaining brand image was our first priority, with the goal to create a site that was both beautiful and easy to navigate given the limitations of the Web. That was also the most challenging point. In order to best show the beauty of the products, graphics were used for text elements; at the same time, we tried not to make the graphics too heavy. Fixed grids are used for more flexible information updates, and much consideration was given to the various categories. We aimed at creating a Web site in which beauty, interface, power to appeal, and operational aspects were fully pursued.

※2000年7月11日現在のデータを使用　As of July 11, 2000

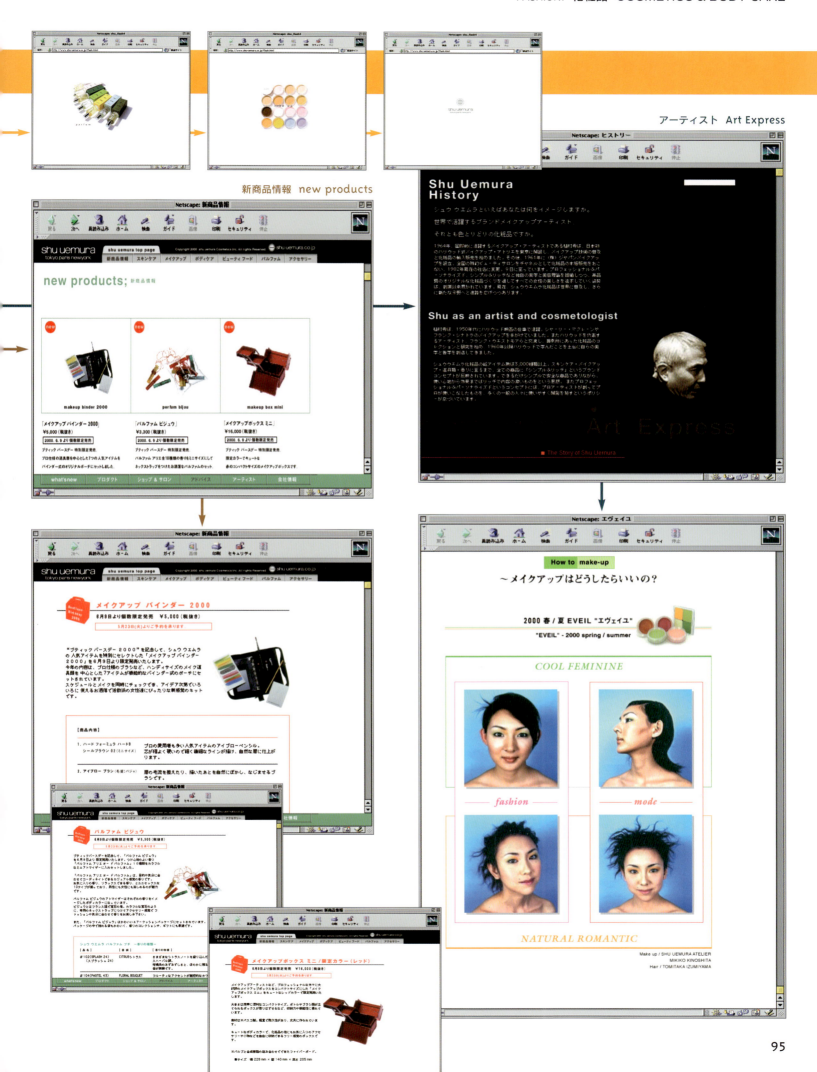

Catalog + Web

shu uemura

プロダクト SHU UEMURA PRODUCTS GUIDE　　　　　　　　　　　Top

化粧品製造・販売
COSMETICS MANUFACTURE & SALES 2000

CL, SB: シュウ ウエムラ化粧品　Shu uemura cosmetics inc.
CD, CW: 太田信子　Nobuko Ohta
AD: 中井 丞太郎（ドーワ・プランニング）
Jotaro Nakai (Dowa Planning Inc.)
D: 中村 稔（ドーワ・プランニング）
Minoru Nakamura (Dowa Planning Inc.)
PR: 関 修武（ドーワ・プランニング）
Osamu Seki (Dowa Planning Inc.)
DF: ドーワ・プランニング　Dowa Planning Inc.
※2000年7月11日現在のデータを使用　As of July 11, 2000

FASHION: 化粧品 COSMETICS & BODY CARE

ショップ&サロン shu uemura shop & salon

Catalog + Web

NIHON L'ORÉAL

中綴 Stapled in the center／210×297mm

"日本ロレアルは、日本とフランス、2つの文化を結んで、人々の美と人生の豊かさに奉仕します"をコンセプトに、日本ロレアル設立時に制作したものです。ロレアル・グループの本拠地であるフランスのエレガンス、そして新会社「日本ロレアル」の誕生の地である日本の美を強く意識しながら、2つの文化の融合と、誰もが持っている"美しくありたい。人生を豊かに彩りたい"という願いに応えてゆくというロレアル・グループ世界共通の使命のビジュアル化を目指しました。

The catalog was created when Nihon L'oreal was established, with the concept that Nihon L'oreal should serve people's beauty and richness of life by connecting the cultures of Japan and France. Maintaining a strong awareness of the elegance of France, the home of the L'oreal group, and the beauty of Japan, where the new Nihon L'oreal is located, the catalog aims to visualize the worldwide mission of the L'oreal Group: fusing the two cultures, while responding to everyone's desire to be beautiful and to paint their life with happiness.

化粧品輸入・製造・販売
COSMETICS IMPORT, MANUFACTURE & SALES 1996

CL, SB: 日本ロレアル NIHON L'ORÉAL K.K
CD, DF: カレ ノアール ジャパン CARRÉ NOIR JAPAN
AD: 柳澤 篤 Atsushi Yanagisawa
P: 佐野 篤 Atsushi Sano

page 4, 5

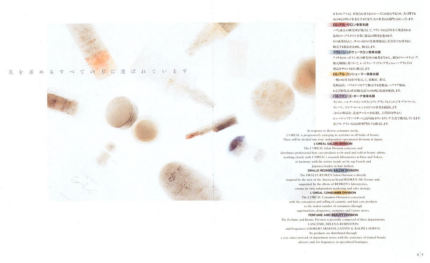

page 8, 9

page 10, 11

98

FASHION: 化粧品 COSMETICS & BODY CARE

Catalog + Web

NIHON L'ORÉAL

www.nihon-loreal.co.jp

1997年1月、「日本ロレアル」の事業内容や組織をより深く理解してもらうためにウェブ版の会社案内を作ろうという意図の元にオープンしました。既にオープンされていた内外の化粧品会社や他業種の膨大な数のサイトを参考に、"化粧品会社である「日本ロレアル」の企業イメージを損なうことのないエレガントなビジュアルにすること"、"動画など重いものは最小限に留め、負荷の大きすぎないユーザーにやさしいサイト、構築が複雑でなく見やすいサイトであること" などを念頭に制作を行いました。1999年4月にリニューアルを行い、現在の形になりました。

The Nihon L'oreal Web site, designed to explain in detail the company's business and organization, made its debut in January 1997. After close examination of a great number of other Web sites, of domestic and foreign cosmetics companies, as well as those of companies from other industries, the site was designed with the following always in mind: First, an elegant visual presentation must not detract from the corporate image of Nihon L'oreal. And the site should be easy for the user to navigate, with a minimum of animation and other graphics that take time to appear on screen. The site underwent a complete renewal in April 1999.

化粧品輸入・製造・販売
COSMETICS IMPORT, MANUFACTURE & SALES
1997 (renewed in 1999)

CL, SB: 日本ロレアル NIHON L'ORÉAL K.K
CD: 日本ロレアル コーポレート・コミュニケーション部
Corporate Communications, NIHON L'ORÉAL
DF: オフィス タント Office TANTO
※2000年7月11日現在のデータを使用 As of July 11, 2000

FASHION: 化粧品 COSMETICS & BODY CARE

製品リリース ライブラリ Products Information

新製品ニュース New Products Information

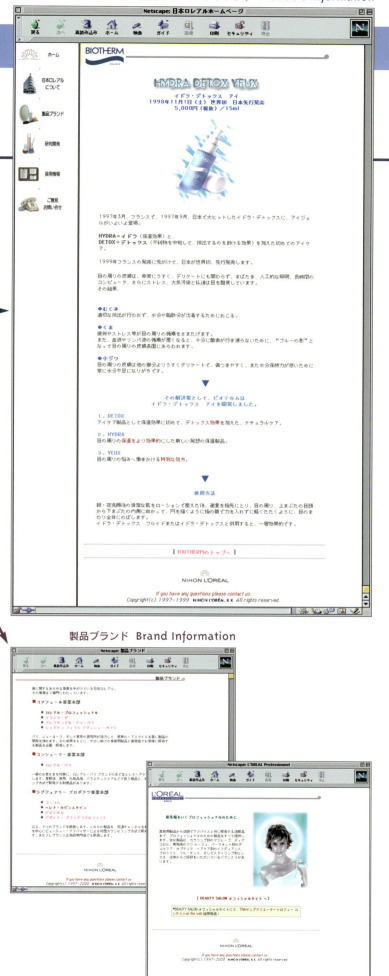

製品ブランド Brand Information

Catalog + Web

L'ORÉAL PARIS

www.loreal-paris.net

- Splash Page
- Top
- ロレアルパリ最前線　the forefront
- 知られざるロレアルパリ　the secret
- ロレアルパリの顔　the spokes person
- ロレアルパリ ザ・コレクション　the collection
- ロレアルパリ的ビューティー講座　the beauty lesson
- What's New
- Present

Splash Page

Top

What's New

世界で初めてモードを意識した本格的なヘアカラーリングを誕生させたロレアル パリの過去、現在、未来の真の姿を、さまざまな角度からアクセス＆分析しています。ページ内では、ロレアル パリのイメージとして、ケイト・モスやアンディ・マクドゥエル、クラウディア・シファー、そして日本のスポークスパーソンたちを一気にご紹介。「ビューティ講座」では、記事やエッセイ、セレブインタビュー等、毎月楽しみながら美容知識を学ぶことができます。また、カンヌ映画祭裏話やアイテムのご紹介、ロレアル パリ製品プレゼント等、見所は満載です。

The Web site of L'oreal Paris, the company that first invented hair coloring with a true fashion consciousness. Various aspects of L'oreal Paris' past, current, and future were analyzed. The site has pages that introduce many of L'oreal Paris' image spokespersons, such as Kate Moss, Andie MacDowell, and Claudia Schiffer, as well as Japanese spokespersons. In the "Beauty Class" corner, customers can learn about beauty by enjoying articles, essays, and interviews with celebrities. There are also entertaining, behind-the-scenes stories from the Cannes Film Festival, product showcases, and giveaways of L'oreal Paris products.

化粧品，香水，トイレタリー剤，美容および頭髪化粧品の輸入・製造・販売およびマーケティング
IMPORT, MANUFACTURING, SALES & MARKETING OF COSMETICS, FRAGRANCES, TOILETRIES & HAIR CARE PRODUCTS 1999

CL: 日本ロレアル　NIHON L'ORÉAL K.K.
CD: Doris Lee
AD: 南 英樹　Hideki Minami
CW, PLANNER: 渡辺佳子　Keiko Watanabe
SB: ロレアル パリ　L'ORÉAL PARIS
※2000年7月11日現在のデータを使用　As of July 11, 2000

FASHION: 化粧品 COSMETICS & BODY CARE

Catalog + Web

THE BODY SHOP

8ツ折 Eightfold／93×225mm
(開いた状態 When fully unfolded：372×450mm)

ザ・ボディショップは、アニータ・ロディックが、1976年英国に第一号店を開店して以来、世界中の女性、男性、子供から大人までご愛用頂ける、自然の原料をベースにしたスキンケア・ヘアケア製品、メイクアップ製品を販売しているお店です。

In the years since Anita Roddick opened her first store in England in 1976, the Body Shop has become well-loved by men, women, and children around the world as a store that sells skin and hair products, and cosmetics, made from natural ingredients.

輸入化粧品販売 INPORT COSMETICS SALES 2000

CL, SB: イオンフォレスト AEON FOREST CO., LTD
CD: 森岩拓子 (DNPメディアクリエイト)
Takuko Moriiwa (DNP MEDIA CREATE Co., Ltd.)
AD: 野上貴志 (ディー・ツウ) Takashi Nogami (d2 inc.)
D: 太田芳絵 (ディー・ツウ) Yoshie Ota (d2 inc.)
P: 中津 粋 (DNPメディアクリエイト) Kiyoshi Nakatsu (DNP MEDIA CREATE Co., Ltd.)
CW: 常松伸子 Nobuko Tsunematsu

front

back

Catalog + Web

THE BODY SHOP

the-body-shop.co.jp

FASHION: 化粧品 COSMETICS & BODY CARE

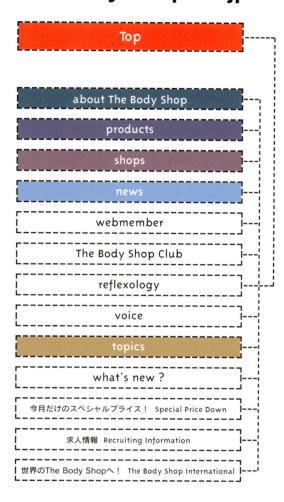

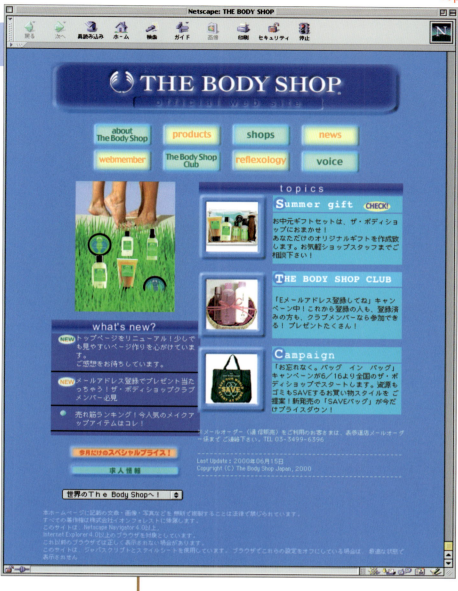

2000年3月の日経ウェブサイト ブランドランキングで12位を頂きました！ホームページでは、プレゼントやモニター募集の企画をどんどん行い、占いやクイズなど楽しいページ作りを目指しています。トップページは季節に合わせて背景の色、デザインを変えたり、新しさを強調するため、フラッシュムービーで新商品をアピールしています。きれいなページを作成しようとすると、画像が増え、データが重くなってしまうため、デザインとデータの大きさのバランスを取るのに苦労しています。

This site ranked 12th in the March 2000 "Nikkei Web site Brand Ranking." With features such as present giveaways, invitations to become a monitor, fortune telling and quizzes, it aims to be a very entertaining site. The top page uses background colors to match the season, page design is continually changing, and Flash movies are used to introduce new products and to keep the site looking fresh. Creating a beautiful page often requires a large number of images and heavy data, so I am always trying hard to find the right balance between design and data.

輸入化粧品販売 INPORT COSMETICS SALES 2000

CL, SB: イオンフォレスト AEON FOREST CO., LTD
CD, D: 本山美保 Miho Motoyama
CD: 大国幸代 (DNPデジタルコム)
Yukiyo Ohkuni (DNP DIGITALCOM Co., Ltd.)
D: 阿久戸 七重 (DNPデジタルコム)
Nanae Akuto (DNP DIGITALCOM Co., Ltd.)
SB: DNPデジタルコム DNP DIGITALCOM Co., Ltd.

※2000年7月11日現在のデータを使用 As of July 11, 2000

Catalog + Web
THE BODY SHOP

Top

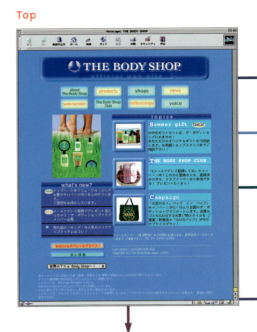

about The Body Shop

shops

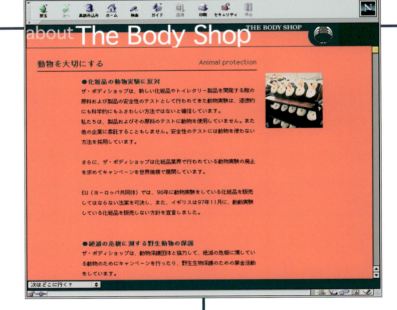

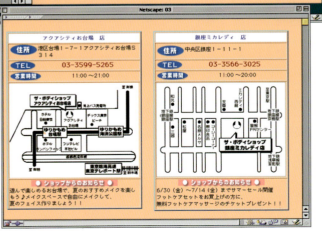

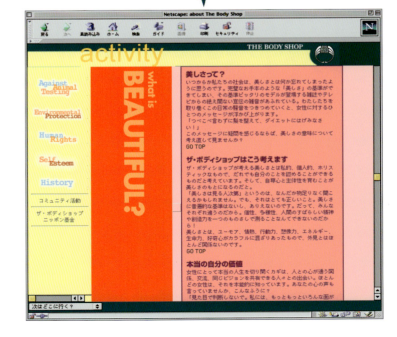

※2000年7月4日現在のデータを使用 As of July 4, 2000

FASHION: 化粧品　COSMETICS & BODY CARE

news

products

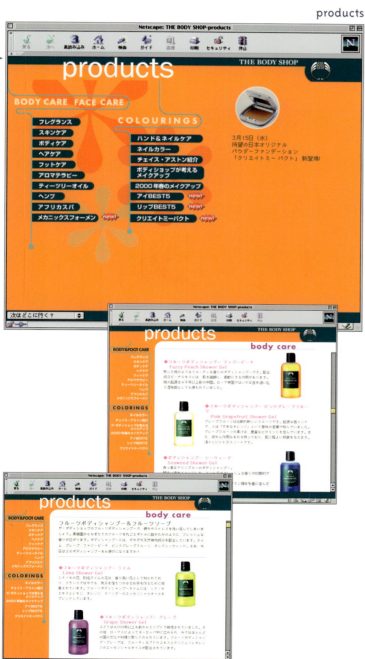

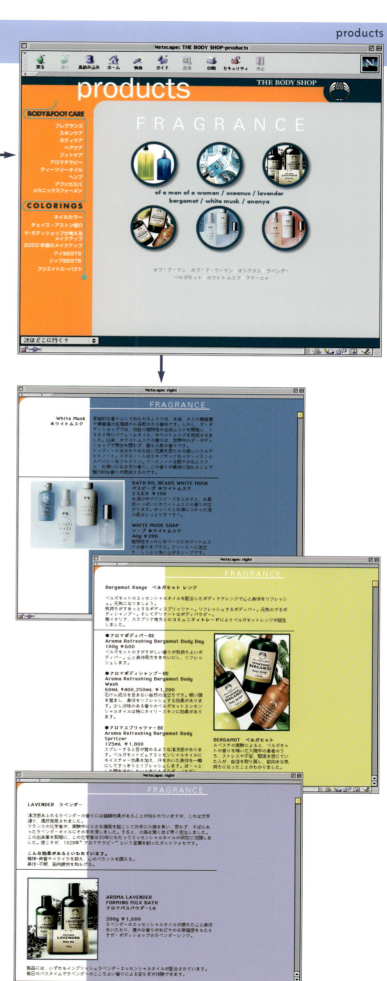

Catalog + Web

Kanebo COSMETICS

kcs.kanebo.co.jp/KC/KCN.htm

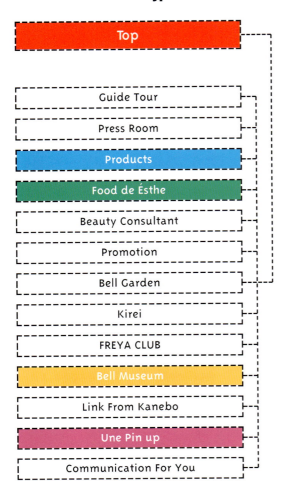
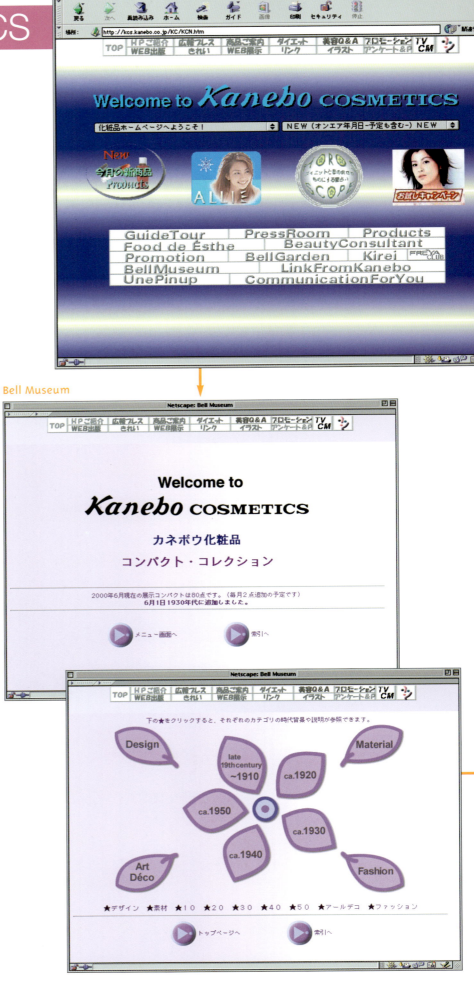

Top

Bell Museum

カネボウ化粧品の商品情報の提供を主目的としています。アクセス件数を分析して、人気のあるページを拡充してきました。新商品（最新3ヶ月分）や、春秋のプロモーション、商品データベースなどに注力する結果になっています。コンテンツを美しくみせるため、イメージを多用。イメージのため、ホームページ表示が遅くなるので、ファイルの軽量化を心掛けています。また、化粧品イメージキャラクター（藤原紀香など）のTVCFオンエアに合わせて、タイムリーに、ホームページにも、関連コンテンツを掲載するようしています。

This Web site's main purpose is to provide information about Kanebo Cosmetics products. By analyzing numbers of accesses to the site, we have been expanding the most popular pages. This has resulted in our focusing on pages such as New Products (from the last three months), spring and summer promotions, and our product database. In order to make the pages look as beautiful as possible, many images are used. To avoid delays in appearance of images, we have tried to make files as small as possible. In addition, when TV commercials are aired using personalities such as Norika Fujiwara, related information is also provided on the Web site in a timely manner.

FASHION: 化粧品 COSMETICS & BODY CARE

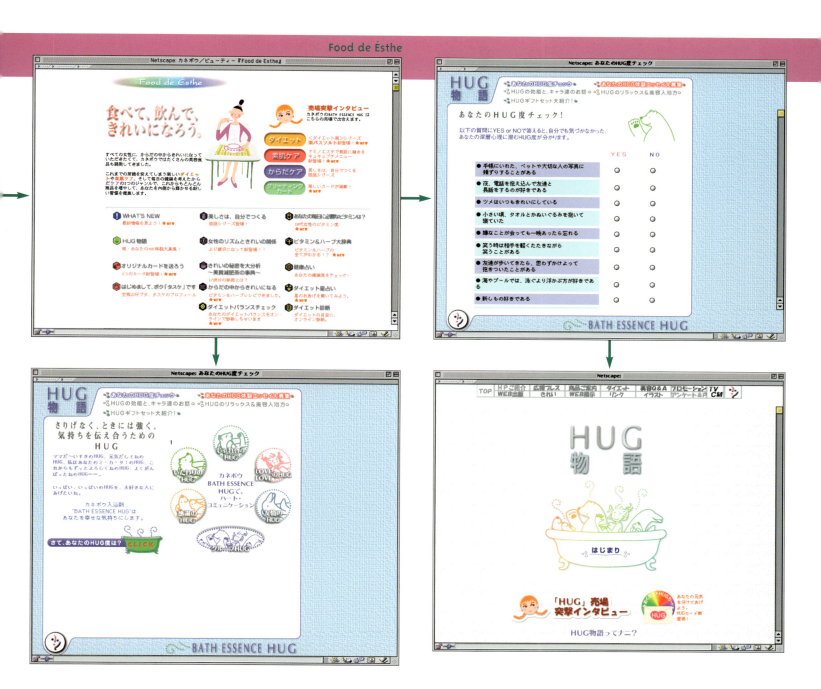

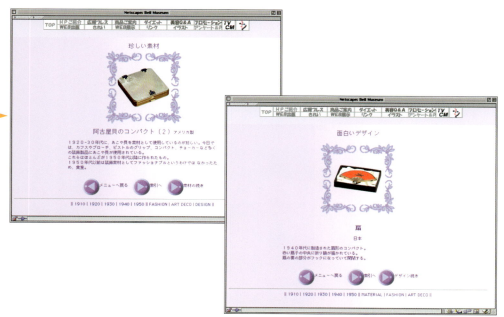

化粧品製造・販売
COSMETICS MANUFACTURE & SALES 2000

CL, SB: 鐘紡 カネボウ化粧品本部
Kanebo.LTD. COSMETICS DIVISION
CD, AD: 林 哲夫 (ウェブマスター)
Tetsuo Hayashi (Web Master) - Top Page
D: 林 哲夫 (ウェブマスター)
Tetsuo Hayashi (Web Master) - Out of Diet Page
DF: 安立デザイン事務所 ANRYU DESIGN - Diet Page
※2000年7月5日現在のデータを使用 As of July 5, 2000

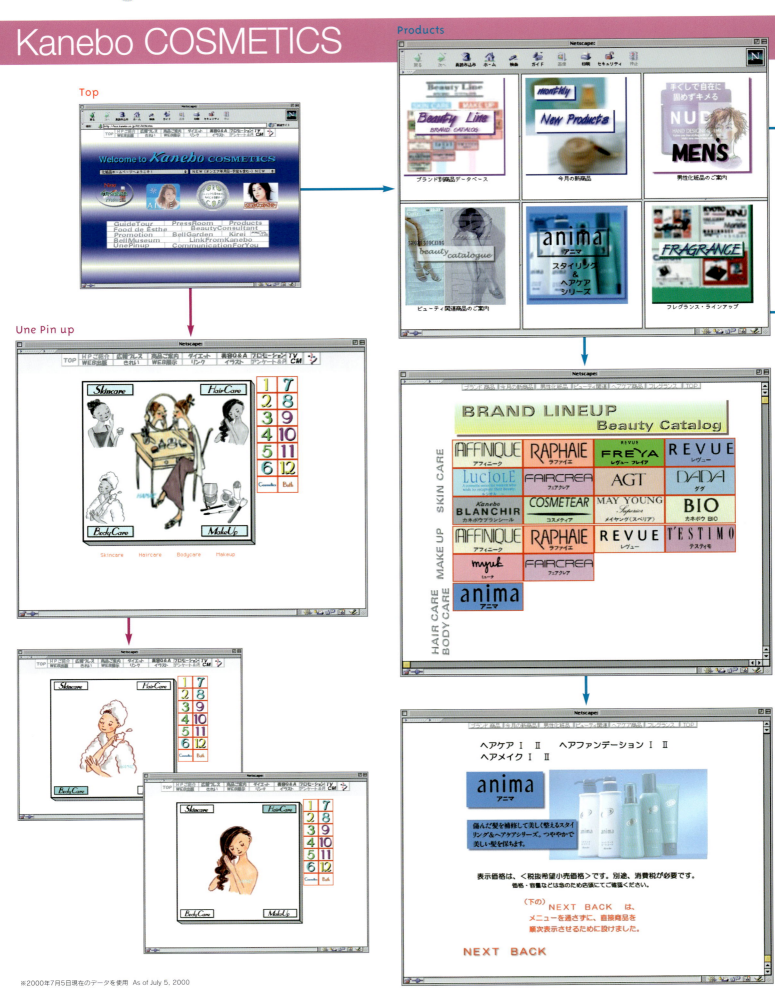

FASHION: 化粧品　COSMETICS & BODY CARE

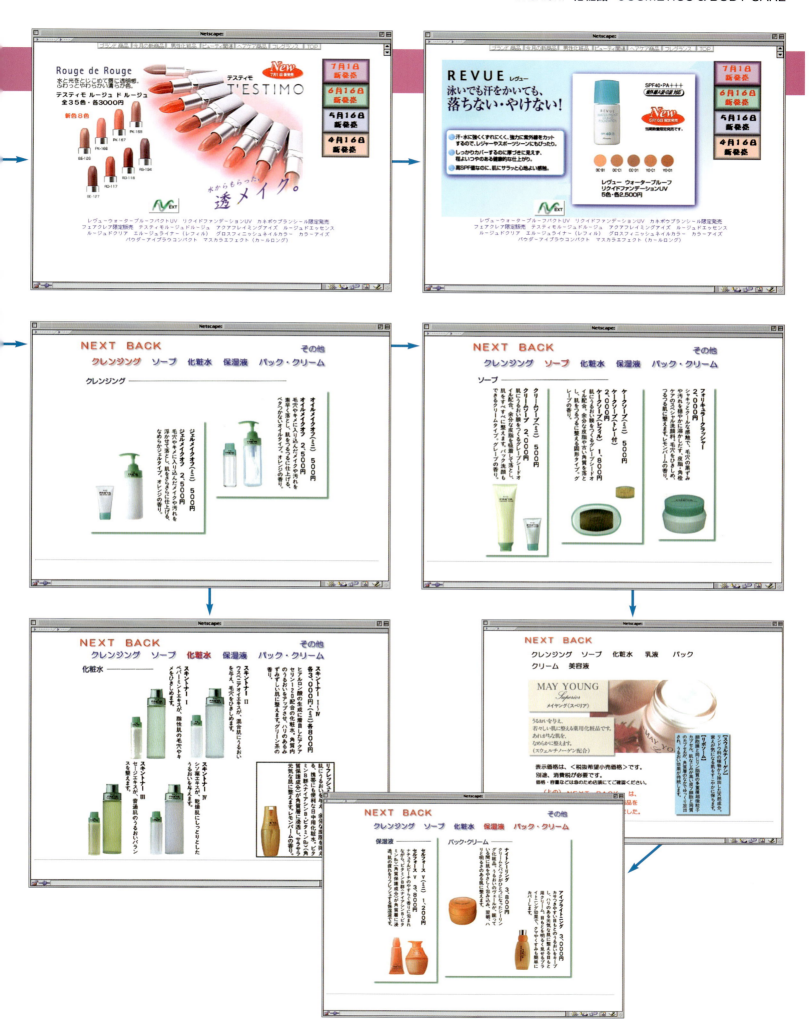

Catalog + Web

MAX FACTOR SK-II

中綴 Stapled in the center／109×184mm

クリアな素肌へ導く、SK-IIのブランドリーフレットです。自然酵母の発酵の過程から生まれたSK-IIの良さを、わかりやすく伝えることに注力して制作しました。SK-IIの持つブランドイメージを大切にしつつ、製品情報までも網羅した紹介パンフレットです。そこでトーン＆マナーとして、①科学的な背景をもつ製品であること。②クリアな素肌をイメージさせること。の2点を、冷たい印象になりすぎないように注意しながら表現しました。

A leaflet that was designed to focus on communicating the benefits of SK-II, a cosmetic for clear skin created by a yeast fermentation process. Paying careful attention to the SK-II brand image, the pamphlet includes detailed product information. The two concepts were that the product has a scientific background, and that clear skin is an important part of the product image. The tone and manner express these concepts in a way that will not leave a cold impression.

化粧品製造・販売
COSMETICS MANUFACTURE & SALES 1999

CL, SB: マックス ファクター MAX FACTOR
CD, CW: 岡田英子 Eiko Okada
AD: 下原秀夫 Hideo Shimohara
D: 冨本成輝 Shigeki Tomimoto／北村誠英 Orihide Kitamura
DF: ジャム・アソシエーツ JAM ASSOCIATES

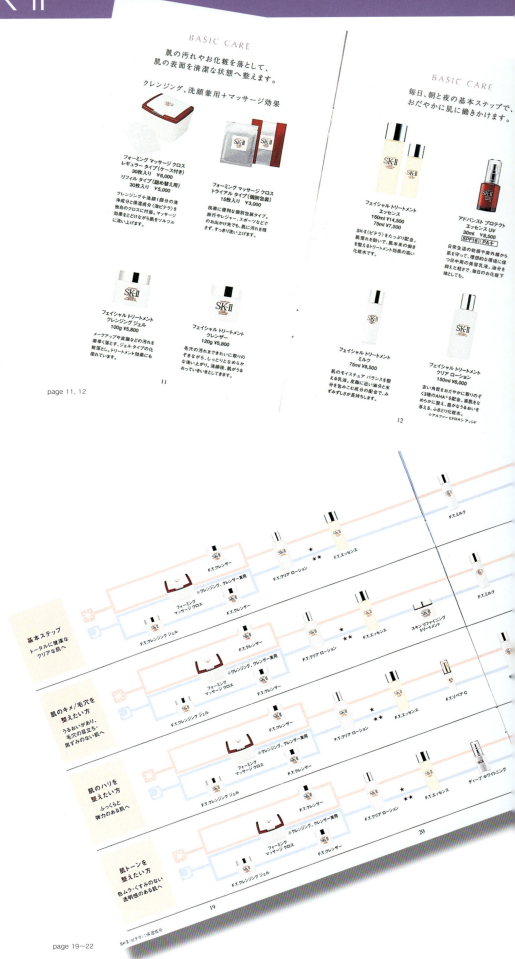

FASHION: 化粧品　COSMETICS & BODY CARE

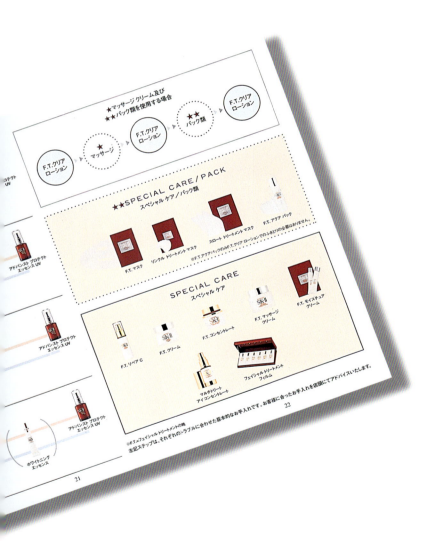

美味しそうに香る発酵の不思議なちから。

ヨーグルトやチーズ、ワイン、ビール、そしてパン類など、発酵という工程を通して生まれてきた発酵食品たち。どれも作りたての時ほど、発酵仕立ての生きた香りはのかに残っていて、とっても美味しそう。そう思うのは、発酵そのものが、酵母や乳酸菌などの微生物の生命活動を利用して、人間に有用な物質を作ってきたから。またそれを私たちの身体が知っていたからかもしれません。

その発酵と酵母にSK-Ⅱが着目したのは、日本の酒蔵でお酒を造る杜氏さんたちの美しい肌に出会ったことから始まります。日本酒はヨーグルトやワインと同じ発酵食品。その発酵をうながす杜氏さんの手の肌はみな、うるおいに満ちて、とても美しかったのです。

page 1, 2

素肌になじみやすいのは酵母と肌が似ていたから。

自然酵母と発酵。SK-Ⅱ〈ピテラ〉はヨーグルトやチーズと同じように、発酵によって生まれてきた自然酵母の発酵代謝液。素肌になじみやすいのは、身体に有用な栄養分を運んでくれる発酵だけの力ではなく、酵母も人間の身体と深いかかわりを持っているから。もともと私たちの身体はいくつもの細胞の集合体。その祖先が、人間の細胞と同じ真核細胞に属している酵母といわれています。また酵母が発酵する過程は私たちの素肌がみずから美しくなろうとする肌細胞の代謝リズムと、とてもよく似ています。だから素肌になじみやすく、足りないものを補いながら素肌本来の働きを整えます。無理なくクリアな素肌へと導くことができるのです。

肌細胞とSK-Ⅱ酵母の類似性

自然酵母と発酵から生まれた生命のエッセンスSK-Ⅱ〈ピテラ〉。

SK-Ⅱ〈ピテラ〉は、ビタミン類やミネラル、アミノ酸、タンパク質などをバランスよく含んでいます。肌に生きた成分を届けることができるから季節や年齢、肌質を問わずに、肌にやさしく働きかけます。

SK-Ⅱ〈ピテラ〉による効果	
水分補給・保持作用	肌の角質層にスムーズに浸透しうるおいを与える
基本の働きを整える作用	健康な肌をつとめ自然に働きかける
肌のキメを整える作用	肌のキメを整えるなめらかにする
pH調整作用	pHを弱酸性の正常な状態へ整える

肌の求める成分をバランスよく含んでいます。

page 3, 4

FACIAL TREATMENT MASK
フェイシャル トリートメントマスク

気持ちまでリラックスするSK-Ⅱ〈ピテラ〉のうるおいパック。

小じわ、肌荒れの原因となる乾燥やカサつき。シミ・ソバカスの原因となる日焼けなどを、素肌に少しでも感じたら、SK-Ⅱ〈ピテラ〉のパックで、素早くうるおいケア。顔全体にSK-Ⅱ〈ピテラ〉をたっぷり実感させること約5分間。素肌以上に気持ちまでリラックスしてきたら、心のトリートメントまで完了です。

〈ご使用法〉
マスクを目の部分からあてがい、指先で顔全体にフィットさせます。約5分間、マスクを取ります。肌に残った液はコットンでふきとります。

page 9, 10

Catalog + Web

MAX FACTOR SK-II

www.sk2.com/

Splash Page

Splash Page 2

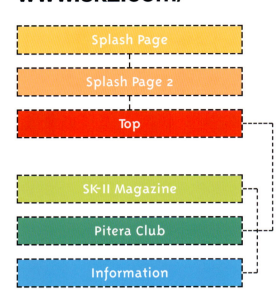

Top

高級化粧品ブランド、「SK-II」のサイト。毎月更新のマガジン型サイトとして独自取材による記事を掲載していますが、コンセプトとしてはマーケティングおよびプロモーション連動サイトとして位置づけています。立ち上げ当初のサンプルプレゼントによるアンケートでは、約5万名の応募者から化粧品関連の情報を集めました。またヴァーチャルとリアルを連動させる試みとして、サイト上で肌診断を行い、結果をプリントアウトして実店舗に持って行くとカウンセリングが受けられるキャンペーンを実施し、新規顧客獲得に成果をあげています。

The Web site of SK-II, a high-quality cosmetics brand. Created as a magazine-like site, updated monthly with original articles, the site is closely linked with marketing and promotional activities. For example, the survey taken with the sample giveaway promotion conducted at the time of the Web site launch collected cosmetics-related information from approximately 50,000 applicants. Additionally, as one of the experiments to link the virtual world with the real one, the site is offering a skin test as part of a promotional campaign, wherein customers can print the specified Web page and bring it to an actual shop to receive counseling. This has been a successful way of acquiring new customers.

化粧品製造・販売
COSMETICS MANUFACTURE & SALES 1999

CL, SB: マックス ファクター MAX FACTOR
CD, D, PR, CODING: ティビーエス・ブリタニカ
TBS-BRITANNICA Co., Ltd.
AD: 森 治樹 (アゾーン アンド アソシエーツ)
Haruki Mori (Azone+Associates)
※2000年7月11日現在のデータを使用 As of July 11, 2000

FASHION: 化粧品 COSMETICS & BODY CARE

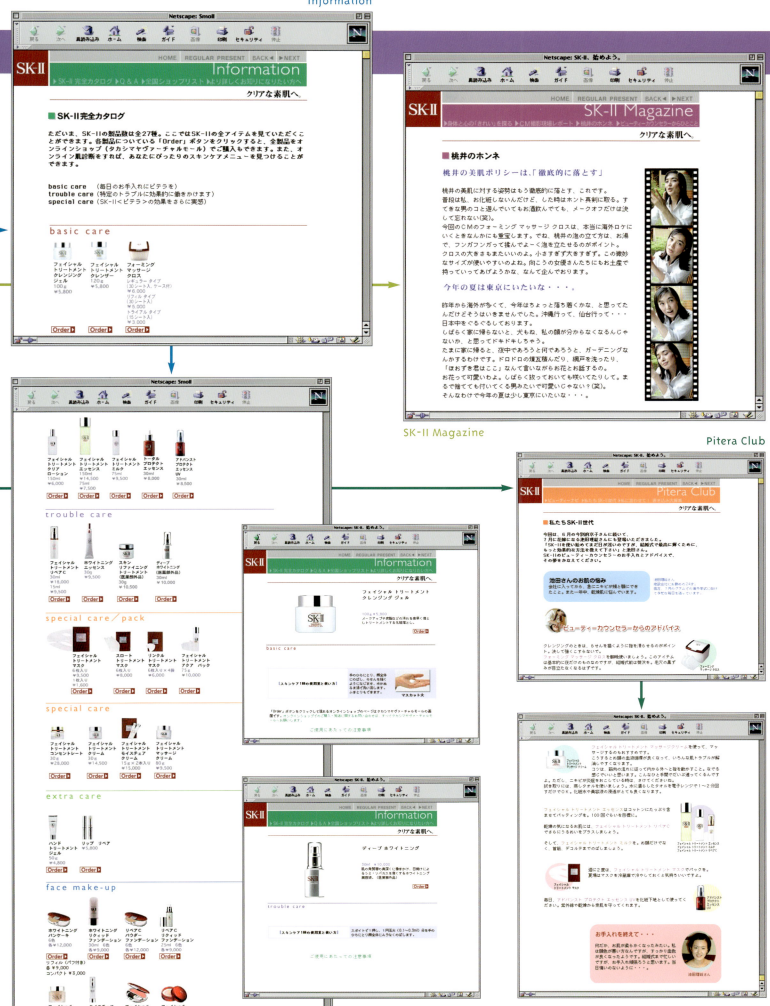

Catalog + Web

BARNEYS NEW YORK

www.barneys.co.jp

- Splash Page
  - Top
    - SPRING 2000 SPORTSWEAR COLLECTION
    - WHAT'S NEW
    - INFORMATION
    - STORES
    - WINDOW DISPLAY
    - HUMAN RESOURCES

バーニーズ ニューヨークの日本店舗（新宿・横浜店）を紹介するホームページ。商品やウィンドウディスプレイの写真等を通じて、バーニーズテイストを発信しています。又、来日デザイナーのトランクショーや、セール情報などのホットなニュースもタイムリーにアップ。シンプルでクオリティの高いバーニーズ ニューヨークの広告クリエイティヴデザインを、ここでも踏襲しています。

This site introduces the Barneys New York stores located in Japan (in Shinjuku and Yokohama). Barneys style is conveyed with photographs of merchandise and window displays. Hot news, such as notice of trunk shows by designers who are visiting Japan, is uploaded on a timely basis, as is sale information. The Web site also follows Barneys New York's creative advertising design, simple and high quality.

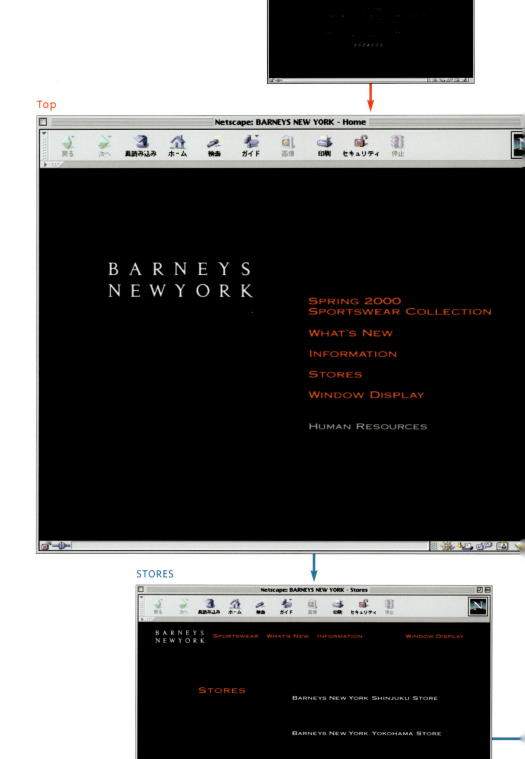

スペシャリティストア　SPECIALITY STORE　1999

CL: バーニーズ ニューヨーク　BARNEYS NEW YORK
CD: バーニーズ ジャパン宣伝部
BARNEYS JAPAN ADVERTISING
AD: 小野 俊太郎　Shuntaro Ono
CW: 小柳二敏　Futoshi Koyanagi
SB: バーニーズ ジャパン　BARNEYS JAPAN CO. LTD
※2000年7月11日現在のデータを使用　As of July 11, 2000

FASHION: 総合 GENERAL FASHION

WHAT'S NEW

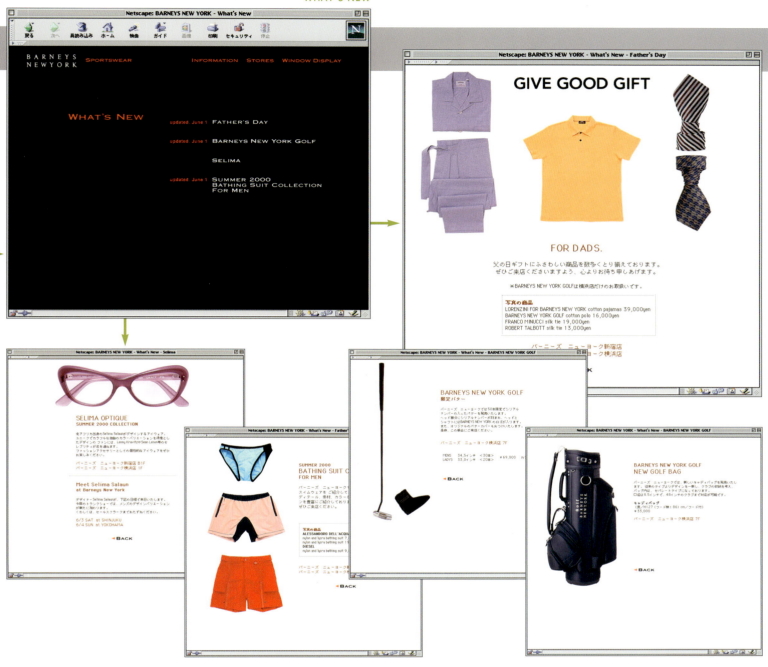
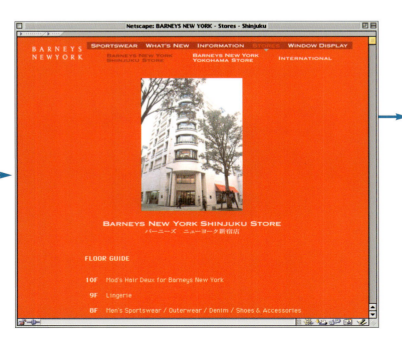
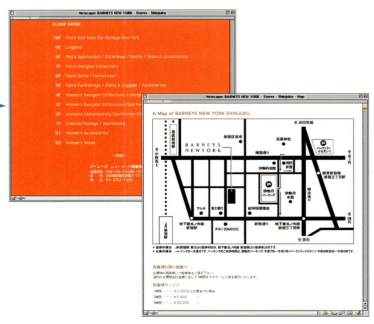

Catalog + Web
BARNEYS NEW YORK

SPRING 2000 SPORTSWEAR COLLECTION

Top

※2000年7月11日現在のデータを使用 As of July 11, 2000

FASHION: 総合 GENERAL FASHION

WINDOW DISPLAY

INFORMATION

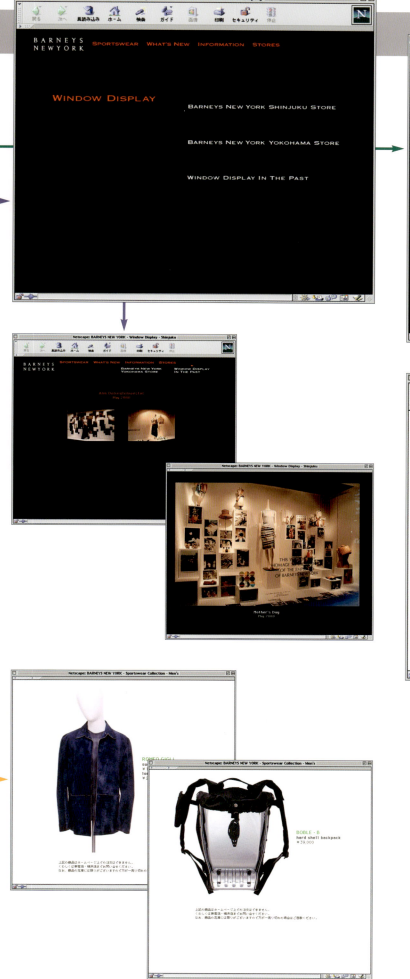
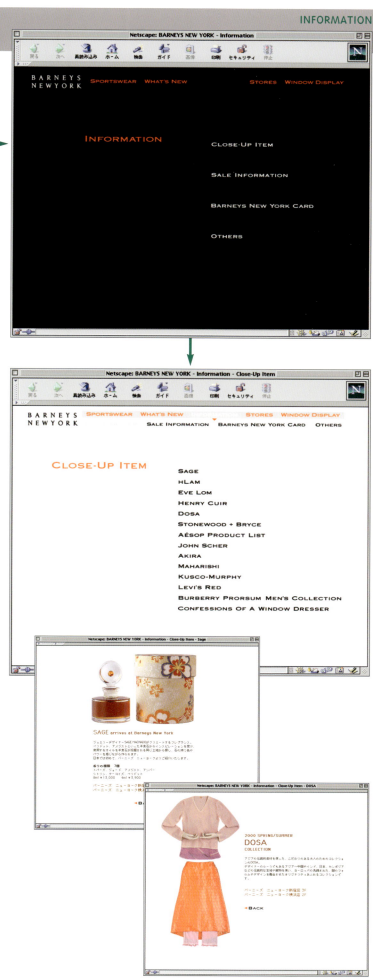

Catalog + Web

LAFORET HARAJUKU

カードセット Set of cards／55×91mm

ラフォーレに来館した人が、来館した瞬間にラフォーレの全ショップの商品を一度に見られることができ、且つ能動的にカードをピックアップするというアクションを起こしてもらうのがコンセプトです。そのために腐心したのが什器まで含めたデザインです。また、良いクライアントの良いデザインで広告用のカードを陳列することにより、カード全体がチャームアップするよう心掛けています。

The concept was that a customer would be able to see at a glance the products carried by every shop in the Laforet fashion building by selecting cards displayed at the entrance. A display unit was even designed specially for this purpose. And by using good designs from good clients on advertising cards, the cards as a whole have more of a charming appeal.

ファッションビル運営
FASION BOUTIQUES MANAGEMENT 2000

CL, SB: ラフォーレ原宿　LAFORET HARAJUKU CO,. LTD
CD: 森 健司 (ラフォーレ)　Kenji Mori (LAFORET)
　　大山ゆかり (ロケットカンパニー)
　　Yukari Ooyama (Rocket Company)
AD: 藤本やすし (キャップ)　Yasushi Fujimoto (Cap)
D: キャップ　Cap
P: 上原たかし　Takashi Uehara (PPI)

120

Catalog + Web

LAFORET HARAJUKU

www.laforet.ne.jp/

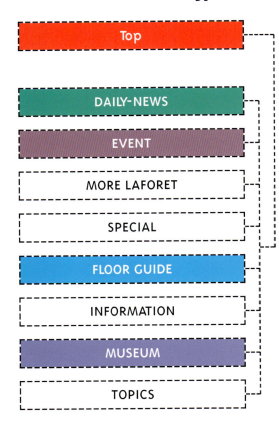

ラフォーレの造りあげてきた「イメージ」を常に意識し、全体的に良質なページデザインを心掛け、また、動きの要素を随所に盛り込むなど、観る側にとって「ラフォーレらしさ」を感じてもらえることに重点を置いています。

Being always conscious about Laforet's established image, we focused on establishing a quality design site by incorporating elements of movement everywhere, to give viewers the Laforet feeling.

ファッションビル運営
FASION BOUTIQUES MANAGEMENT 1999

CL, SB: ラフォーレ原宿 LAFORET HARAJUKU CO,. LTD
CL: ラップネット LAPNET
AD: 勅使河原 一雅 Kazumasa Teshigawara (TOPKNOT)
※2000年7月11日現在のデータを使用 As of July 11, 2000

Top

DAILY-NEWS

FASHION: 総合 GENERAL FASHION

FLOOR GUIDE

EVENT

MUSEUM

Catalog + Web

Spiral

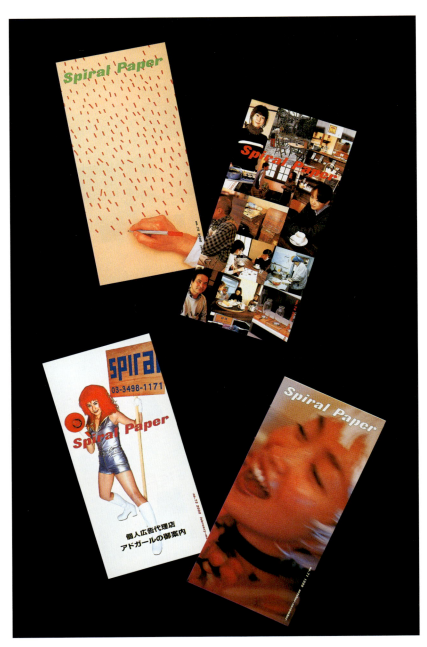

ジャバラ Accordion fold／100×210mm （開いた状態 When fully unfolded：700×210mm）

複合文化施設運営・企画
FASHION BOUTIQUES MANAGEMENT　1999-2000

CL, SB: ワコールアートセンター　Spiral / Wacoal Art Center
AD: 伊丹友広　Tomohiro Itami
D: イット イズ デザイン　It Is Design
P: 市川勝弘　Katsuhiro Ichikawa
CW: カワイイファクトリー　Cawaii Factory

スパイラルペーパーは、スパイラルが隔月で発行している広報誌です。「生活のなかにアートを見る」をコンセプトに、スパイラルからのメッセージ／情報と、アーティストとのコラボレーションによるオリジナルアートワークで構成しています。顧客への郵送とスパイラル館内で配布しています。「もの」や「場所」の提供とともに、人々の様々な出会いが日々生まれる場として活動するスパイラルから、成熟したコミュニケーションこそが都市生活を豊かにしていくということを提案していきたいと考えます。

Spiral Paper is published bimonthly by Spiral, a culture complex. With its concept of "Looking at art in life," it is a quality catalog suggesting possibility of rich urban life with identity. The catalogs are mailed directly to customers, and are also distributed in the Spiral building. Contents include a message from Spiral, information, and original artwork created in collaboration with the artists. Seeing that Spiral offers "things" and "places," and is a place where people meet daily in a variety of ways, we would like to propose that only communication in mature manner will enrich our urban lives.

FASHION: 総合　GENERAL FASHION

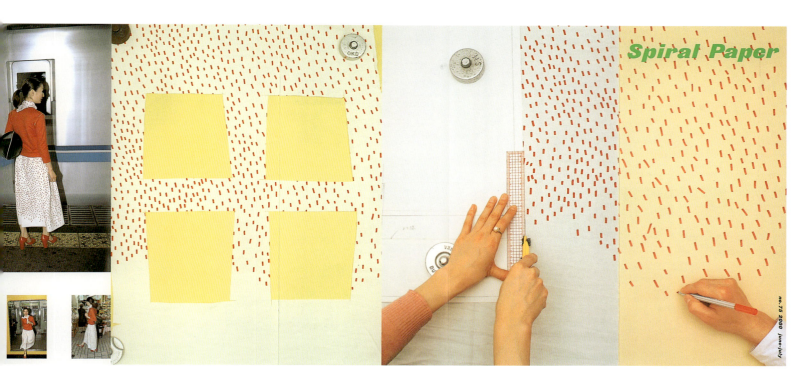

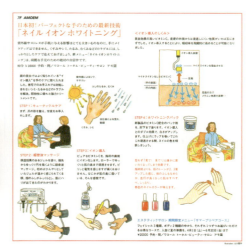

Catalog + Web

Spiral

www.spiral.co.jp/

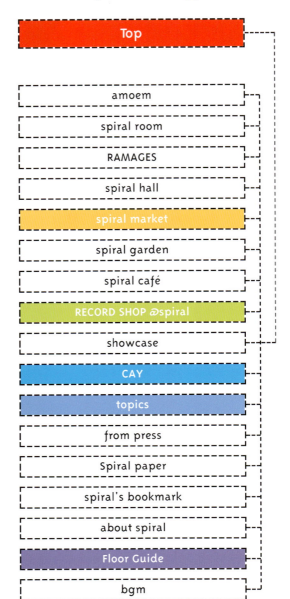

Floor Guide

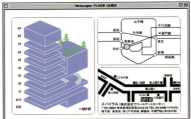

RECORD SHOP @spiral

Top

スパイラルとは、東京南青山にある、現代アートシーンを紹介する複合文化施設です。ホームページではギャラリー、レストラン、生活雑貨ショップなど様々なスタイルで活動するスパイラルをわかりやすく紹介することに力を入れています。イベントや新商品などの館内のニュースを中心に、各フロアの営業を紹介するフロアガイドを基本とした構成にしています。さらに館内スタッフのコラムやインタビューを掲載し、読み物としても楽しめる要素を追加。また、館内のBGMや自社レーベルの音楽を視聴できるページ、期間限定でのBBSを作成するなど、ウェブならではの情報発信／交換の場として幅広い可能性を探っています。2000年10月には、リニューアルを予定。

Spiral, located in Tokyo's popular Minami-Aoyama district, is a culture complex where the latest in the contemporary art scene can be found. The Web site presents the various aspects of Spiral, including galleries, restaurants, and lifestyle accessory shops, in a clear and simple manner. The Web site takes the form of a floor guide; priority is given to upcoming events and new products, and Spiral staff columns and interviews add entertaining reading elements. We are always looking for ways to make the site the type of place for information dissemination and exchange that can only be found on the Web, such as including pages where one can listen to the complex's BGM and music from Spiral's own label, and a limited-time BBS. There are plans to renovate the site in October 2000.

FASHION: 総合 GENERAL FASHION

spiral market

CAY

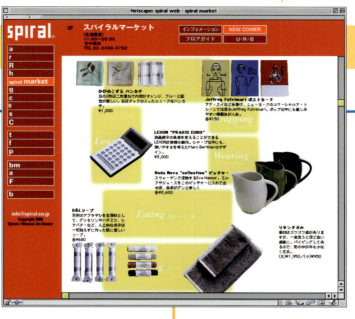

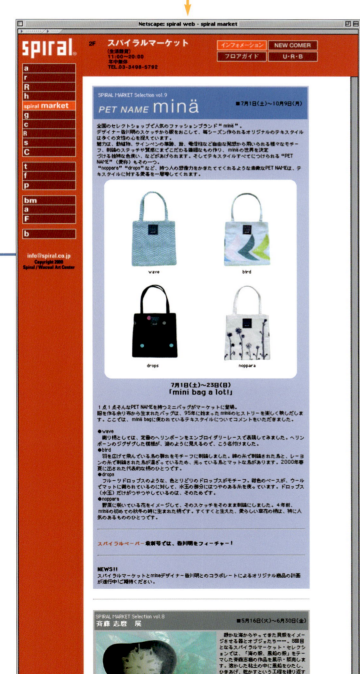

topics

複合文化施設運営・企画
FASHION BOUTIQUES MANAGEMENT 1999

CL, SB: ワコールアートセンター Spiral / Wacoal Art Center
CD: 尾島由郎 Yoshio Ojima
AD, D: 武者小路 実政 Sanemasa Mushakoji
CW: 榊原輝子 Teruko Sakakibara

※2000年7月13日現在のデータを使用 As of July 13, 2000

Catalog + Web

不二家

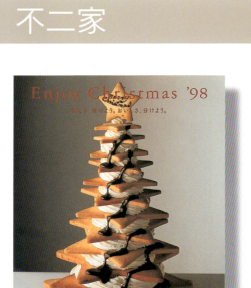

中綴 Stapled in the center／210×265mm

みんなが揃ったら切り分けるケーキ。ひときれの幸せを分け与えるファミリークリスマス。その真ん中に不二家のクリスマスケーキ。30度を越す真夏の撮影、冷蔵設備のないフランスのスタジオ。毎日市場で新鮮なイチゴの買い出し、突然の停電。果たして冷蔵庫の生クリームは大丈夫か？エビアンの硬水でジェリーは固まるか、ケーキの目を出すための特別仕様のカッターをどう作るか。すべてケーキとの戦いでした。それを見事にフランスのカメラマンはこなしてくれました。

Cake to be served when everyone gets together. A family Christmas that shares a slice of happiness. In the center, there is Fujiya's Christmas cake. Shooting this photo was really a battle with the cake: A mid-summer photo session with temperatures exceeding 30 degrees Centigrade, in a French studio with no air conditioning. Buying fresh strawberries every day at the market; sudden power failures. Is the cream in the refrigerator OK? Will the jelly harden if we use mineral water? How can we best show delicate holes of the sponge cake? The French photographer solved all of these problems splendidly.

洋菓子製造・販売　CONFECTIONERY 1998

CL: 不二家　FUJIYA Co., Ltd.
CD, AD: 阿部 博　Hiroshi Abe
D: 深澤幸子　Sachiko Fukasawa
P: Jean Jouis Bloch-Laine
CW: 佐藤宏史　Hirofumi Sato
SB: 阿部博デザイン事務所　Hiroshi Abe Design Office

page 13, 14

page 17, 18

FOOD: 菓子　CONFECTIONERY

page 1, 2

page 5, 6

page 15, 16

Catalog + Web

不二家

www.fujiya-peko.co.jp/

- Splash Page
- Top
- ペコちゃんサマーグッズ　PEKO GOODS
- まっ赤なミニ冷蔵庫プレゼント　Present
- Peko Mints
- ミルキーハッピークローバー　Milky Happy Clover
- GOTHAM DELI
- CMコレクション　CM Collection
- ペコポコランド　Peko Poko Land
- Good F series
- Recommended
- Quick access
- What's new
- PEKOTOWN WALKER

ペコちゃん、ポコちゃんでおなじみの不二家の公式ホームページです。不二家のお店でお買い上げいただけるケーキの数々、スーパー、コンビニでお求めいただけるチョコレート、キャンディ等、そして様々なキャンペーン等、耳よりな情報がいっぱいです。さらにペコちゃんの歴史やプロフィール、ペコちゃんグッズの数々もご覧いただけます。お菓子が大好きな方、ペコちゃんファンの方必見のこのサイト、ぜひ一度遊びに来て下さい。ペコちゃんが皆様をご案内いたします。

The official site of Fujiya, known for their characters Peko-chan and Poko-chan. The site provides information about the varieties of cakes that can be purchased at Fujiya shops, and the chocolates and candy available at convenience stores, as well as event information. Additionally, Peko-chan's history and profile, as well as character goods, can be viewed. We invite everyone who likes candy, and of course Peko-chan's fans, to come visit the site. Peko-chan will be your guide.

洋菓子製造・販売　CONFECTIONERY 1997

CL, SB: 不二家　FUJIYA Co., Ltd.

※2000年7月5日現在のデータを使用　As of July 5, 2000

Splash Page

Top

ペコポコランド　Peko Poko Land

FOOD: 菓子 CONFECTIONERY

Recommended

Peko Mints

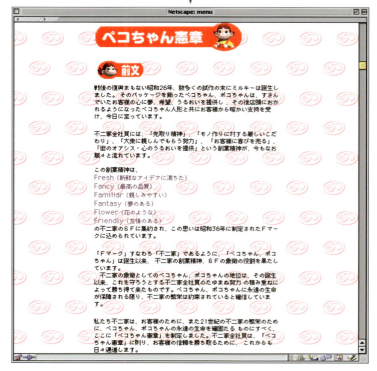

Catalog + Web

不二家

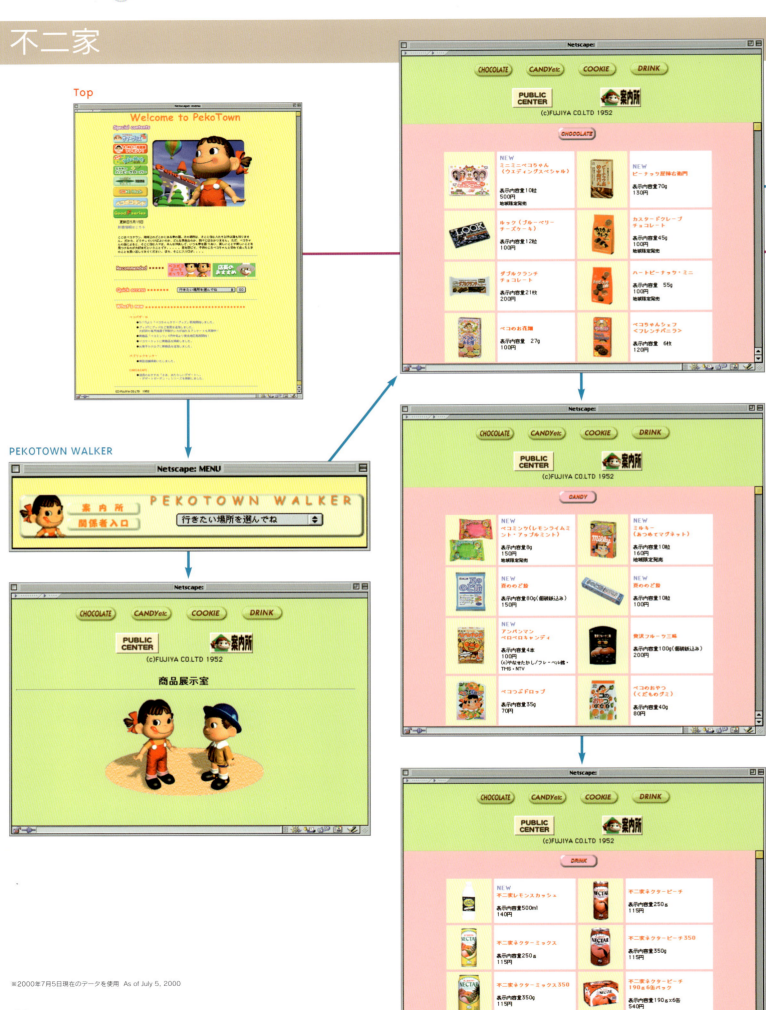

※2000年7月5日現在のデータを使用 As of July 5, 2000

FOOD: 菓子 CONFECTIONERY

Catalog + Web

Morozoff

中綴 Stapled in the center／116×220mm

モロゾフは「ロマンのあるスイーツ」を企業テーマとし、各種洋菓子の製造・販売を通して、豊かな暮らしの提案を行っております。スイーツにそそぐ限りない愛情、積み重ねた伝統。深い思いとともに丹精込めて作り上げたモロゾフのスイーツは、人々の暮らしに素敵なひとときを演出します。そんなスイーツがいっぱい詰まった2000 SPRING SUMMER COLLECTIONカタログ。商品カタログとしての商品の見やすさ、選びやすさはもちろんのこと、各商品の特徴を最大に表現し、スイーツの美味しさがお客様に少しでもお伝えできればと工夫をしております。

Morozoff's corporate theme is "Romantic Sweets," proposing a rich lifestyle through the manufacture and sale of various kinds of confectionery. Unlimited love of sweets, and years of tradition. Morozoff's sweets, created with care and years of experience, will help stage wonderful moments in people's lives. The "2000 Spring Summer Collection" catalog is full of such sweets. The catalog was created with consideration given to presentation of products and ease of product selection, as well as to detailed explanations of each product's distinctive qualities, trying to communicate the deliciousness of the sweets to our customers.

洋菓子製造・販売 CONFECTIONERY 2000

CL, SB: モロゾフ Morozoff Ltd.
CD: 三浦啓子 (モロゾフ) Keiko Miura (Morozoff Ltd.)
AD: 林 政司 (ヴィイ) Masashi Hayashi (VIE INC.)
D: 多田裕子 (ヴィイ) Yuko Tada (VIE INC.)
P: 山田 案希良 (スタジオジャップス) Akira Yamada (STUDIO JAPS)
CW: 京田義久 (ヴィイ) Yoshihisa Kyoda (VIE INC.)

FOOD: 菓子 CONFECTIONERY

自然の豊かな風味と
香ばしさ。やさしい甘さに
包まれる、くつろぎの時間。

ARCADIA
アルカディア

GOURMET SWEETS
グルメスイーツ

目持ちのするケーキ
ブロードランド

GIFT SELECTION
ブロードランド詰合せ

Catalog + Web

Morozoff

www.morozoff.co.jp/

1931年、神戸で創業以来、洋菓子の製造販売をしてきたモゾロフ(株)の公式サイトです。企業テーマである「ロマンのあるスイーツ」を軸に、単なる商品紹介にとどめずに、商品開発にかける意気込み、こだわりといったものまでお伝えできるよう心がけています。インターネットの持ち味の双方向通信を生かし、文字、画像、音声の活用によって、タイムリーな情報提供を行い、インターネットならではの構成を目指しています。女性の訪問が多いのも特徴で、これからも女性に喜ばれるデザイン、画面、ページ構成となるよう努めます。

The official site of Morozoff Co., Ltd., a manufacturer and retailer of confectionery founded in Kobe in 1931. Based on the company's theme of "Romantic Sweets," the site tries to convey the company's enthusiasm and particularity regarding product development. By utilizing the type of interactive communication that is possible with the Internet, timely information is provided using characters, images and sounds. We try to develop our site with designs, views and page structures that appeal to women, who comprise the majority of visitors to our site.

洋菓子製造・販売　CONFECTIONERY 2000

CL, SB: モロゾフ　Morozoff Ltd.
CD: 高木英智 (モロゾフ)　Hidetomo Takagi (Morozoff Ltd.)
AD: 荻野 優 (モロゾフ)　Masaru Ogino (Morozoff Ltd.)
D: 畑 智子 (パワー・インタラクティブ)
Tomoko Hata (Power Interactive Corp.)
CW: 山名恵子 (パワー・インタラクティブ)
Keiko Yamana (Power Interactive Corp.)

※2000年7月11日現在のデータを使用　As of July 11, 2000

FOOD: 菓子 CONFECTIONERY

Online Sweets Boutique

Spring Summer Collection 2000

Sweets of Romance

Catalog +Web

HENRI CHARPENTIER

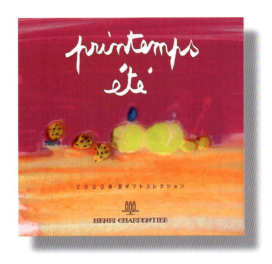

中綴・シート
Stapled in the center・Sheet

中綴 Stapled in the center／150×150mm
シート Sheet／140×140mm

アンリ・シャルパンティエがめざす商品づくりの基本、それは「本物の探究」と表現することができるでしょう。売れることだけを考えて、本当によいものをつくるために必要なことを見逃したり、妥協したりするのではなく「いいものを最良の状態でつくりだし、それを認めてくださるお客様にお届けしたい」。これがアンリ・シャルパンティエの考え方です。

Henri Charpentier's basic concept regarding the making of their products is, "the spirit of inquiry for that which is real." Thinking only about sales can lead one to compromise or overlook something essential. Henri Charpentier strives to create good things of the highest quality possible, for the sake of those customers who appreciate our philosophy.

洋菓子製造・販売／カフェ
CONFECTIONERY/CAFE 2000

CL, SB: アンリ・シャルパンティエ
HENRI CHARPENTIER CO., LTD.
DF: カレノアール CARRENOIR

page 5, 6

 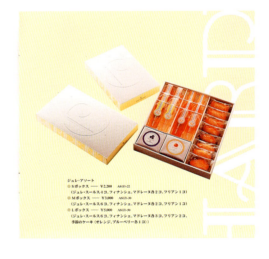

page 9, 10

page 17, 18

FOOD: 菓子 CONFECTIONERY

スプランドゥール
昔からのファンも、今のファンも、この3つの味。

飾ることなく、飾らないこと。
誰からも愛されている焼菓子の原点。
3つの味わいを詰め合わせました。
アーモンドが香ばしいフィナンシェ、
レモンとラム酒がほんのり香るマドレーヌ、
アーモンドの香ばしさとピターの風味を抽出した
コクのあるフリアン。
いずれも素材に、焼き加減に徹底してこだわった味、
そして何よりもしっとりとした上品なおいしさが、
支持され続ける理由です。

- SSボックス ¥900 SD-9
  (フィナンシェ2コ、マドレーヌ2コ、フリアン2コ)
- Sボックス ¥2,000 SD-20
  (フィナンシェ4コ、マドレーヌ4コ、フリアン4コ)
- Mボックス ¥3,000 SD-30
  (フィナンシェ7コ、マドレーヌ7コ、フリアン6コ)
- Lボックス ¥4,000 SD-40
  (フィナンシェ9コ、マドレーヌ9コ、フリアン9コ)

page 21, 22

仏蘭西クッキー街道
クッキーのふるさとをめぐる旅、贈ります。

フランスの各地方には、そこに暮らす人々が、
長きにわたってつくりあげてきた
自慢のクッキーがあります。
それは今なお修道院や農家の台所で
出会うことができます。
そんなかくれたおいしさをそっくり再現しました。
丸く、平らく、古代のコインの形をした
素朴で温かみのあるおいしさばかりです。
おいしいフランスの旅、あの方へお贈りしてみませんか。

・ノルマンディ地方の〈チーズ・サブレ〉
・ボルドー地方の〈サブレ・ド・ボルドー〉
・ロレーヌ地方の〈マカロン・ド・ナンシー〉
・ブルターニュ地方の〈ガレット・ブルトンヌ〉
・アキテーヌ地方バイヨンヌの〈チョコレート・クッキー〉
・シャンパーニュ地方ランスの〈ビスキュイ・ド・ランス〉
・ロワール地方ナントの〈ナンテ〉
・プロヴァンス地方の〈アーモンド・クッキー〉

仏蘭西クッキー街道
- Sボックス (30枚入り) ¥2,000 C-20
- Lボックス (30枚・19本入り) ¥3,000 C-30

page 29, 30

Royal Class

ロイヤルクラス
芳醇なボルドーワインが香る。

かつてマリー・アントワネット王妃のお気に入りだった
フランス アルザス地方のお菓子、クグロフ。
素材もレシピも一新してつくりました。
オリジナル・クグロフの味わい。
ボルドーワインでしっかり風味づけ。
独特の陶磁器型を使い、
紙型でじっくり焼き上げました。
ホームパーティや記念日などのご贈答にも喜ばれています。

- ロイヤルクラス1箱 (フランス アルザス民芸〈陶磁 クグロフ型〉付き)
  ¥6,500 RC-65

page 33, 34

139

Catalog + Web

HENRI CHARPENTIER

www.henri-charpentier.com/

- Top
- 会社プロフィール PROFILE
- アンリ・シャルパンティエ HENRI CHARPENTIER
- シーキューブ charpentier contemporary cuisine
- オンラインショッピング ONLINE SHOPPING

〜ワンシーンを演出〜私たちは、人と人との結びつきを大切にし、生活文化に貢献できる企業として、いつもお客様に喜び・感動していただけることに、積極的に取り組んでいます。そして、アンリ・シャルパンティエのお菓子が、より多くの方々の"ワンシーン"を素敵に演出できるように願っています。

〜One-Scene Productions〜 Henri Charpentier, a company that values the importance of personal relationships and aims to be a company that can contribute to creating a life culture, is trying positively to give our customers joy and excitement. We hope that Henri Charpentier's confectioneries will help make those special "one scene" occasions a success for many.

洋菓子製造・販売／カフェ
CONFECTIONERY/CAFE 2000

CL, SB: アンリ・シャルパンティエ
HENRI CHARPENTIER CO., LTD.
DF: ジャパンデザインサービス　Japan Design Service
※2000年7月11日現在のデータを使用 As of July 11, 2000

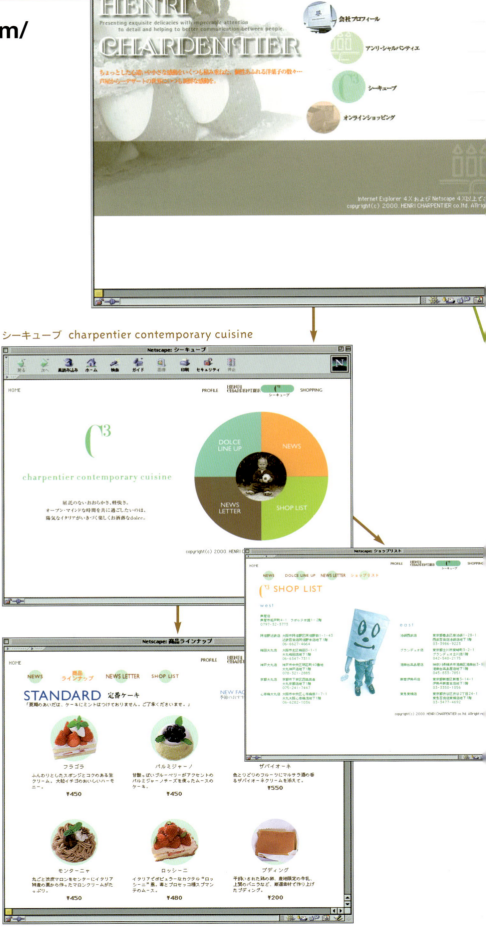

FOOD: 菓子 CONFECTIONERY

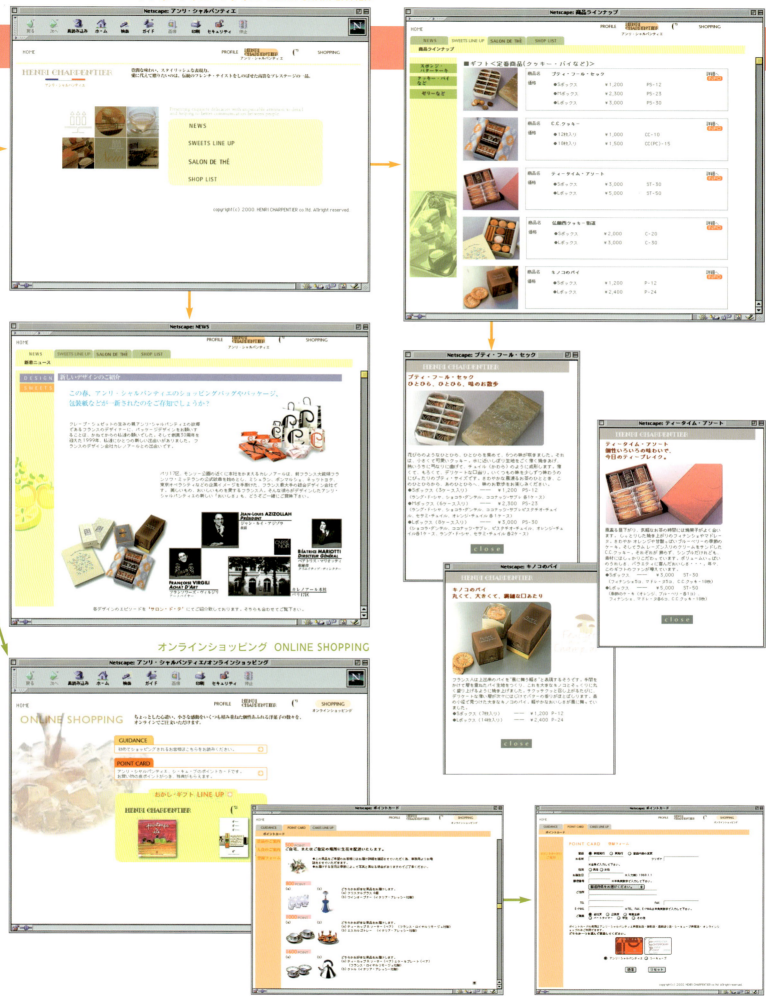

Catalog + Web

La Calline de Verl

www.sun-inet.or.jp/~colline/

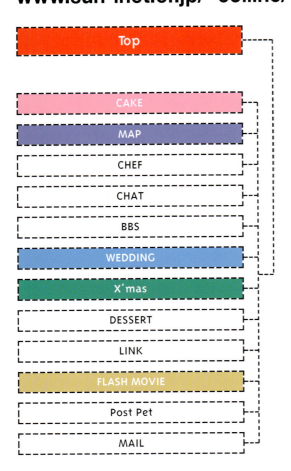

ホームページを立ち上げたのは5年前です。勿論、私自身もその様な知識もなく、知人に制作して戴きました。半年もしないうちに、ただ見ているだけのホームページではつまらないと思い、本やウェブ上で勉強しました。お陰で現在は、Java・ダイナミックhtml・ショックウエーブ等を使用し、見ていただいている方に飽きさせないよう更新したりしています。お菓子のことに興味のない方にも見ていただきたいというコンセプトで制作しました。

Our Web site was established five years ago. As I knew nothing of Web design, an acquaintance created the site for me. After about six months, though, just looking at Web sites started to bore me. I read books, and studied using the Web itself. Now I can use Java, dynamic HTML, Shockwave, and other Web tools, updating the contents to keep viewers' interest. My aim is to make our Web site attractive even to someone who is not that interested in confectionery.

洋菓子製造・販売 CONFECTIONERY 1995

CL, SB: フランス菓子・喫茶コーリンベール
Fransukashi Kissa Kolin Berl
※2000年7月11日現在のデータを使用 As of July 11, 2000

FOOD: 菓子 CONFECTIONERY

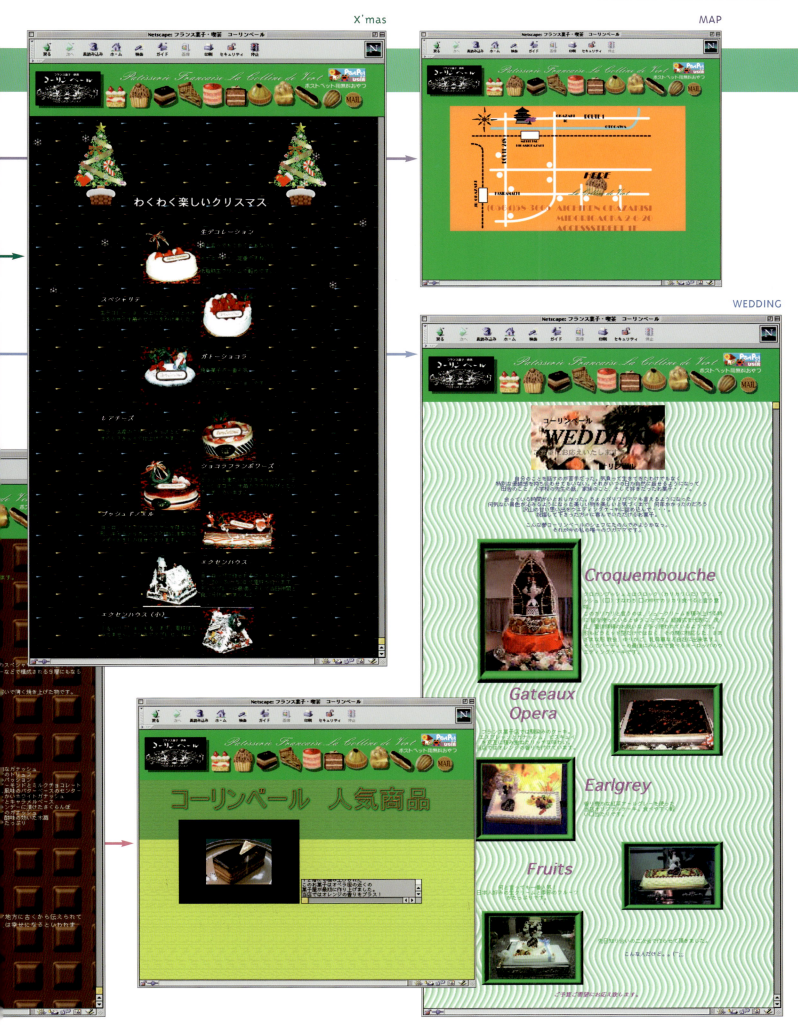

143

Catalog+Web

CLUB HARIE

中綴 Stapled in the center／100×197mm

『クラブハリエ』は、建築家「メレル・ヴォーリズ」と菓子舗「たねや先々代山本久吉」との出会いから生まれました。明治38年より昭和39年まで湖東近江八幡に居を構え、こよなく日本を愛した著名な建築家であり 敬虔な伝道師「メレル・ヴォーリズ」。彼から、洋菓子の本来の素朴さと、手づくりのあたたかさを教わったのが『クラブハリエ』の出発点でした。

CLUB HARIE was established after the meeting of Merel Voliz, an architect, and Hisakichi Yamamoto, the president of Taneya two generations ago. Merel Voliz, a well-known architect and pious missionary who deeply loved Japan, lived in Ohmi Hachiman on the east side of Lake Biwa from 1905 to 1964. He taught us about the original simplicity of western cakes, and showed us the warmth that can be found in handmade cakes. That is how CLUB HARIE came to be.

洋菓子製造・販売 CONFECTIONERY 2000

CL, SB: クラブハリエ CLUB HARIE Co., Ltd.
CD, AD, D: 山本昌仁 Masahito Yamamoto
P: エクボスタジオ Ekubo Studio
CW: 川島民親 Tamichika Kawashima

page 1, 2

page 13, 14

page 7, 8

Catalog + Web

FOOD: 菓子 CONFECTIONERY

www.taneya.co.jp/

- Top
- Adoption Information
- Company Outline
- 最新情報 What's New!!
- 工房直送便 Direct Delivery Service
- 菓子教室 Classroom
- 環境対策 Environment
- 何でもメール Mail

明治5年、近江に創業した菓子舗『たねや』のサイト。日本人の大切な心の種でもある四季の移ろいの美しさを彩り豊かに表現する和菓子や、たねやの洋菓子専門店『クラブハリエ』の商品情報のチェック、そしてネットショッピングが楽しめます。また、たねやの店舗、催し物情報、毎週更新の『たねや』のキャラクター「福童子」のイラストと、そのイラストに関するお話や、月刊の情報誌「くらしのしるべ」のデジタル版（PDFデータ）など、魅力あるコンテンツが盛りだくさんです。

The Web site of Taneya, a Japanese confectionery maker founded in Ohmi in 1873. It includes a wealth of information about Japanese confectionery, a colorful expression of the beauty of the changing seasons that provides spiritual nourishment to the Japanese. There is also information about CLUB HARIE, a western cake specialty shop established after the meeting of Hisakichi Yamamoto, the president of Taneya two generations ago, and architect Merel Voliz. In addition to offering on-line shopping, the site's other interesting contents include illustrations of "Fuku-warabe (lucky boy)," Taneya's symbol character, which are updated weekly with stories about the illustrations, and a digital version (PDF) of monthly magazine "Kurashi-no-shirube."

洋菓子製造・販売　CONFECTIONERY 2000

CL, SB: クラブハリエ　CLUB HARIE Co., Ltd
CD: 大山 真　Makoto Ohyama
AD: 松本 徹　Toru Matsumoto
D: 吉田 佐江子　Saeko Yoshida
CW: 川島民親　Tamichika Kawashima
PR: 永本哲夫　Tetsuo Nagamoto
DF: 山元勇樹　Yuuki Yamamoto

※2000年7月5日現在のデータを使用　As of July 5, 2000

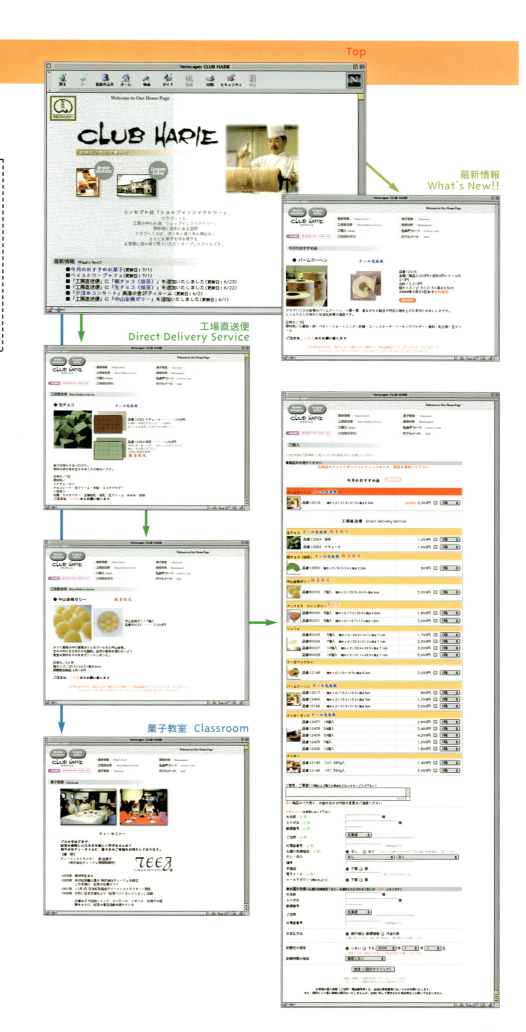

Catalog + Web

たねや

中綴 Stapled in the center／210×197mm

『たねや』は明治五年、近江に創業した菓子舗です。『たねや』の屋号は江戸時代、穀倉地帯でもある近江湖東を中心に幅広く作物の種子（たね）を販売していたところからそのまま『たねや』となりました。菓子舗『たねや』は、日本人の大切な心の種でもある四季の移ろいの美しさを彩りゆたかに表現した和菓子に加え、より美味しくいただけるよう開発された工夫豊かな和菓子が豊富です。

TANEYA is a manufacturer of Japanese Confectioneries, established in Ohmi in 1873. TANEYA was named after the traditional commerce that was based in Ohmi's eastern district during the Edo Era, the selling of seeds (tane) for crops nationwide. TANEYA offers a wide-ranging variety of Japanese confectioneries; not only those that colorfully express the beauty of the changing seasons that provide spiritual nourishment to the Japanese, but also those full of ideas, originally created and presented for the best of taste.

和菓子製造・販売
JAPANESE CONFECTIONERY 2000

CL, SB: たねや　TANEYA Co., Ltd.
CD: 山本昌仁　Masahito Yamamoto
AD, D: 宇田川哲弥　Tetsuya Udagawa
P: エクボスタジオ　Ekubo Studio
CW: 川島民親　Tamichika Kawashima

page 1, 2

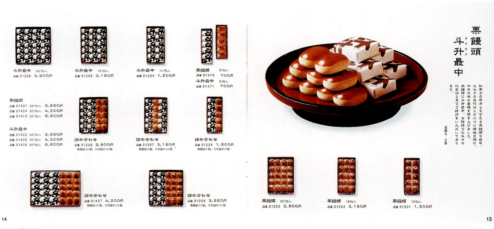

page 13, 14

page 19, 20

Catalog + Web

www.taneya.co.jp/

- Top
- 新しいお知らせ　News
- ご購入・近江直送便　Order
- 今週のおすすめ品　Recommendation
- 素材のお話　Materials
- たねっと倶楽部　Member's club
- 各店のご案内　Shop Information
- お問い合わせ　Inquiries
- カタログ請求　Printed Catalog Order
- リンク　Links
- 会社概要　Corporate Outline
- 採用情報　Recruiting Information
- CLUB HARIE

明治5年、近江に創業した菓子舗『たねや』のサイト。日本人の大切な心の種でもある四季の移ろいの美しさを彩り豊かに表現する和菓子や、たねやの洋菓子専門店『クラブハリエ』の商品情報のチェック、そしてネットショッピングが楽しめます。また、たねやの店舗、催し物情報、毎週更新の『たねや』のキャラクター「福童子」のイラストと、そのイラストに関するお話や、月刊の情報誌「くらしのしるべ」のデジタル版（PDFデータ）など、魅力あるコンテンツが盛りだくさんです。

The Web site of TANEYA, a Japanese confectionery maker founded in Ohmi in 1873. It includes a wealth of information about Japanese confectionery, a colorful expression of the beauty of the changing seasons that provides spiritual nourishment to the Japanese. There is also information about CLUB HARIE, a western cake specialty shop established after the meeting of Hisakichi Yamamoto, the president of TANEYA two generations ago, and architect Merel Voliz. In addition to offering on-line shopping, the site's other interesting contents include illustrations of "Fuku-warabe (lucky boy)," TANEYA'S symbol character, which are updated weekly with stories about the illustrations, and a digital version (PDF) of monthly magazine "Kurashi-no-shirube."

FOOD: 菓子　CONFECTIONERY

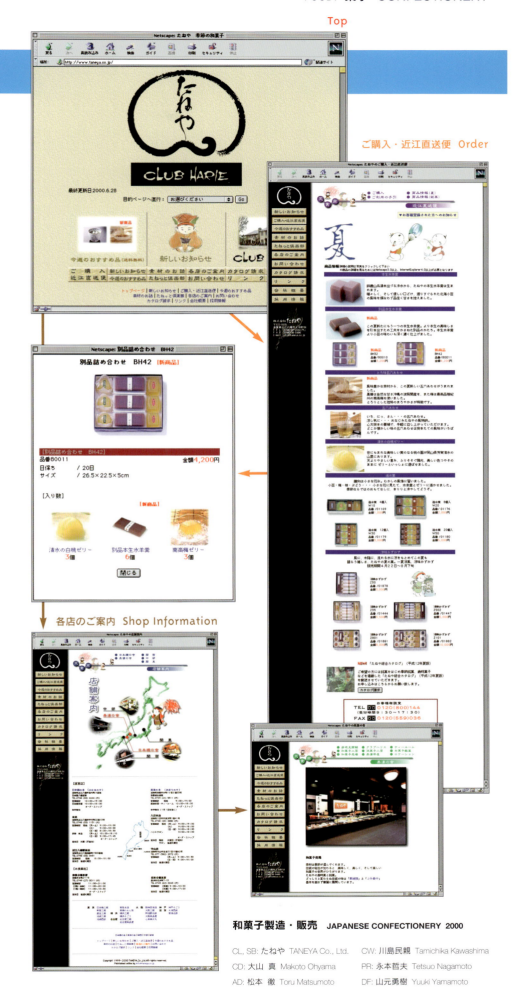

和菓子製造・販売　JAPANESE CONFECTIONERY 2000

CL, SB: たねや　TANEYA Co., Ltd.　CW: 川島民親　Tamichika Kawashima
CD: 大山　真　Makoto Ohyama　PR: 永本哲夫　Tetsuo Nagamoto
AD: 松本　徹　Toru Matsumoto　DF: 山元勇樹　Yuuki Yamamoto
D: 吉田佐江子　Saeko Yoshida

※2000年7月11日現在のデータを使用　As of July 11, 2000

Catalog+Web

叶匠寿庵

2ツ折・中綴・6ツ折
Single-fold・Stapled in the center・sixfold

2ツ折 Single-fold／148×210mm・中綴 Stapled in the center／100×200mm・6ツ折 sixfold／87×129mm
（開いた状態 When fully unfolded：261×258mm）

叶匠壽庵は、昭和33年9月、芝田清次によって、「多くのお客様に感動を与えられるお菓子作りをしよう」という信念のもと創業されました。昭和60年には、農工一体の郷づくりを目標に大津市大石龍門の広大な地に「寿長生の郷」を完成。和菓子作りの理想の姿を実現させています。

With a conviction to "make confectioneries that can touch the hearts of many customers," Seiji Shibata established Kanou syoujuan in September 1958. In 1985, "Sunai-no-Sato" was completed on a large tract of land in Daikokuryumon, Ohtsu City, Shiga Prefecture, aiming to be a village that unifies agriculture and industry and realizing an ideal style of Japanese confectionery-making.

和菓子製造・販売
JAPANESE CONFECTIONERY 2000

CL, SB: 叶匠寿庵　Kanou syoujuan

page 1, 2

page 5, 6

FOOD: 菓子 CONFECTIONERY

寿長生の郷

こころづくり楽しく集う 寿長生の郷

大きく支える　悠久の地
すっぽり包みこむ　原生の林
木達が
歳を重ねてむすびゆく
果樹の園
野の花観音さまに
みちびかれ
ひらく花草
そんな中での
ものづくりの日暮し
土を耕し　木をそだて
菓子をつくる
みんな　みんな　正直
よろこび働く
寿長生の郷
倉然として
欽びに
みちて

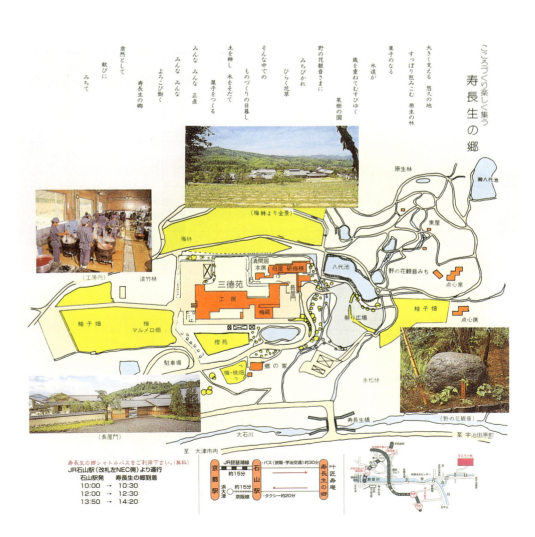

叶匠寿庵　寿長生の郷本社工場

149

Catalog + Web

叶匠寿庵

www.kanou.com

Splash Page

Top

寿長生の郷 SUNAINOSATO

叶匠寿庵は、和菓子作りの理想の姿を実現する為に、農工一体の郷づくりを目標に滋賀県大津市大石龍門の広大な地（6万3千坪）に「寿長生の郷」を造りました。郷では、菓匠たちが丹精込めて、日本の美しい風土から生まれた恵みを、美しい和菓子につくりあげています。又、広大な郷には、桜や梅、椿などが原生し、四季折々には美しい日本の彩りを楽しむことができます。このホームページでは、叶匠寿庵の和菓子作りと寿長生の郷の考え方、又イメージ発信を最大のテーマにまとめあげました。

Kanou syoujuan has established "Sunai-no-Sato" on a large tract of land (approx. 208,000 square meters) in Daikokuryumon, Ohtsu City, Shiga Prefecture, unifying agriculture and industry with the goal of making an ideal style of Japanese confectionery manufacturer. In the village, confectionery masters are making every effort to make exquisite Japanese confectioneries from the fruits found in Japan's beautiful nature. Around the vast area, cherry blossoms, Japanese apricots, and camellia can be seen, creating a joy of beautiful seasonal Japanese colors. This web site was created with Kanou syoujuan's confectionery production as the main theme, as well as presenting Sunai-no-Sato's corporate philosophy and image.

和菓子製造・販売
JAPANESE CONFECTIONERY 2000

CL, SB: 叶匠寿庵 Kanou syoujuan
CD, COPYWRITE DIRECTOR, PLANNER:
漆畑銑治（クー・レジェント） Senji Urushibata (COU LEGENDS)
D: 関根慎一 Shinichi Sekine／古関正彦 Masahiko Koseki
PLANNER: 宇野恒和（叶匠寿庵）Tsunekazu Uno (Kanou syoujuan)
※2000年7月11日現在のデータを使用 As of July 11, 2000

FOOD: 菓子 CONFECTIONERY

健康和菓子 寿長生菓 SUNAIKA

商品のご紹介 Products Information

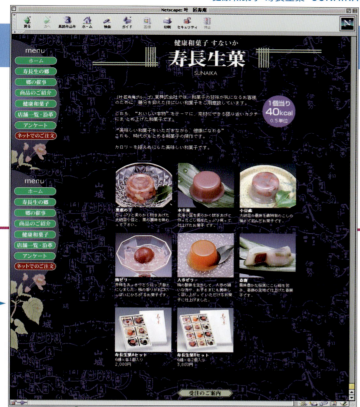

店舗一覧・沿革 Shop Information・History

Catalog +Web

亀屋万年堂

中綴 Stapled in the center／109×220mm

（株）亀屋万年堂のもつ「高級大衆和菓子店」という
コンセプトに基づき、「和」の持つ風合いを「筆文字」
（カリグラフィー）と「和紙」、「器」などにて演出し、
アピールしています。また各ページの商品も「和」の
パターンである「市松模様」で構成して、「和」の中
に和洋菓子をレイアウトし、各商品をより見やすくし
ています。

Based on Mannendo Kameya's concept of being a "quality confectioner for the masses," Japanese calligraphy, paper, and chinaware are used to provide a sense of traditional Japanese style. Products on each page are presented in a traditional Japanese ichimatsu checkerboard pattern, which makes for easier viewing of the products.

菓子製造・販売　CONFECTIONERY 1999

CL, SB: 亀屋万年堂　KAMEYA-MANNENDO.COMPANY
AD: 加藤祐司　Yuji Katoh
D: 土坂 浩　Hiroshi Dosaka
P: 石丸 諭　Satoshi Ishimaru
CALLIGRAPHER: 箱守弘道　Hiromichi Hakomori
CW: 山田慎一　Shinichi Yamada

FOOD: 菓子 CONFECTIONERY

Catalog+Web

亀屋万年堂

village.infoweb.ne.jp/~navona/

- Top
- 創業の歴史　History
- 御用命はこちら　Order
- 特選菓子せいぞろい　Products Information
- 店舗のご案内　Shop Information
- 会社概要・事業内容　Company Information

昭和十三年創業の亀屋万年堂のホームページです。コンテンツを「創業の歴史」「御用命はこちら」「特選菓子せいぞろい」「店舗のご案内」「会社概要・事業内容」という5項目に絞り込み、ムダのない、わかりやすいレイアウトにしています。特に「店舗のご案内」ページでは、電車の路線図を配し、その路線上から店舗の検索ができるようになっており、とても利用しやすい作りとなっています。

The web site of Kameya Mannendo, a company established in 1938. The table of contents was limited to five headings: "History," "Order," "List of Selected Confectioneries," "Shop Information," and "Corporate Outline and Business," making the layout trim and easy to navigate. The Shop Information pages are especially easy to use, with a search system that uses a train map to select a route.

菓子製造・販売　CONFECTIONERY 2000

CL, SB: 亀屋万年堂　KAMEYA-MANNENDO.COMPANY
※2000年7月5日現在のデータを使用　As of July 5, 2000

Top

創業の歴史　History
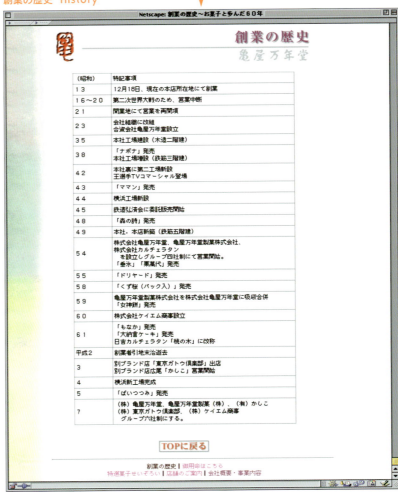

FOOD: 菓子　CONFECTIONERY

御用命はこちら　Order

特選菓子せいぞろい　Products Information

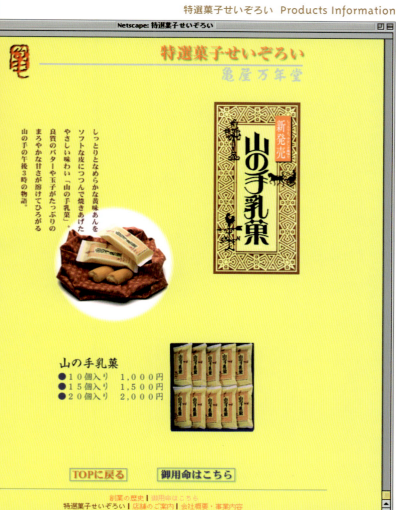

店舗のご案内　Shop Information

会社概要・事業内容　Company Information

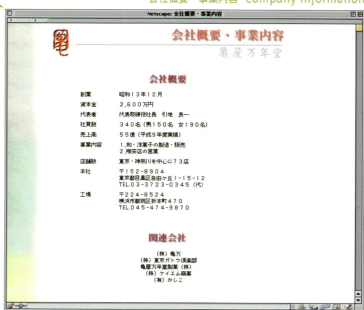

Catalog + Web

文明堂

中綴 Stapled in the center／110×220mm

文明堂は、明治33年に創業。初代、中川安五郎が長崎・丸山を中心とする菓子製造販売業を開始しました。文明堂がつくるカステラは、厳選した素材を丁寧に仕上げる伝統の味です。またカステラ以外にも豊富な商品をラインナップしています。

Bunmeido was established in the year 1900. Yasugoro Nakagawa, the first president of Bunmeido, began as a confectionery maker and retailer based in Maruyama, Nagasaki. The traditional flavor of Bunmeido's castella was attained through careful selection of ingredients. In addition to the castella, we also offer a variety of other confectioneries.

菓子製造・販売 CONFECTIONERY 1999

CL, SB: 文明堂 新宿店 Bunmeido Shinjuku-Ten Co., Ltd.
CD: 新井 喬 (ロフトハウス) Takashi Arai (Loft House)
D: 久門博美 (ロフトハウス) Hiromi Kyumon (Loft House)
P: 安部謙一 Kenichi Abe
CW: 石月秀二 Shuji Ishizuki
PRODUCTION: 協同広告 Kyodo Koukoku

FOOD: 菓子 CONFECTIONERY

三笠山

抹茶の味も喜ぶだろうな。
抹茶味も大好評です。
休みには帰るから、
待っててね。

さらに上品に、まろやかに。文明堂ならではの隠し味を調合して、卵の香りふかふかなふんわりと焼き上げました。中身は北海道産の小豆を使用して、ふっくらと炊き上げた「和」菓子としてのクオリティ。そして上品な甘さにじっくり仕上げ、抹茶のコクをさらに引き立たせています。ハーモニーをお楽しみください。

和菓子

甘いものに目のない、私。
ダイエットにも気をつけています。

文明堂和菓子の人気の秘密は、洗練された日本の味と心にあります。

アニバーサリー

「ありがとう」の言葉も
口ではちょっと
言いにくいけれど…。

母の日
敬老の日
七五三
子供の日

カステラ

「このデザート、キミがつくったの？
カレったら、失礼しちゃうわ。
カステラをベースにひと工夫。
ちょっぴりオシャレなデザートを
つくってみませんか。

素材にこだわり、伝統の技で磨きあげた文明カステラの深い味わい。そのままでもおいしいですが

Catalog + Web

文明堂

www.tokyo-bunmeido.co.jp

- Top
- ニュース News
- 商品カタログ Products Information
- 店舗のご案内 Shop Information
- カステラ博物館 Kasutera Museum
- グルメの館 Recipe
- 文明堂CM年鑑 CM History
- カロリーカフェ BUNMEIDO CALORY CAFE
- 文明堂 Company Information

テレビCMでおなじみの熊のダンスをアニメ化して、「文明堂カステラ劇場」の舞台のイメージをトップページにおいた、ファミリーで楽しめるサイトとしました。階層下には、Javaで作成したカロリー・カフェ、CM年鑑（動画）、グルメの館、カステラ博物館など充実したコンテンツがいっぱい。貴重な資料も入っています。今後、オンラインでカステラ等を販売する予定。更に海外版も検討中です。

This Web site is fun for the whole family. Bunmeido's top page represents the stage of the Bunmeido Castella Theater, featuring the animated dancing bears from their well-known TV commercials. Inside pages boast a variety of rich content, such as the Java-created "Calorie Cafe," "Commercial Annual" (animation), "the House of Gourmet", and the "Castella (sponge cake) Museum." Valuable reference materials are also available. There are plans to sell the cake online in the future, and an overseas version of the site is currently being considered.

菓子製造・販売　CONFECTIONERY 2000

CL, SB: 文明堂 新宿店 Bunmeido Shinjuku-Ten Co., Ltd.
CD: 山崎 徹 （協同広告） Toru Yamazaki (Kyodo Koukoku)
AD: 古賀 祥 （アーバン・トランスレーション）
Sachi Koga (Urban Translation)
PRODUCER: 荒井 浩 （協同広告） Hiroshi Arai (Kyodo Koukoku)
※2000年7月11日現在のデータを使用 As of July 11, 2000

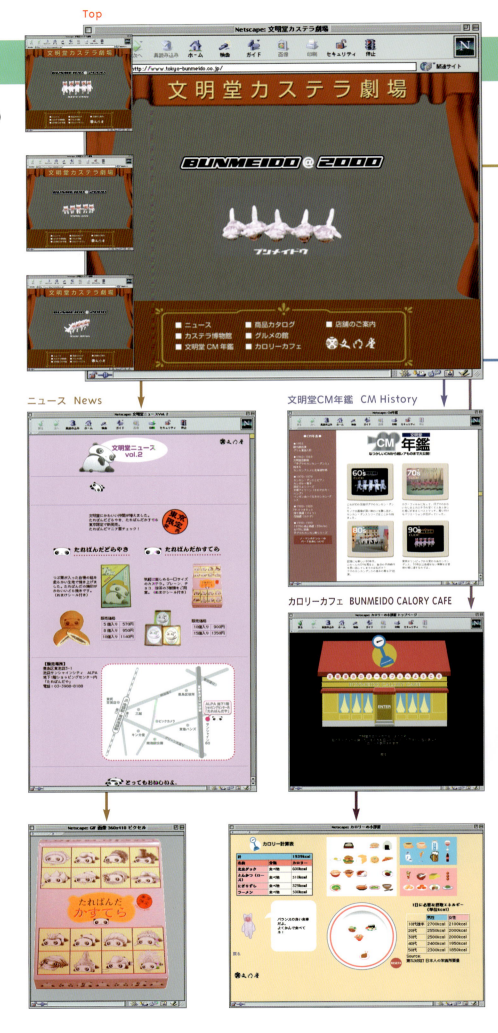

FOOD: 菓子 CONFECTIONERY

商品カタログ Products Information

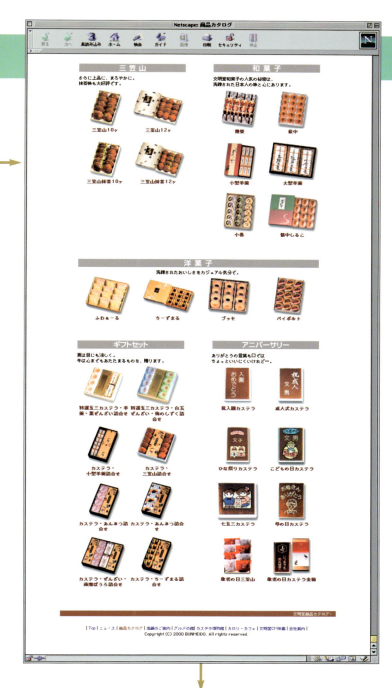

グルメの館 Recipe

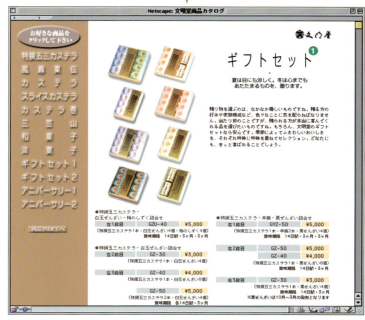

Catalog + Web

おかめ堂

3ツ折観音開き・シート
French Threefold・Sheet

3ツ折観音開き French Threefold／75×100mm
シート Sheet／紫 Purple：65×129mm & ピンクPink：63×133mm

「伊那の梅衣」は、あら粉のらくがんタイプの生地の中に、漬け込んだ梅を含ませた白あんと、漬けて細かく刻んだ紫蘇の葉を混ぜ合わせた短冊型の銘菓です。ほのかな梅の酸味と、しその香りを漂わせた味覚が、お茶席のお菓子にはぴったりとご好評を頂いております。

The "Ina Ume Goromo" is a well-known oblong cake, with dough made from a type of coarse flour, and a filling of white bean paste mixed with well-pickled plums and finely sliced salted shiso leaves. With its faint fragrance of sour plums and scent of shiso, this cake is favorably received as a perfect confectionary for Japanese teatime.

菓子製造・販売　CONFECTIONERY 2000

CL, SB: おかめ堂　Okamedo

Catalog+Web

FOOD: 菓子 CONFECTIONERY

www.valley.ne.jp/~okamedo/

おかめ堂のスタッフは、お菓子の一番おいしい時は、"作りたて"と考えております。当店のPRではいつでも焼きたてをお客様に発送できる「かぼちゃパイ」に的を絞ってホームページ文を更新しております。次にホームページで工夫をこらした点ですが、リンク時にクリックするホットイメージをページ毎に変えております。商品代金等が一目でわかるページもあります。菓子教室のページは毎月更新ですが、画像を使い、わかりやすい説明に心掛けました。当店のラジオコマーシャルを音声で貼り付けたページもあります。伝言板のページにおかめ堂のホームページのご感想をお寄せ下さい。

The staff of Okamedo believes that a confectionery is most delicious when freshly made. On the company's Web site, we feature pumpkin pies that can be delivered to customers in "just out of the oven" condition, with promotional copy updated periodically. There is also a page where customers can find price information at a glance. The confectionery-making class pages, updated monthly, use images to make the explanations easy to understand. There is also a page where customers can listen to our radio commercial. Please write comments on our Web site's bulletin board.

菓子製造・販売 CONFECTIONERY 2000

CL, SB: おかめ堂 Okamedo

※2000年7月7日現在のデータを使用 As of July 7, 2000

Catalog + Web

山本海苔店

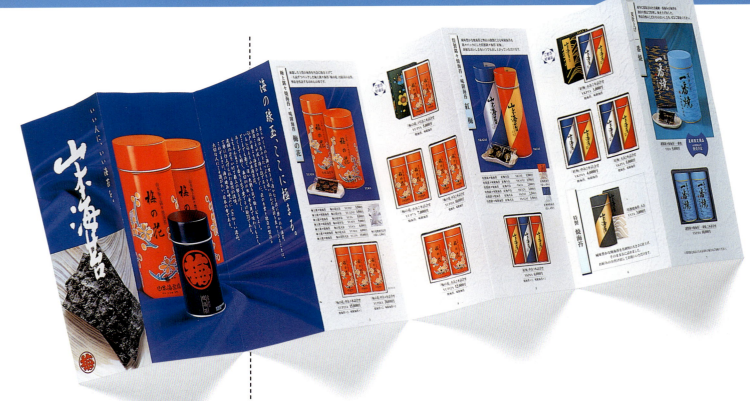
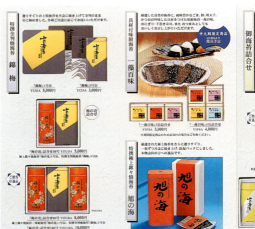
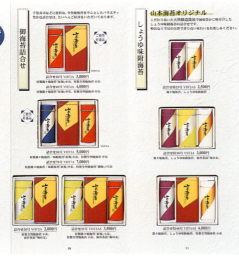
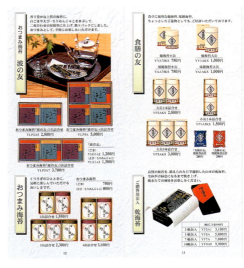
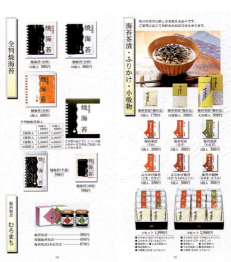

ジャバラ Accordion fold

104×224mm
(開いた状態 When fully unfolded：918×225mm)

中元といえば夏。海苔といえば海。こうしたイメージを、表紙でどう表現するかを念頭に置きました。そこで青い布を波のように敷き、その上に商品を配置して涼感を出しています。お中元ということもあり、包んであった布がハラリと落ちたように見せることも狙いました。

Mid-summer gifts; nori from the ocean. We focused on how to best express these images on the cover. For a solution, a blue cloth was spread to look like waves, and the products were displayed on the cloth to produce a cool atmosphere. To make it look like a Chugen (summer gift), we tried an effect that the wrapping cloth was just untied and fell open naturally.

海苔・海苔加工品販売 SEAWEEDS SALES 1999

CL: 山本海苔店 YAMAMOTO NORITEN Co., Ltd.
CD, AD: 青木一男 Kazuo Aoki
D: 吉田浩樹 Hiroki Yoshida
P: 鈴木武男 Takeo Suzuki
CW: 多々良 憲一郎 Kenichiro Tatara
SB: 朝日広告社 ASAHI ADVERTISING INC.

Catalog + Web

FOOD: 食品 FOOD

www.yamamoto-noriten.co.jp/

- Top
- WEB店長ご挨拶 Greeting
- マルトク情報 Special Information
- お役立ち情報 Cooking recipe
- catalog
- shopping
- gift
- cooking recipe
- health
- 全国店舗MAP Shop Map
- 山本海苔店紹介 History
- 事業案内 Company Information
- お問い合わせはこちら Inquiries

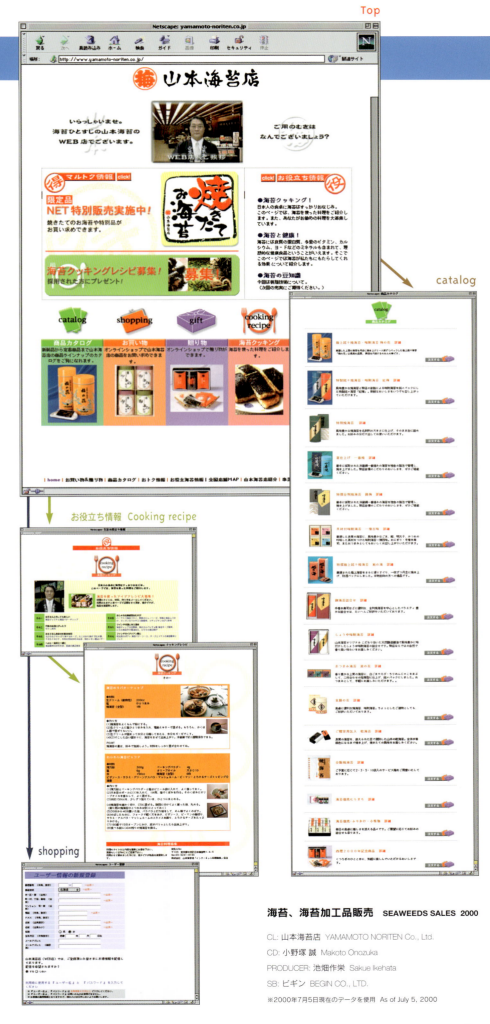

「海苔のすばらしさをお届けする楽しいホットライン」がコンセプト。150年の伝統ある老舗のウェブ店と位置づけ、"ネット店長"を設けるなど、親しみやすく実用的なコンテンツをめざしました。またシステム構成上も、拡張性を考慮しました。随時、更新と見直しを重ね、将来的には「日本一役立つ楽しい海苔サイト」にする予定です。さらにユーザーに「贈答先リスト作成プログラム」を提供する、という新しい試みも実施しています。こちらも改良を加える中で、より実用的な"使える"ホームページにしていきます。

The goal of Yamamoto Noriten's Web site is "to become a hot line for delivering wonderful nori." For the Web shop of this retail business with a 150-year history, we created friendly and useful contents, including providing the Net Shop with a manager. We also took into consideration the need to be able to expand system configurations. We are planning to make it "the most useful web site about nori in Japan" in the future, by continually updating and revising its pages. Additionally, the site has a trial service with a program that allows customers to making their own list of gift recipients. By improving this service, we hope to make this site even more practical.

海苔、海苔加工品販売 SEAWEEDS SALES 2000

CL: 山本海苔店 YAMAMOTO NORITEN Co., Ltd.
CD: 小野塚 誠 Makoto Onozuka
PRODUCER: 池畑作栄 Sakue Ikehata
SB: ビギン BEGIN CO., LTD.

※2000年7月5日現在のデータを使用 As of July 5, 2000

Catalog + Web

伊藤ハム

2ツ折 Single-fold／210×297mm

伊藤ハムでは、毎年お中元の他に、同様のパンフレットをお歳暮の時期にも制作しております。弊社のギフト商品は、常にナンバーワンブランドとして、広くお客様にご愛用頂き、発行部数も数万枚にのぼります。ただし、掲載している商品はエリアによって異なるため、様々な種類のものを制作し、常にお客様に満足して頂けるものを目指して、毎年、内容を検討しております。弊社は昭和3年の創業以来の実績と信頼を築き上げて参りましたが、ミレニアムイヤーとなる本年を新たな飛躍の年として、取り組んでいます。

Ito Ham produces summer gift catalogs as well as year-end catalogs. As a number one brand, our gift line-ups are always very popular, and tens of thousands of catalogs are distributed. Because product selection for the catalog differs by area, we produce several types of catalogs. Every year, we seriously consider the contents, in order to give our customers the fullest satisfaction. Since its establishment in 1928, Ito Ham has firmly established both business achievements and trust, and in this millennium year we are trying harder than ever.

ハム・ソーセージ及び肉類製造・販売
MEAT PROCESSER 2000

CL, SB: 伊藤ハム ITOHAM FOODS INC.

Catalog + Web

FOOD: 食品 FOOD

www.itoham.co.jp/

ホームページの立ち上げ当初から、伊藤ハムの購買層である女性を意識し、色使いや構成内容を出来るだけわかりやすく伝えられるよう心がけて制作しています。例えば、ホームページ専用のファミリーを設定して、キャラクターを開発し、そのキャラクターを使って、食にまつわる特集ページを制作。企業ホームページにありがちな堅苦しさを解消しています。また、サイト全体もカラフルながらデータの読み込みが遅くならないよう各所に工夫を凝らしています。オープン懸賞ではサイトの安定した運営が出来るよう、プログラム開発において工夫しました。

Since the launch of the Web site, content and color usage have been designed to appeal to Ito Ham's predominantly female customers, and designed for easy navigation and understanding by the visitor. For example, we have developed a family of characters especially for the site, and included special pages that feature food topics. In this way, we have avoided the formality that is a stereotype of corporate sites. The entire site has been designed to be very colorful, with care taken so that data downloads without delay. Programs for contests are fully developed for stable site operation.

ハム、ソーセージ及び肉類製造・販売
MEAT PROCESSER 1997

CL: 伊藤ハム ITOHAM FOOD INC.
CD: 武藤英樹 Hideki Muto
AD: 北岡壮介 Sosuke Kitaoka
D: 猪野世利香 Serika Ino
I: 近藤みずほ Mizuho Kondo
PR: 三野健 Ken Mitsuno
SB: ディー・エヌ・ピー・デジタルコム
DNP DIGITALCOM CO., LTD.

※2000年7月11日現在のデータを使用 As of July 11, 2000

165

Catalog + Web

村田合同

page 1, 2

page 3, 4

page 45, 46

カタログキット（箱・中綴7冊）
Catalog kit (Box・Stapled in the center×7)

箱 Box／212×203mm
中綴 Stapled in the center／210×200mm

毎年2月に発売されるニュープロダクトと同時に、全国取扱店頭で配付されるコンシューマ向けのカタログです。各ブランド別に分けて編集されているが、全体として一冊のスタイル・ブックの様な構成がされています。BOXケースの他にバインダー式のカタログにしたりと、使う場面においてその形式がアレンジ出来る工夫もされています。プロダクトがわかりやすく美しく見える様なカット（写真）と、イメージを自由に発想させる事が出来そうなビジュアル構成は、他業者のカタログの手本としても注目されています。

Distributed nationwide at stores that carry Murata furniture, this consumer catalog is issued once a year when new products go on sale in February. Edited and categorized by brand, the catalog in its entirety will work as a stylebook. The format can be altered according to usage; without its box case, it can be arranged in a binder catalog. The catalog has received attention from companies in other fields as a model for their own catalogs, with photographs taken in a way that make the products look clear and beautiful, and a visual layout that allows viewers to create images freely.

Catalog + Web

村田合同

www.murata-godo.co.jp

「ショップイノベーター＆カサブランカ」をはじめ、北欧のモダンカジュアルな家具「イノベーター」、ラタン家具の「カサブランカ」、独自のセレクションを集めた「ワンプラスワン」などを展開する村田合同のウェブサイトです。スタンダードな手法が見やすく利用しやすいのか、ウェブショップの売上も業界No1です。

The Web site of Murata Godo. Starting with "Shop Innovators & Casablanca," the company offers brands such as "Innovator," Scandinavian modern casual furniture; "Casa Blanca," rattan furniture; and "One plus One," a line of originally selected items. Thanks to the convenience of our standard way of navigation, our Web shop can boast top sales for this type of business.

家具輸出入・製造・販売
FURNITURE MANUFACTURE & SALES 2000

CL, SB: 村田合同 Murata Interior Design Inc.
※2000年7月11日現在のデータを使用 As of July 11, 2000

HOME: 家具・インテリア FURNITURE & INTERIOR GOODS

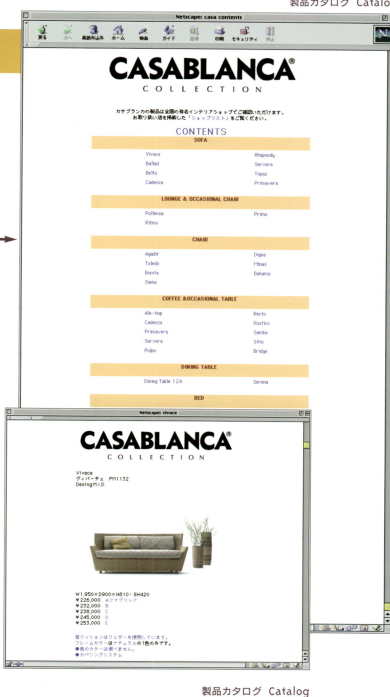

Catalog + Web

SHOP innovator & CASABLANCA

www.innovator.co.jp

見やすく、そしてネットショップも利用しやすく、買いやすい。カタログとの完全リンクなので、どこでも製品の確認ができるという、スタンダードなコンテンツが家具業界のお手本となっています。

Easy to navigate, this useful online shop has been designed to make shopping easy. As the site is completely parallels our catalogs, customers can look closely at the products no matter where they are. Such standard practices have become good examples for furniture industry sites.

家具輸出入・製造・販売
FURNITURE MANUFACTURE & SALES 2000

CL, SB: 村田合同 Murata Interior Design Inc.
※2000年7月11日現在のデータを使用 As of July 11, 2000

HOME: 家具・インテリア FURNITURE & INTERIOR GOODS

innovator COLLECTION

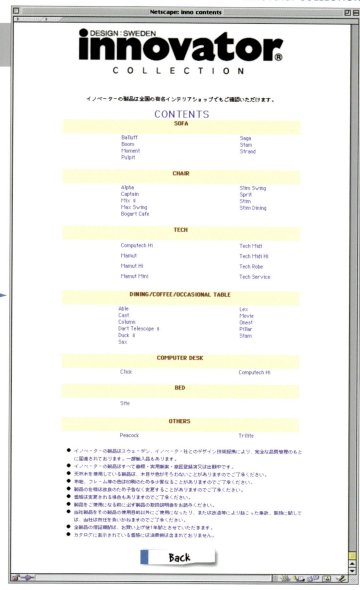

WEB SHOP!!

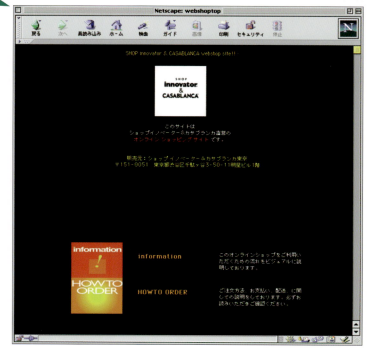

Catalog + Web

PROJECT CANDY

カタログキット（パッケージ・カード）
Catalog kit (Package・Card)

パッケージ Package／223×112mm
カード Card／218×110mm

プロジェクトキャンディのカタログは、1枚に1商品のカード式になっています。商品の写真が見やすく、また裏面にはデザインコンセプト、サイズ、材質等の情報を掲載しています。1枚1枚がカードになっていますので、ポストカードの様に飾って頂けます。

Project Candy's catalog is in card format, with a card for each product. Product photographs are attractive; the back of the card provides such information as design concept, size and materials. Because each card is individual, they can be displayed like postcards.

家具企画・販売　FURNITURE SALES　1994

CL, SB: 東京三都屋　Tokyo Mitoya Co., Ltd.

HOME: 家具・インテリア FURNITURE & INTERIOR GOODS

Catalog + Web
PROJECT CANDY

www.projectcandy.com

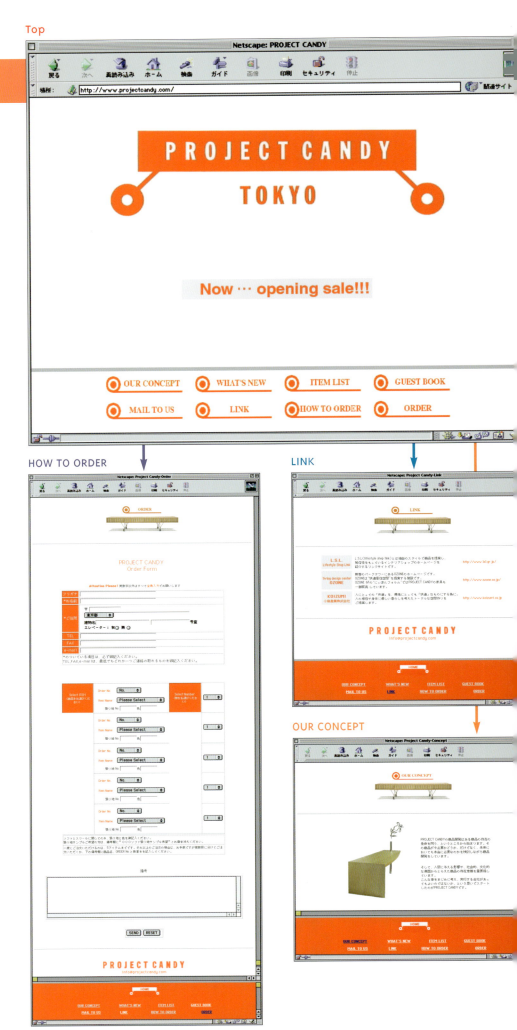

道具としてだけでなく、わずかな遊び心で人を優しく包む家具。そんな家具を多くの人に知って頂く為、プロジェクトキャンディのホームページは開設されました。全アイテムをご覧頂く為に写真だけでなく、イラストを用いる事で興味をもって頂けるよう工夫したのと同時に、イラストにする事で容量を軽くし、ロード時間の短縮に配慮しました。シンプルでありながらも単調にならないページを目指しました。

Furniture with a hint of playfulness: not just something to be used but designed to make people feel relaxed. Project Candy's Web site was created to tell people about that type of furniture. In order to show all products, illustrations as well photographs were used to keep the viewer's interest. Also, illustration data files are small, ensuring that images will appear quickly. We aimed to be simple without being boring.

家具企画・販売　FURNITURE SALES　2000

CL, SB: 東京三都屋　Tokyo Mitoya Co., Ltd.

※2000年7月11日現在のデータを使用　As of July 11, 2000

HOME: 家具・インテリア FURNITURE & INTERIOR GOODS

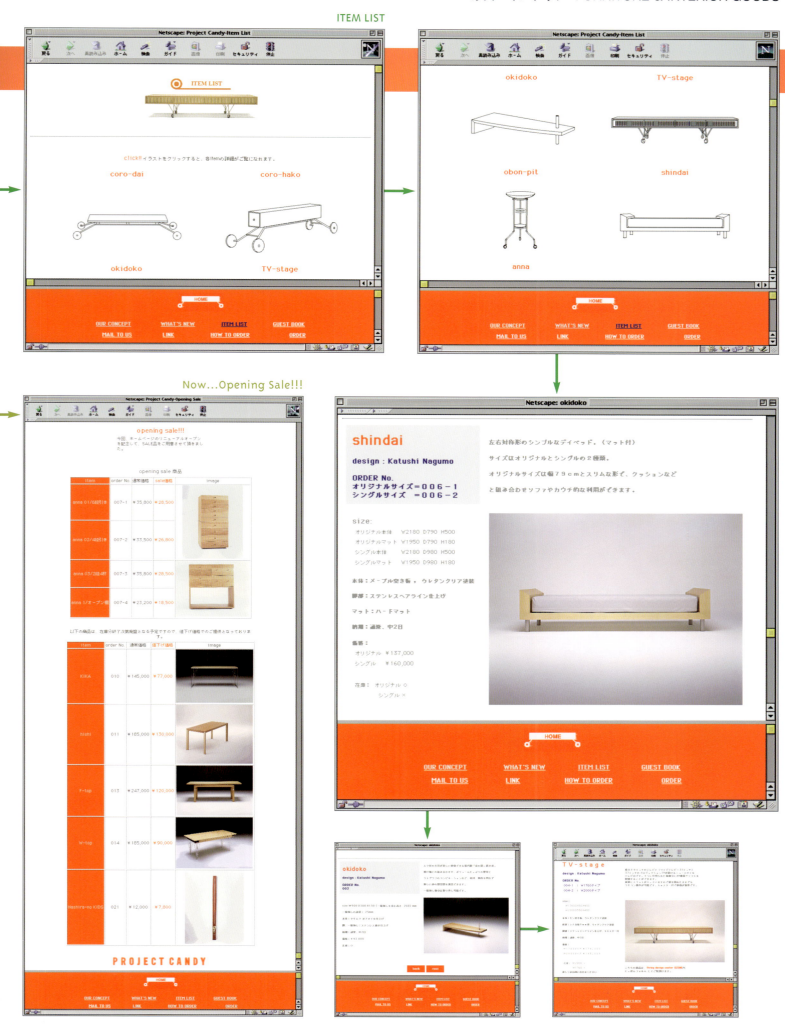

Catalog+Web

Y's for living

中綴 Stapled in the center／210×280mm

ブランドコンセプトであるシンプルでベーシックなイメージを、カタログにも反映させています。カタログはベッドウェアをメインとするコーディネートされたイメージページと、商品紹介ページとで構成されています。前半のイメージページは、シーズン商品を自然光の入るスタジオにて、爽やかな雰囲気で撮影しています。商品紹介ページ、及び後半の定番商品ページでは、通販でもお買い求め頂けるよう、価格、サイズ、カラーなどの情報を盛り込み、見やすくレイアウトしています。

Simplicity and basic brand image were incorporated into the catalog, which consists of two sections: image pages that show coordination primarily of bedding, and product information pages. In the image pages in the first half of the catalog, seasonal products were photographed in fresh settings, in a naturally lighted studio. In the product information pages and regular all-season product pages toward the end of the catalog, layouts clearly indicate price, size, and color information, for the purpose of catalog shopping.

寝装、寝具、家具、下着、生活雑貨企画・製造・販売　INTERIOR MANUFACTURE & SALES 2000

CL, SB: ワイズフォーリビング　Y's for living
CD: 杉浦久夫 (スタジオ スーパーコンパス)
Hisao Sugiura (Studio Super Compass)

HOME: 家具・インテリア　FURNITURE & INTERIOR GOODS

page 1, 2

page 13, 14

page 19, 20

177

Catalog + Web

Y's for living

www.ysforliving.co.jp

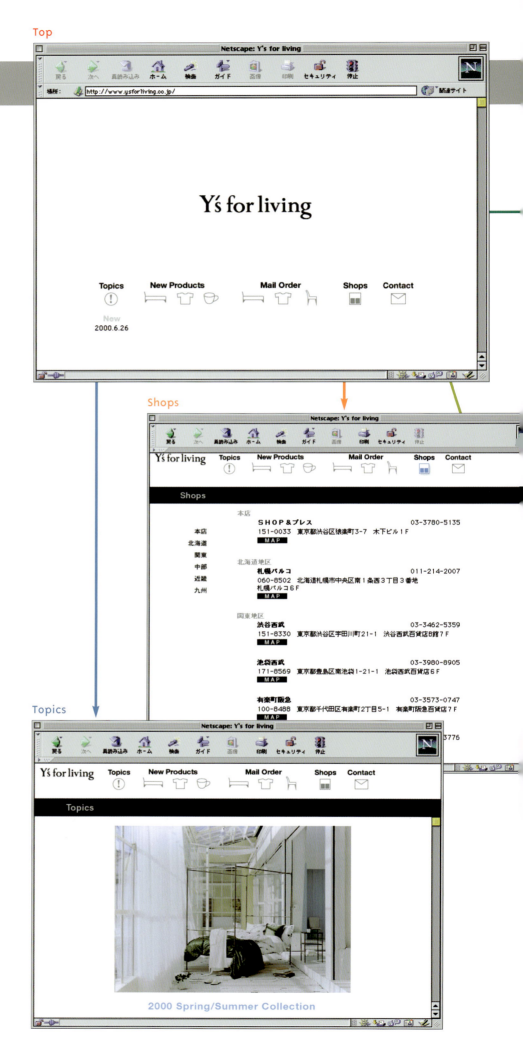

ワイズフォーリビングのシンプルなイメージと、操作の分かり易さなどの機能面を最小限の要素で両立させています。大きく分けて、タイムリーな情報を提供するトピックス、新作紹介、メールオーダー、店舗案内と4つのカテゴリーで構成しています。工夫点はサイト内のどのページを見ていても、全体のボリュームと自分の場所の把握という、紙媒体では当然のことが認識できること、ユーザーに不必要なストレスを感じさせずに最大限の演出効果を狙うこと、サイトの独自性をグラフィック／インタラクション一体で表現したことです。

The Web site of Y's for living characterizes, with a minimum number of elements, the brand's simple image, with functionality designed for easy operation. There are four roughly separated categories in the site: Topics, which provides timely information; New Products; Mail Order; and Shops. The most challenging aspects of designing this site were ensuring that the viewer would always be aware of his location within the site, something that is taken for granted with paper media; attaining maximum production effectiveness without making the viewer feel unnecessary stress; and expressing the site's originality by unifying its graphics and interactive features.

寝装、寝具、家具、下着、生活雑貨企画・製造・販売　INTERIOR MANUFACTURE & SALES　1999

CL, SB: ワイズフォーリビング　Y's for living
CD: 辻村哲也 (ツジムラ デザインスタジオ)
Tetsuya Tsuzimura (Tsuzimura Design Studio)
※写真はカタログから流用しています。
Photos from the printed catalog were used on the Web site.
※2000年7月11日現在のデータを使用　As of July 11, 2000

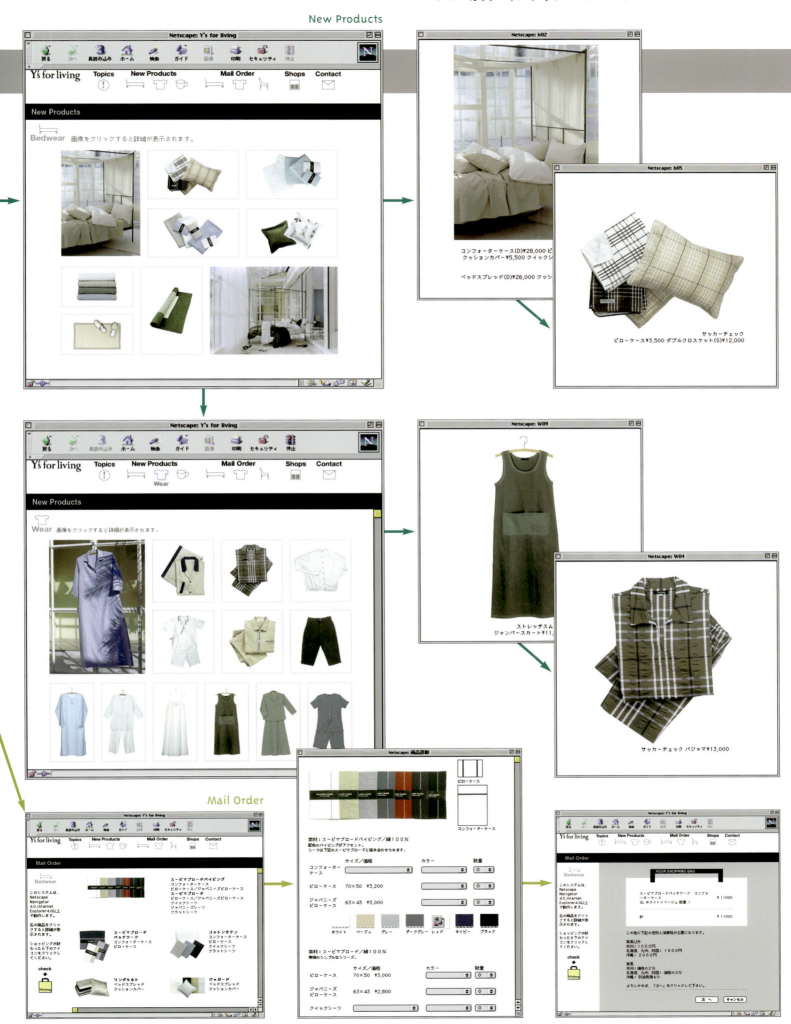

Catalog + Web

THE CONRAN SHOP

www.conran.ne.jp

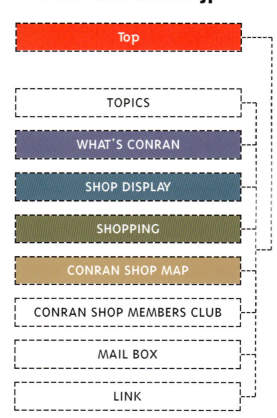

Top

WHAT'S CONRAN

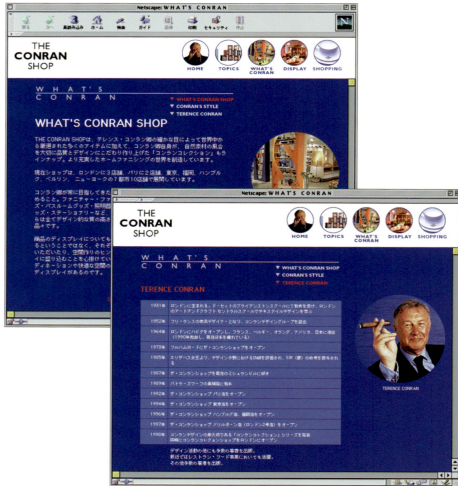

「ザ・コンランショップ」は、テレンス・コンラン卿の確かな目によって世界中から選りすぐられた、幅広いラインナップとそのディスプレイで、美しく楽しい生活をご提案します。このサイトでは、そのコンラン・スタイルを広く皆様にお伝えすると共に、ショップにお越しになれない方でもお買い物を楽しんで頂けたり、トピックスやディスプレイを、高い鮮度でご覧頂くことができます。今迄コンランをご存知なかった方は勿論、既にご存知の方まで、きっとご満足頂けると思います。是非ご覧ください。

The Conran Shop offers suggestions for a beautiful and entertaining lifestyle, presenting a beautifully displayed wide range of products selected from all over the world by the discerning eyes of Sir Terence Conran. This site was created not only to convey the Conran style to many, but also to provide shopping enjoyment for people who can not visit an actual shop, and a close look at hot product displays. We believe that everyone can enjoy our site, those who are not already familiar with the Conran Shop, as well as those who are. Please visit.

インテリア販売　INTERIOR SALES 1999

CL, PRODUCTION, SB:
ザ・コンランショップ　THE CONRAN SHOP
※2000年7月11日現在のデータを使用 As of July 11, 2000

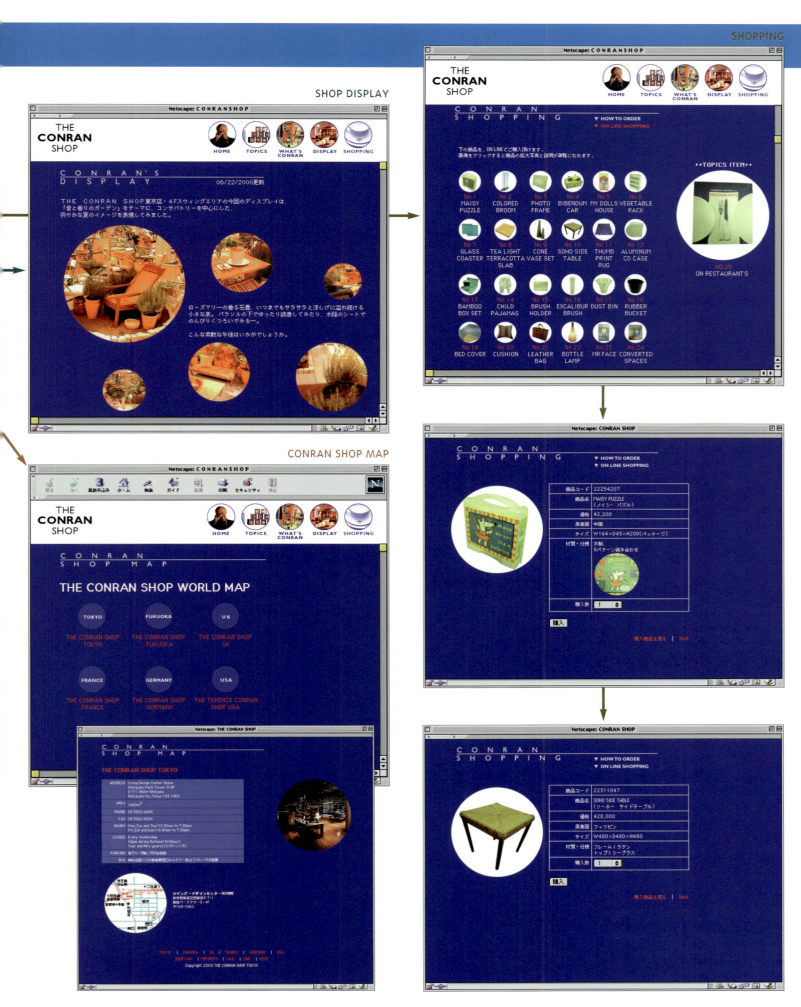

Catalog + Web

abode

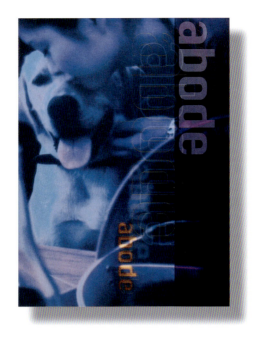

カタログキット(中綴・シート・ポストカード)
Catalog kit (Stapled in the center・Sheet・Postcard)

中綴 Stapled in the center／256×363mm
シート Sheet／210×296mm・ポストカードPostcard／
105×150mm

アボードでは選りすぐりの洗練された新鮮なデザインであると同時に、柔軟でシンプルかつ多面的で、現代の生活に欠かせない機能性を持った作品をご提供しています。優れた品質に裏打ちされたエキサイティングな作品の数々を、お客様のライフスタイルに合わせてご提案しています。

Abode offers select, sophisticated products of original design that are flexible and simple but versatile, with the functionality necessary for today's lifestyles. We offer a variety of exciting, quality products that will fit every lifestyle.

インテリア販売　INTERIOR SALES 1997

CL, SB: アボード 協和木工　abode - Kyowa Mokko
CD: 美川千秋　Chiaki Mikawa (abode MD)
AD: 橋本 弘　Hiroshi Hashimoto
D: 入交真由　Mayu Irimagiri／大貫雅子　Masako Ohnuki

HOME: 家具・インテリア　FURNITURE & INTERIOR GOODS

page 2, 3

page 30, 31

Catalog + Web

abode

www.abode.co.jp

- Top
- About us
- Information
- Cataloque
- Order
- Kyowamokko Co., Ltd.
- Press Release
- LIFESTYLE SHOP LINK

ショップの商品コンセプトを表現するべく、硬派に、甘くなり過ぎないデザインを心掛けました。単に家具や小物を紹介するだけでなく、それらを軸にしたライフスタイルの提案を意識して制作しました。

To express the shop's product concepts, I tried to make the design fairly straightforward. On that basis, I designed the site to not only introduce furniture and accessories, but to make life style suggestions as well.

インテリア販売　INTERIOR SALES　2000

CL, SB: アボード 協和木工　abode - Kyowa Mokko
CD: 美川千秋　Chiaki Mikawa (adobe MD)
AD: 橋本 弘　Hiroshi Hashimoto
D: 入交真由　Mayu Irimagiri
※2000年7月11日現在のデータを使用　As of July 11, 2000

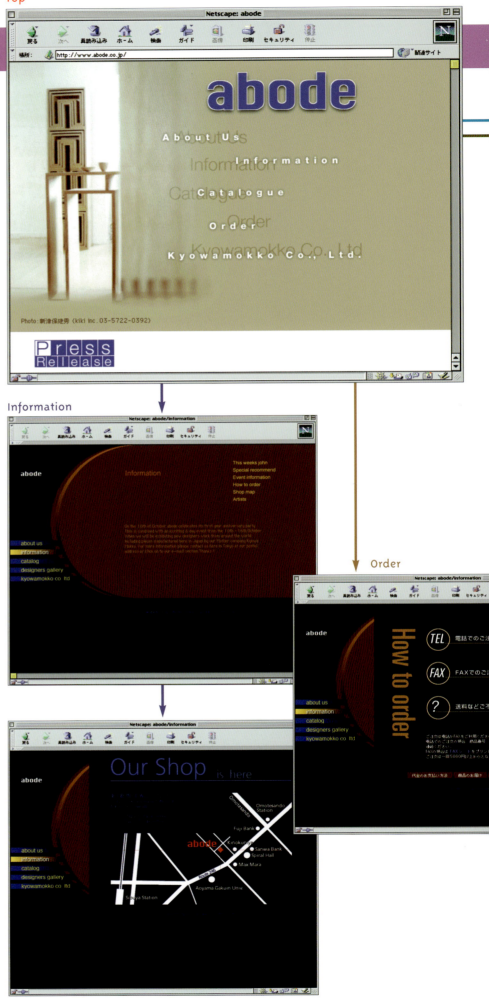

HOME: 家具・インテリア　FURNITURE & INTERIOR GOODS

Cataloque

LIFE STYLE SHOP LINK

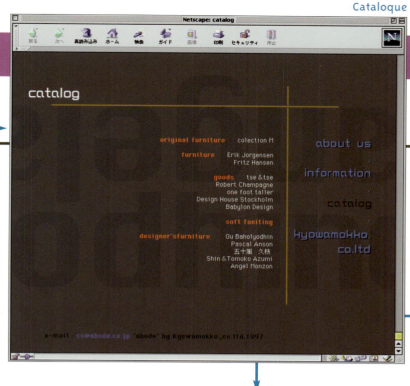

185

Catalog +Web

ACTUS

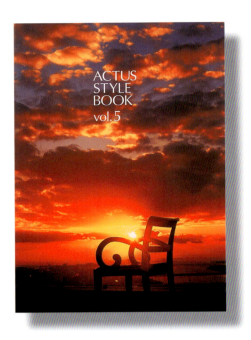

平綴 Bound／210×297mm

約1年じっくりと時間をかけて社内スタッフで作っています。日本の四季と素晴らしい空間、そしてインテリアとのコラボレーションをテーマにしています。
今回で5号目となるスタイルブックは、有料カタログとしては、異例の15万部発行され、読者の期待も年々大きくなっています。やはり1番の苦労はクォリティとして少しずつ上げていかなければならないことと、良い空間をみつけることにつきますね。やはりインテリアの撮影は体力的にも精神的にも大変な作業です。

The catalog was produced in-house, taking almost a year to complete. The theme is a collaboration of interiors, Japan's four seasons, and wonderful spaces. 150,000 copies of stylebook issue #5 were published, an unusually high amount for a catalog that is not distributed free of charge, indicating that reader expectations are growing from year to year. The greatest challenge is to improve quality with each issue and find good, new locations. Shooting interiors is extremely hard work, physically as well as mentally.

輸入家具販売
IMPORT FURNITURE SALES 1999-2000

CL, SB: アクタス ACTUS CORPORATION
CD: 荒木正則 Masanori Araki
AD: 大重 亨 Toru Oshige
P: 渡瀬良和 Yoshikazu Watase／森 曼好 Nobuyoshi Mori
CW: 伊東裕子 Yuko Ito／柳沢真澄 Masumi Yanagisawa

page 46, 47

page 174, 175

HOME: 家具・インテリア　FURNITURE & INTERIOR GOODS

page 1

page 20, 21

page 138, 139

Catalog + Web

ACTUS

www.actus-shop.co.jp

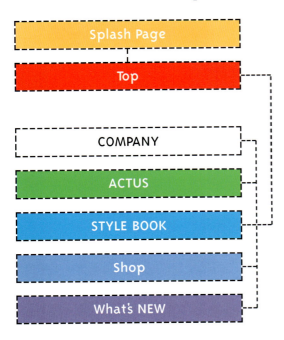

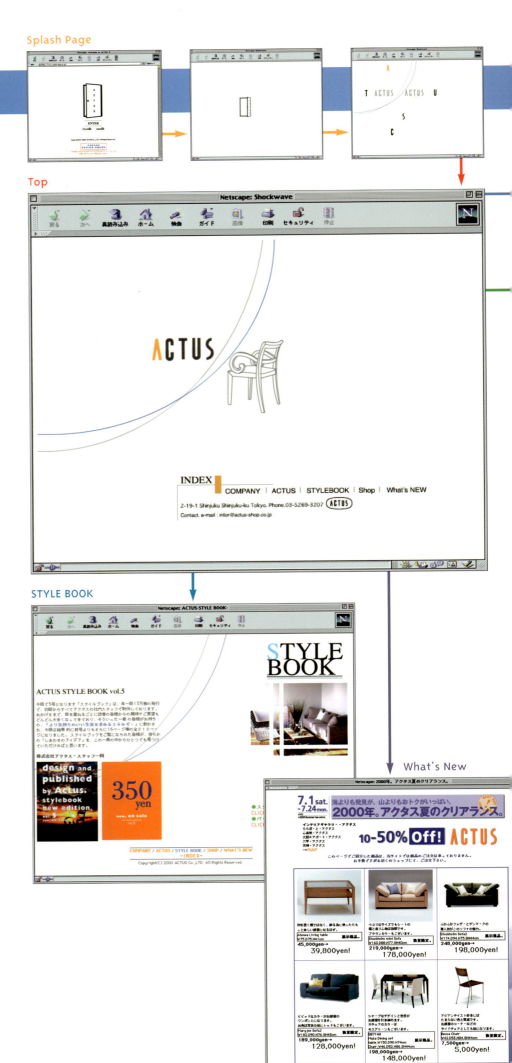

オールカラー212ページのインテリアカタログ「アクタス・スタイルブック」は、約15万部を発行しており、「アクタス」という企業の思想やスタイルを表現する媒体として、おかげさまで毎年読者も増え好評をいただいていますが、一年に一回の発行であるため、様々なイベントなど毎月のように新しく生み出されている、お客様とアクタスとのコミュニケーション活動の新鮮な情報は残念ながら表現できないことが多くありました。印刷媒体である「アクタス・スタイルブック」に、常に新鮮な情報を提供できるウェブを加えることにより、お客様に、より深くアクタスのことを理解していただければと考えております。実際にはウェブサイトは今年からのスタートでまだ第一フェーズですので、未完成な部分もありますが、今後さらに内容の充実をはかっていく予定です。

150,000 copies of the latest Actus Style Book, with 212 full-color pages, were printed. As a medium of expression of corporate ideas and style, it has been well received, with readership increasing each year. However, as it is published just once a year, the style book is not able to convey the latest information about Actus's activities, such as monthly events, to customers. By adding a Web site, which can provide fresh information, to the printed catalog "Actus Style Book," we hope that our customers can gain a better understanding of Actus. The web site is still in its initial phase, launched only this year; there are still some areas that are incomplete. There are plans to expand and enrich the site's contents in the future.

輸入家具販売　IMPORT FURNITURE SALES 2000

CL, SB: アクタス　ACTUS CORPORATION
CD: 早田 剛　Tsuyoshi Souda
D: 須永知子　Tomoko Sunaga
P: 渡瀬良和　Yoshikazu Watase
CW: アクタス　ACTUS CORPORATION
DF: アスタリック　ASTERIC

※2000年7月11日現在のデータを使用　As of July 11, 2000

HOME: 家具・インテリア FURNITURE & INTERIOR GOODS

Catalog + Web

Formio

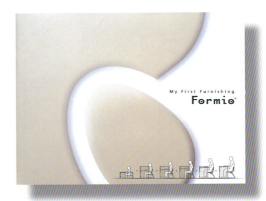

中綴 Stapled in the center／270×210mm

幼児から使いはじめ、成長とともに大人まで使える家具というこれまでにないジャンルの商品『フォルミオ』を紹介するカタログです。今までの子供家具と違ってなぜ幼児から使うのか、なぜ北欧で作られたのか、なぜ天然素材にこだわったのか、はじめてふれる消費者にも分かり易く伝えることを考慮しました。商品コンセプトは、子供を持つ親の願い、教育専門家のアドバイス、開発スタッフのねらいやデザインに込めた思いなど商品が生み出されるまでの経緯と背景になった思想を、ストーリーとして表現しています。

The catalog introduces Formio, a new category of furniture which can be used from infancy through adulthood. The catalog is designed to make first-time customers understand easily how the furniture can be used by an infant, why it is made in Scandinavia, and why only natural materials are used. To express product concepts, process and background thoughts of creation, such as the dreams of parents, the advice of educational specialists, the aims of product development staff, and ideas brought into the designs, are told in story form.

page 5, 6

page 9, 10

総合商社 TRADING COMPANY 1999

CL, SB: 三栄コーポレーション　SANYEI CORPORATION
CD, AD: 阿久津 雄一　Yuichi Akutsu
D: 松本 学　Manabu Matsumoto
P: 鏑木高人　Takato Kaburagi
DF: GKプランニング アンド デザイン
GK PLANNING AND DESIGN INC.

HOME: 家具・インテリア　FURNITURE & INTERIOR GOODS

遊んだら片づける。
基本的な生活習慣の一つです。
自分のお気に入りのものを飾りながら、遊びの一環として楽しく片づけることができれば、自然と片づけの習慣は身につきます。

子どもが小さいときは両親と同室がほとんど。
日本の習慣だった「川の字寝」が見直されてきています。
フォルミオのベッドは伸長可能。
パパとママのベッドのすぐそばに置くことができます。

STORAGE BOX
●ストーレッジボックス

OPEN WAGON
●オープンワゴン

CHEST WAGON
●チェストワゴン

HIGH CHEST WAGON
●ハイチェストワゴン

LAMP
●ランプ

HOOKS KF-201

HANGER KF-202

REPAIR KIT KF-203

BOARDS
●ボード

BOARD 3 KF-204

BOARD 4 KF-205

BOARD 5 KF-206

BOARD 6 KF-207

page 15, 16

page 17, 18

191

Catalog + Web

Formio

www.formio.co.jp

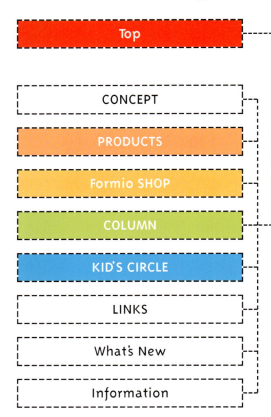

Top

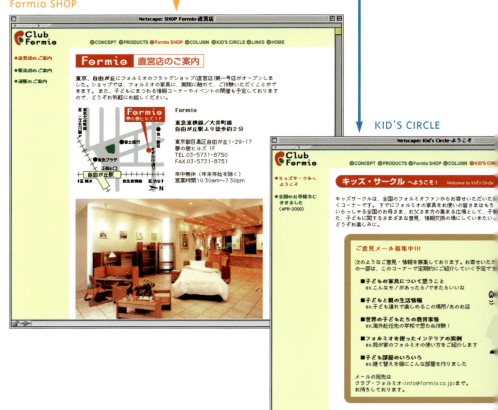

Formio SHOP

KID'S CIRCLE

日本の子供のための北欧製特選家具シリーズ「フォルミオ」を紹介するサイト。従来の子供家具という範疇を超えた同製品の特長を多面的に紹介し、親しみのなかにもハイエンド感を訴求することが求められました。既にカタログをお持ちのお客様からのアクセスも想定し、関連情報やユーザーの声の紹介など、ウェブ独自のコンテンツも多くとり入れています。制作上の留意点は、シンプルでわかりやすいナビゲーション、画像の減色や使いまわしによる読み込み時間の軽減、更新作業の省力化への配慮などです。常に成長を続けるサイトに育つことを願っています。

This site showcases the Formio series of Scandinavian furniture, selected especially for Japanese children. We were asked that the site introduce special features of the products, which go beyond the traditional classifications of children's furniture, emphasizing the high-end quality and at the same time its familiarity. Considering that the site might be accessed by customers who already have our catalog, we incorporated many original Web contents, such as related information and user comments. When designing the site, some of our priorities were simple and easy navigation, reducing time of appearance by using fewer colors and reusing images, and making the site easy to update. We hope that the quality of the site will continue to improve.

総合商社 TRADING COMPANY 2000

CL, SB: 三栄コーポレーション SANYEI CORPORATION
CD, AD: 阿久津 雄一 Yuichi Akutsu
D: 牧野奈緒（アールプラント） Nao Makino (R-PLANT)
DF: GKプランニング アンド デザイン
GK PLANNING AND DESIGN INC.
※2000年7月11日現在のデータを使用 As of July 11, 2000

HOME: 家具・インテリア　FURNITURE & INTERIOR GOODS

PRODUCTS

COLUMN

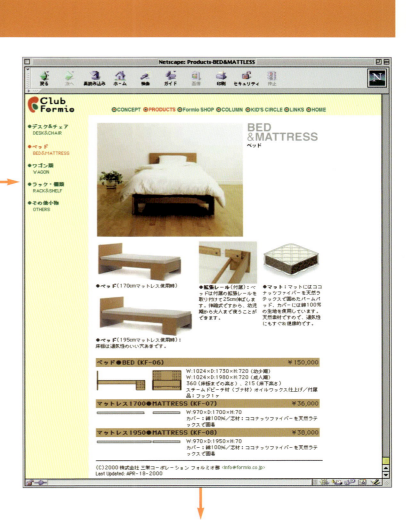

Catalog +Web

都倉インターナショナル

3ツ折観音開き French Threefold／183×256mm

デザインのシンプルさが日本人にも定評の高い北欧のモダンカジュアル家具を、日本の住居で快適に取り入れられるよう細部にわたるメーカーとの協同設計により、年齢を問わず予算と空間の広がりに応じてアレンジできる商品を提供しています。SOHO関連商品においては、グッドデザイン選定商品を受賞した"GRANRIK""PROEFORM"の各シリーズが、名実共に大好評です。またチェア、ベッド、チェスト等住居空間のアクセントになるようなデザインアイテムも登場。ウェブショップからの直接購入も可能です。秋からは多くの新商品の紹介も予定されています。

Tokura International offers Scandinavian modern casual furniture, the simplicity of design of which has gained a reputation among Japanese people. The products were designed and developed in detail together with the manufacturer, ensuring that they would comfortably fit Japanese homes. Selections can be made depending on considerations of either space or budget, and the furniture appeals to all age groups. Among our SOHO products, the Granvik and Preform series are both very popular; they boast good sales, and have received Good Design Awards. There are also new items, such as chairs and bed chests, which can be used as accent items in living spaces. Products can be purchased online. There are plans to introduce a range of new items in the fall.

家具、雑貨輸入・販売
FURNITURE・SUNDRIES IMPORT & SALES　2000

CL, SB: 都倉インターナショナル　TOKURA INTERNATIONAL CO., LTD.

HOME: 家具・インテリア　FURNITURE & INTERIOR GOODS

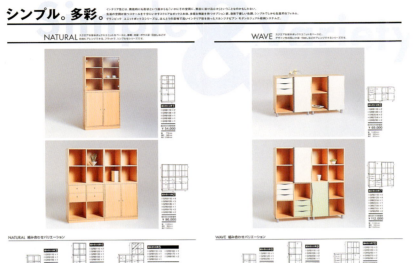

GRANVIK SERIES
ユニットボックス

GRANVIK SERIES
ウォールシェルフ

Zamat Tower System
タワーシェルフがひとつの結論を出した。

1. 二ツ折　2. 三ツ折観音開き　3. シート
1. Single-fold　2. French Threefold　3. Sheet

3種共 All／210×296mm

家具、雑貨輸入・販売
FURNITURE・SUNDRIES IMPORT & SALES　1998

CL, SB: 都倉インターナショナル
TOKURA INTERNATIONAL CO., LTD.
DF: アドヱヌエイ　AD NA

Catalog + Web

都倉インターナショナル

www.tic-concept.com/

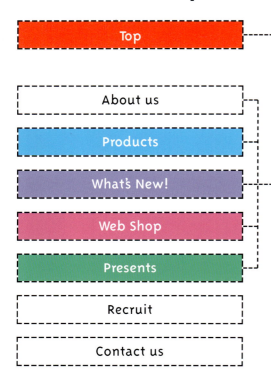
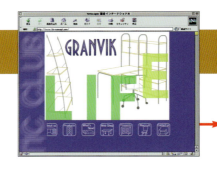
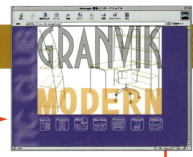

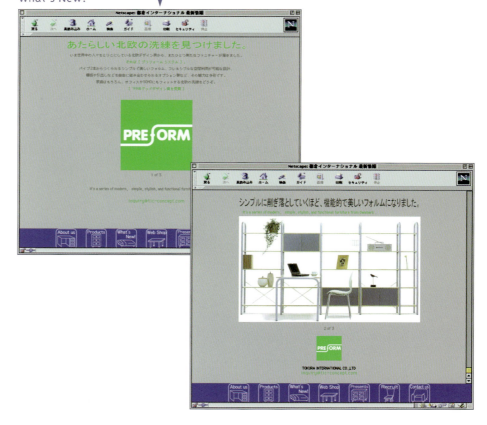

同業種のサイトとの差別化を図る為、思い切って背景をブルーにし、トップページではフラッシュを予告無しで開くよう配慮しました。動的素材ではない「家具」をインパクトある表現にする為に、ロゴがサウンドに合わせて動く様、施策しました。制作過程では、数十秒のバックサウンドも長く感じました。サイト内は主に、メーカー別商品紹介の形態を取っており、今後メーカー別オープニングムービーを制作し、公開していく予定です。

We wanted our Web site to be different than the sites of similar companies. Set against a blue background, a Flash movie opens automatically on the opening page. Logos dancing to sound give more impact to the expression of the furniture, which themselves are inanimate objects. During production, we felt that the opening background music should not be much longer than 10 seconds. The site is structured to introduce products classified by manufacturer, and we are planning to create a unique opening movie for each company.

家具、雑貨輸入・販売
FURNITURE・SUNDRIES IMPORT & SALES 2000

CL, SB: 都倉インターナショナル
TOKURA INTERNATIONAL CO., LTD.
DF: 時計人 TOKEIJIN
※2000年7月11日現在のデータを使用 As of July 11, 2000

HOME: 家具・インテリア　FURNITURE & INTERIOR GOODS

Presents

Products

Web Shop

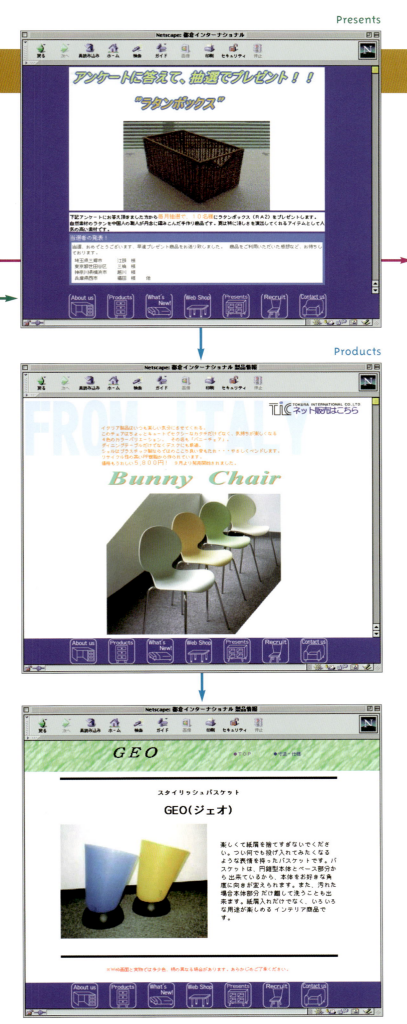

Catalog + Web

SCANDEX

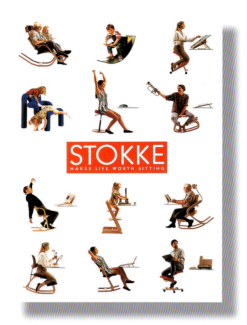

4ツ折観音開き・中綴・シート・ジャバラ
French Fourfold・Stapled in the center
Sheet・Accordion fold

ジャバラ Accordion fold／140×194mm
（開いた状態 When fully unfolded：840×194mm）
その他 Others 210×297mm

森と湖に囲まれたスカンジナビアの、長い冬と短い夏。長くつらい冬は、健康や快適さを大切にするシンプルさと機能性を、短い夏は、生命と自然の美しさを活かす精神を育んできました。そうした北欧の、生活の豊かさに対する意識の高さは、私たちがご紹介する北欧家具の底流に脈々と受け継がれています。私たちスキャンデックスは、北欧家具をはじめ、世界の家具・調度品を通じて、住空間のニーズにお応えするとともに、より高いご満足を みなさまにお届けします。

The long winters and short summers of Scandinavia, a region abundant in forests and lakes. The long winters developed a mentality that maintains good health and comfort, while short summers developed an appreciation of life and the beauty of nature. This high awareness of the richness of life has been continuously introduced in our Scandinavian furniture. We at Scandex will respond to the needs of living spaces, and provide higher satisfaction through furniture and interior products of the world, and of Scandinavian furniture in particular.

家具輸入・販売
FURNITURE IMPORT & SALES 2000

CL, SB: スキャンデックス SCANDEX CO.,LTD.
D: 福田良一 Ryoichi Fukuda

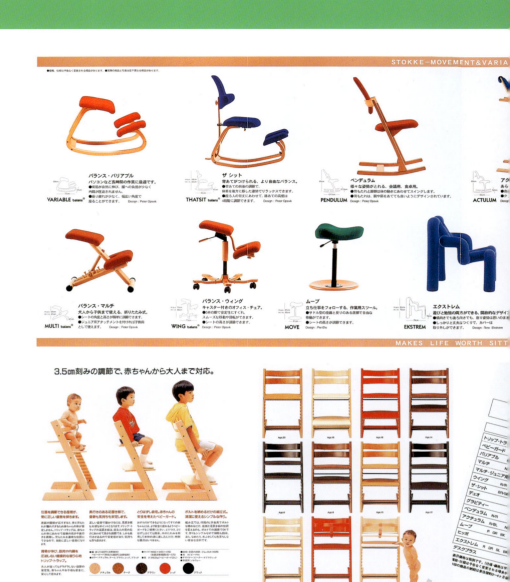

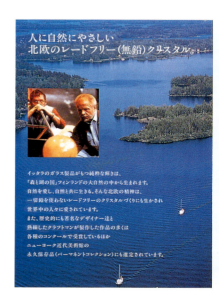

HOME: 家具・インテリア　FURNITURE & INTERIOR GOODS

page 7, 8

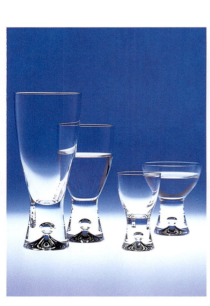

Catalog + Web

SCANDEX

www.SCANDEX.co.jp/

- Splash Page
- Splash Page 2
- Top
- LE KLINT
- iittala
- STOKKE
- 会社概要 Corporate Outline

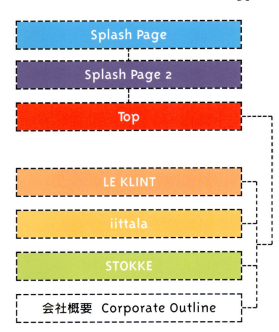

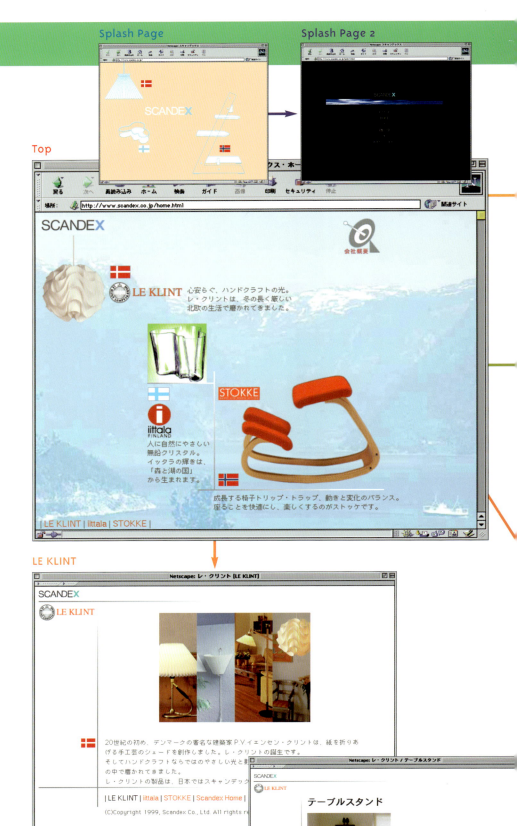

北欧商材を扱うスキャンデックス社の紹介サイトです。ストッケ社商品の使い方と調整の仕方などを、動画を使うことにより表現しました。他にイッタラ社のガラス、クリント社のランプシェードなど北欧の良さを日本の人々にお伝えする目的で製作しました。

The Web site of SCANDEX Co., Ltd., a dealer in Scandinavian products. Animations provide instruction on use and adjustment of STOKKE Inc. products. The site was created for introducing the quality of Scandinavian products to Japanese people, including such products as iittala glassware and LE KLINT lamp shades.

家具輸入・販売
FURNITURE IMPORT & SALES 2000

CL, SB: スキャンデックス SCANDEX CO.,LTD.

※2000年7月5日現在のデータを使用 As of July 5, 2000

HOME: 家具・インテリア FURNITURE & INTERIOR GOODS

iittala

STOKKE

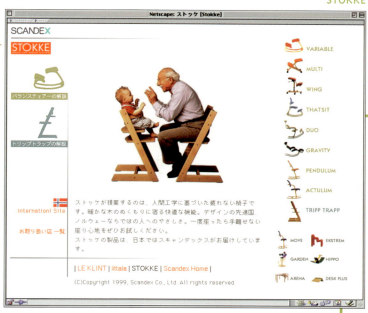
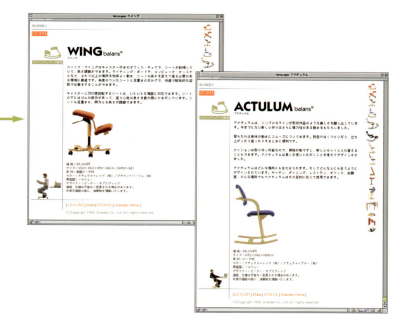

LE KLINT

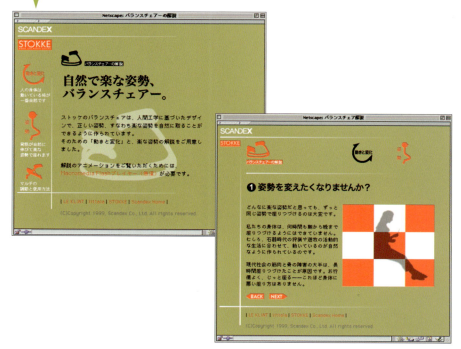

Catalog+Web

T·FACTORY

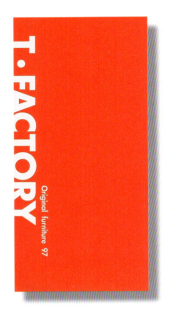

3ツ折観音開き・2ツ折
French Threefold・Single-fold

2種共 All／100×210mm

家具を中心に、インテリア商品の企画製造販売をしています。アートを融合させたT·FACTORYらしいオリジナルを目指し、生活の提案をしています。墨田区のショップは、工房を兼ねているため、製作者と購入者が直接、対話できるようになっています。店頭販売以外にウェブやDMでの販売も行っており、それぞれの広告デザインには、イメージが伝わるよう工夫しています。

T·FACTORY designs, manufactures, and sells interior products, with an emphasis on furniture. T·FACTORY proposes a lifestyle, with originals that incorporate art. In our workshop and retail shop located in Tokyo's Sumida Ward, consumers can communicate directly with the craftsmen. In addition to sales at our shop, we offer sales by mail order and our web site. We try to convey the company's image in each advertising design.

家具製造・販売
FURNITURE MANUFACTURE & SALES 1997

CL, SB: ティー・ファクトリー T·FACTORY

Catalog+Web

HOME: 家具・インテリア FURNITURE & INTERIOR GOODS

www.t-factory.org

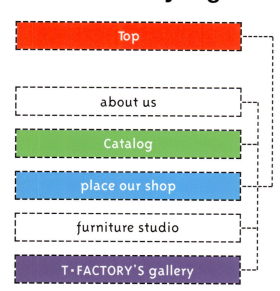

通販的なウェブショップというよりも、私たちがやっている、やりたいことをホームページ全体で表現しています。個人でやっている為、広告費はほとんどかけられませんので、T・FACTORYを知って頂くのに、ホームページを開くという手段は近道と思っています。ただ、普通の家具屋のホームページを見る感覚で開くとインパクトがありません。そこで特長である工房兼ショップであるということや、アート感覚を主張して、新しい形をウェブショップで表現して行きたいです。

Rather than being an online shop, we use our Web site to express what we do and what we want to do. Because we are a small company, we do not have a large advertising budget. Having a Web site is a quick way to let people know about T・Factory. However, most furniture stores have Web sites with little impact. By emphasizing our strong points - our shop and studio, and our art sensibility - we hope to find new ways for a Web store to manifest itself.

家具製造・販売
FURNITURE MANUFACTURE & SALES 2000

CL, SB: ティー・ファクトリー T・FACTORY
※2000年7月11日現在のデータを使用 As of July 11, 2000

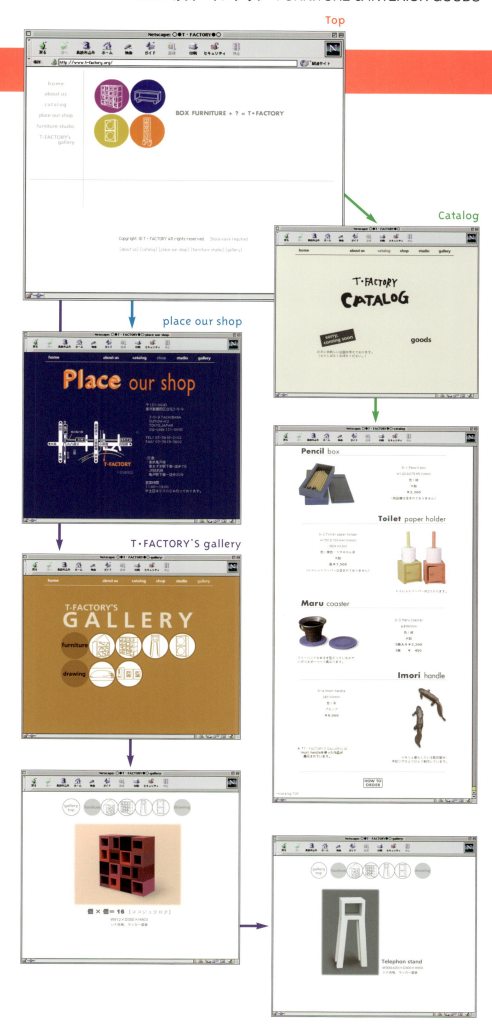

203

Catalog + Web

無印良品

page 4, 5　　　　　　　　　　　　　　page 40, 41

page 18, 19　　　　　　　　　　　　　page 44, 45

1980年、西友のPB商品として開発された無印良品。このネーミングには、私たちの生活哲学そして商品開発のすべての意味が集約されています。実質本位の商品をより安くという思想は、既存商品に見られる無駄（必要外機能・必要以上の装飾・過剰包装等）を排除し、また生活者の合理的価格志向をよりよく反映するという方向に展開され、時代感覚にマッチした商品づくりが丹念に続けられてきました。店舗は、1983年の「無印良品青山」オープンを皮切りに全国主要都市に展開して、現在では、海外にも広がり、深い共感をもって受け入れられています。

Mujirushi Ryohin was developed as a Seiyu private brand in 1980. The name, literally "no-brand good products," contains our philosophy for life, and the concepts behind product development. The idea of making practical products cheaper, and eliminating unnecessary features often seen in existing products (unnecessary functions or decorations, over-wrapping, etc.), was developed in a direction that better reflects consumers' price-oriented rationale. Product development sensitive to our times has been undertaken painstakingly. The first Mujirushi Ryohin shop opened in Aoyama in 1983, and there are now popular stores in major cities nationwide, as well as in foreign countries.

HOME: 生活用品・雑貨　LIFESTYLE PRODUCTS & SUNDRIES

自転車
無印良品 2000 夏

3

キッチン・テーブル　バス・トイレ用品
無印良品 2000 夏

4

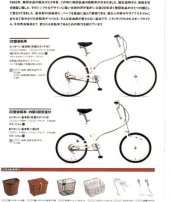
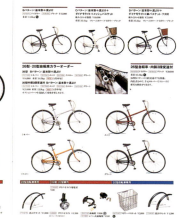

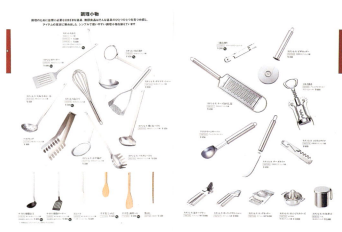

page 6, 7

page 20, 21

1、2、4、中綴 Stapled in the center／190×257mm
3、4ツ折観音開き French Fourfold／190×257mm

日用品製造・販売
HOUSEHOLD GOODS MANUFACTURE & SALES　2000

CL, SB: 良品計画　RYOHIN KEIKAKU CO., LTD.
CD: 田中一光　Ikko Tanaka
AD: 廣村正彰　Masaaki Hiromura
D: 伊藤幸子　Sachiko Itoh (1, 4)／木住野 英彰　Hideaki Kishino (2, 3)
P: 中本徳豊　Tokutoyo Nakamoto (1)／楢木野 修　Osamu Narakino (2, 3)／横井隆喜　Takaki Yokoi (4)
CW: 梅本洋一　Yoichi Umemoto

Catalog + Web

無印良品

1

2

page 2, 3

page 2, 3

page 14, 15

page 30, 31

1、2、中綴 Stapled in the center／190×257mm

日用品製造・販売
HOUSEHOLD GOODS MANUFACTURE & SALES 2000

CL, SB: 良品計画　RYOHIN KEIKAKU CO., LTD.
AD: 斎藤隆郎　Takao Saito
D: 眞根井 靖嘉　Yasuyoshi Manei／水野佳史　Yoshifumi Mizuno
P: アズ・ライフ　AZU LIFE
CW: 土屋幸裕　Yukihiro Tsuchiya
DF: バウハウス　BAU HOUSE

HOME: 生活用品・雑貨　LIFESTYLE PRODUCTS & SUNDRIES

page 8, 9

page 2, 3

page 44, 45

page 6, 7

3、4、中綴 Stapled in the center／190×257mm(3), 220×300mm (4)

日用品製造・販売
HOUSEHOLD GOODS MANUFACTURE & SALES　2000

CL, SB: 良品計画　RYOHIN KEIKAKU CO., LTD.
CD: 田中一光　Ikko Tanaka
AD: 廣村正彰　Masaaki Hiromura
D: 水野佳史　Yoshifumi Mizuno
P: 大山 高　Takashi Ohyama (3)／中本徳豊　Tokutoyo Nakamoto (4)
CW: 梅本洋一　Yoichi Umemoto

Catalog + Web

無印良品

www.muji.co.jp

- Top
- キャンペーン情報 Campaign Information
- 店舗情報 Shop Information
- 商品紹介 Products Information
- キャンプ場情報 Campground Information
- その他 Others
- カタログ一覧 List of Catalog
- 採用情報 Recruiting Information
- 会社概要 Corporate Outline
- 業績推移 Changes in Company Business
- 決算情報 Company Information

「無印良品」の商品イメージに準じた、シンプルで、わかりやすい構成を第一に考え、商品情報・店舗情報・決算情報などをご紹介しています。店頭にて配付されているカタログをPDF化し、ネット上でも閲覧できるようにしています。不必要に最新技術に走ることはしませんが、商品または、店舗をご紹介するのに効果的と思われるものについては、積極的に取り入れるようにしています。

The Web site of Mujirushi Ryohin, providing product and shop information, as well as corporate financial reports, within a simple and easily navigable structure. Catalogs, which are distributed at the retail stores, are converted into PDF files, so that people can look at them on the Net. We don't usually rush to adopt unnecessary cutting-edge technologies, but we do tend to utilize those techniques that seem that they will help us introduce our products and shops.

日用品製造・販売
HOUSEHOLD GOODS MANUFACTURE & SALES 2000

CL, SB: 良品計画　RYOHIN KEIKAKU CO., LTD.
CD: 小澤康子　Yasuko Ozawa
AD, D: 飯盛雅子　Masako Iimori
PR: 車谷浩愛　Hiroyoshi Kurumatani
　　中村彩子　Ayako Nakamura
DF: DNPデジタルコム　DNP DIGITALCOM Co., Ltd.
TECHNICAL DIRECTOR: 小島直人　Naoto Kojima
※2000年7月5日現在のデータを使用　As of July 5, 2000

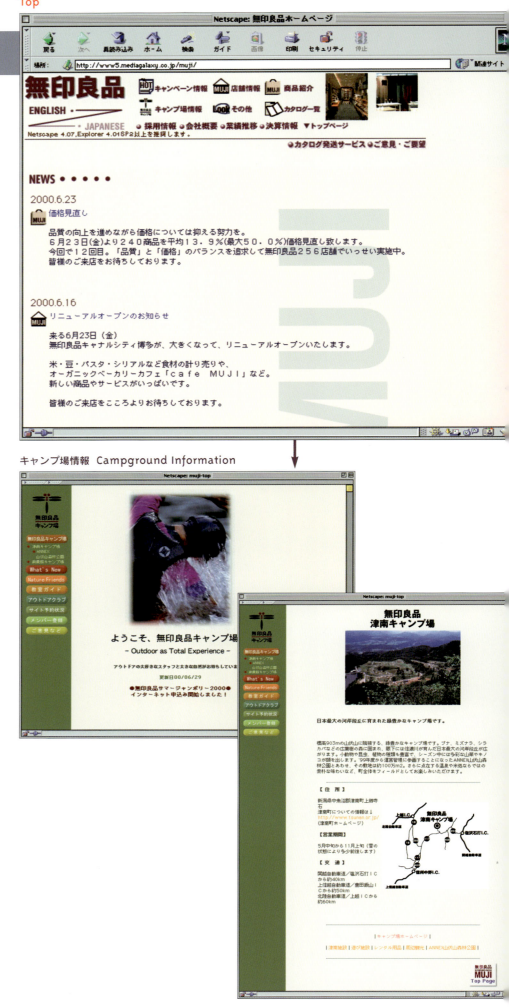

Top

キャンプ場情報 Campground Information

HOME: 生活用品・雑貨　LIFESTYLE PRODUCTS & SUNDRIES

商品紹介　Products Information

店舗情報　Shop Information

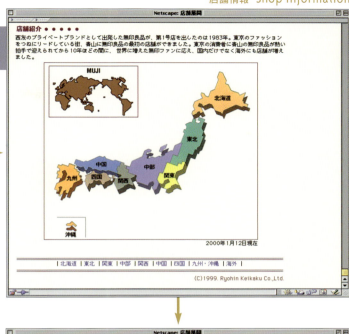

Catalog + Web

無印良品

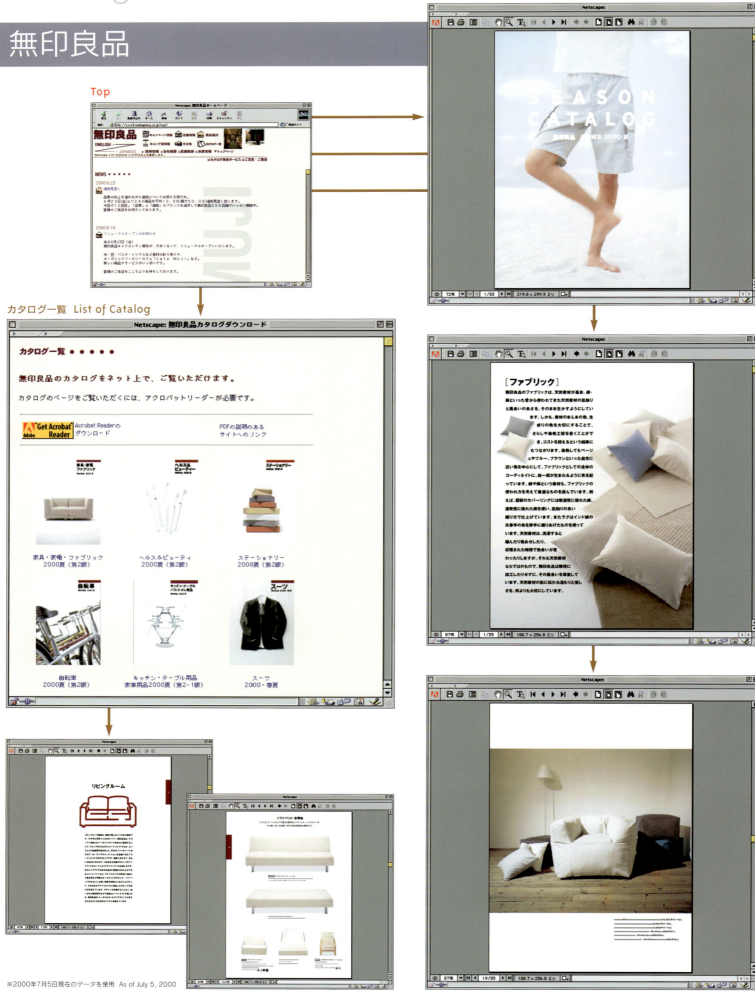

※2000年7月5日現在のデータを使用 As of July 5, 2000

HOME: 生活用品・雑貨　LIFESTYLE PRODUCTS & SUNDRIES

カタログ一覧　List of Catalog

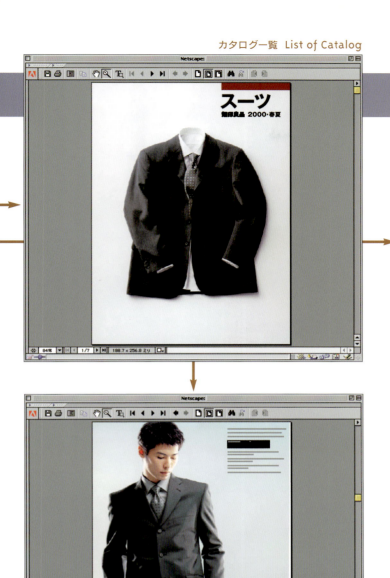

カタログ一覧　List of Catalog

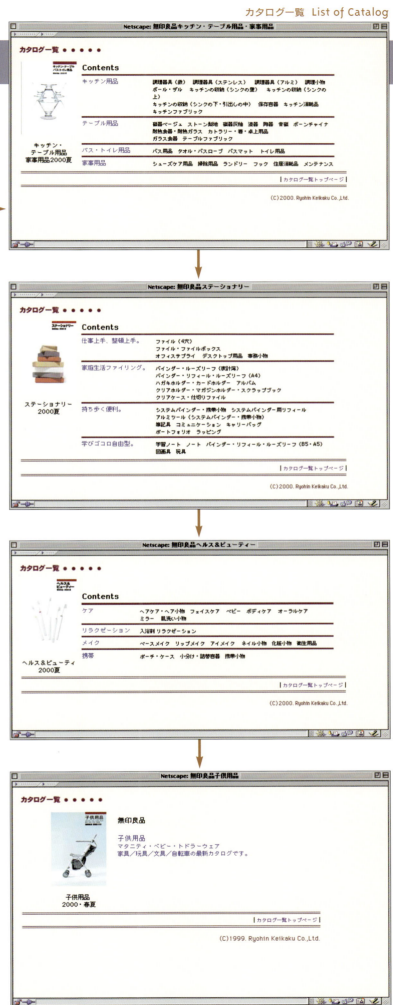

Catalog +Web

WiLL

中綴 Stapled in the center／120×120mm

『WiLL』の全商品が紹介されたカタログを作る事により、各社個別の売り場や流通事情を超えて商品を紹介する場づくりが可能となりました。『WiLL』のコンセプトを紹介したうえで、最新の全ラインナップを紹介。各社の流通事情を配慮した上で『WiLL』のロゴをあしらった正方形のカタログに仕上げました。また、さらに『WiLL』の魅力を理解していただく為にウェブ "willshop.com" のアドレスを紹介しています。

This is the complete catalog of all "WiLL" items, a brand created to enable participating companies to introduce products in areas that are beyond their usual sales and distribution reach. The catalog displays the latest, complete product lineup, and includes an introduction of the concept behind WiLL. After considering the distribution circumstances of each company, the catalog was designed in a square format, displaying the brand logo. The web site address of willshop.com is included, for further explanations of WiLL's appeal.

異業種合同プロジェクト
COMBINED BRAND STRATEGY WITH PARTICIPATION FROM DIFFERENT INDUSTRIES 2000

CL: WiLL委員会 WiLL PROJECT
CD: 永井一史 (博報堂) Kazufumi Nagai (HAKUHODO Inc.)
AD: 宮崎稔己 (スカット・コーポレーション) Toshiki Miyazaki (scatto corporation)
D: 下田 佳代子 (スカット・コーポレーション) Kayoko Shimoda (scatto corporation)
P: 中川昌彦 Masahiko Nakagawa
CW: 斉藤賢司 (博報堂) Kenji Saito (HAKUHODO Inc.)
後藤 学 Manabu Goto／薄井 富士子 Fujiko Usui
SB: 博報堂 HAKUHODO Inc.

page 1. 2

page 5. 6

212

HOME: 生活用品・雑貨　LIFESTYLE PRODUCTS & SUNDRIES

page 7, 8

005　WiLL Vi　IN COLLABORATION WITH TOYOTA

007　WiLL RANGE　IN COLLABORATION WITH National

006　WiLL FRIDGE　IN COLLABORATION WITH National

008　WiLL TOUR CITY&RESORT HOTEL（東京／関西）

page 9, 10

013　WiLL COSMiCFiZZ　IN COLLABORATION WITH KOKUYO

015　WiLL BIKE　IN COLLABORATION WITH Panasonic

014　WiLL MD　IN COLLABORATION WITH Panasonic

016　WiLL オンタイム チョコレート　IN COLLABORATION WITH Glico

page 17, 18

Catalog + Web

WiLL

www.willshop.com

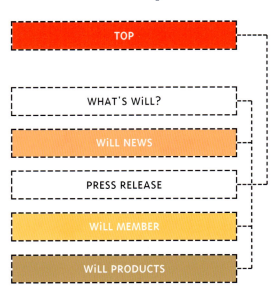

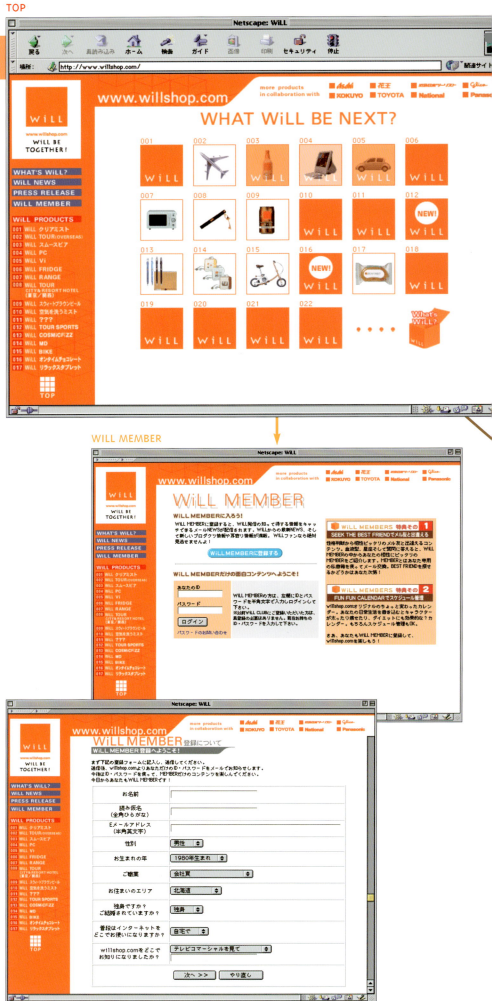

『WiLL』の全商品を一堂に紹介する場として機能することを目指しました。『WiLL』の最新情報を掲出し、「What's WiLL」というコーナーを設け、『WiLL』のコンセプトを紹介。各社の商品情報は『WiLL』のラインナップとしてナンバーを設け、共通のトーンで統一。また、希望者にはメンバー登録をしていただき、『WiLL』の最新ニュースを配信しています。

This Web site was intended to be a place where all of the items in the WiLL product line could be introduced. The latest information about WiLL can be found, and the brand concept is explained in the "What's WiLL?" corner. Item numbers are included as part of product information, and common design tones were used for each company. After they have registered, members will receive WiLL updates and information.

異業種合同プロジェクト
COMBINED BRAND STRATEGY WITH PARTICIPATION FROM DIFFERENT INDUSTRIES 2000

CL: WiLL委員会 Will PROJECT
AD: 斉藤久生 Hisao Saito
(キッズ・コーポレーション KIDS Corporation)
D, I: 村上 健 Ken Murakami, 中野 徹 Toru Nakano
(キッズ・コーポレーション KIDS Corporation)
P: 中川昌彦 Masahiko Nakagawa
CW: 斉藤賢司 (博報堂) Kenji Saito (HAKUHODO Inc.)
後藤 学 Manabu Goto／薄井 富士子 Fujiko Usui
PR: 大月真人 Masato Otsuki, 田邉敬弘 Takahiro Tanabe
(キッズ・コーポレーション KIDS Corporation)
SB: 博報堂 HAKUHODO Inc.

※2000年7月7日現在のデータを使用 As of July 7, 2000

HOME: 生活用品・雑貨　LIFESTYLE PRODUCTS & SUNDRIES

WiLL PRODUCTS

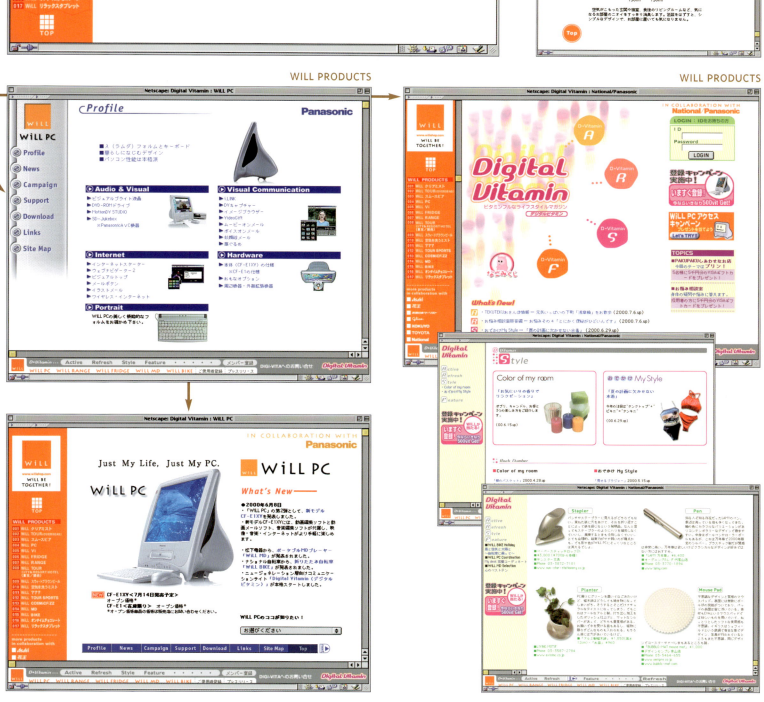

Catalog + Web

loft

中綴 Stapled in the center／210×297mm

ロフト・インテリアカタログは、インテリア生活雑貨全般を網羅したトータルインテリアカタログです。制作コンセプトは、「都市生活者の等身大のカジュアルなライフスタイルの表現」を提案しています。

The Loft Interior Catalog, a comprehensive interior catalog with everything from interior goods to everyday products. The catalog proposes the concept of "expression of a life-size urban casual lifestyle."

page 21, 22

日用品、雑貨販売
LIFESTYLE PRODUCTS SALES 2000

CL: ロフト　LOFT
CD: 富田貞彦（スコープ）
　　Sadahiko Miyata (SCOPE INC. CO.)
AD, D: 清水一博（清水広告事務所）
　　Kazuhiro Shimizu (Shimizu Advertising Office)
P: DNPメディアクリエイト　DNP MEDIA CREATE
CW: 太田 千代江　Chiyoe Ohta
SB: スコープ　SCOPE INC. CO.

Catalog+Web

HOME: 生活用品・雑貨　LIFESTYLE PRODUCTS & SUNDRIES

www.loft.co.jp

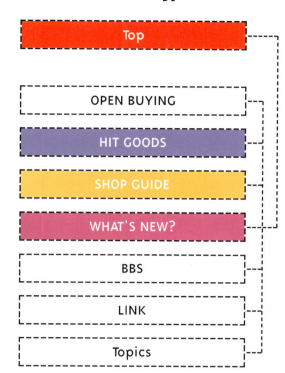

企業のイメージカラーである"ロフトイエロー"をどう新しく見せるかというポイントは、いくつかのアイデアを考えました。技術的には、誰にでもストレスなく見られる様に、プラグインを必要とするムービーなどは多用せず、グラフィック的表現だけでブラウザを設計しました。デザインが押しつけにならない様に気をつかい、商品である雑貨が主役になれるよう、スペースを工夫しています。シンプルであり、イメージを強く残すホームページの一つだと思います。

We came up with several ideas to present the company's image color, "Loft Yellow," in new ways. In order to make it possible for anyone to easily view the site's pages, we did not include such features as movies that require plug-ins, but planned the site using only graphics for expression. We took into consideration the fact that the products must be the main characters, given sufficient space, and that the design would not be overwhelming. We believe that this is one of the simpler homepages, but one with a strong image impact.

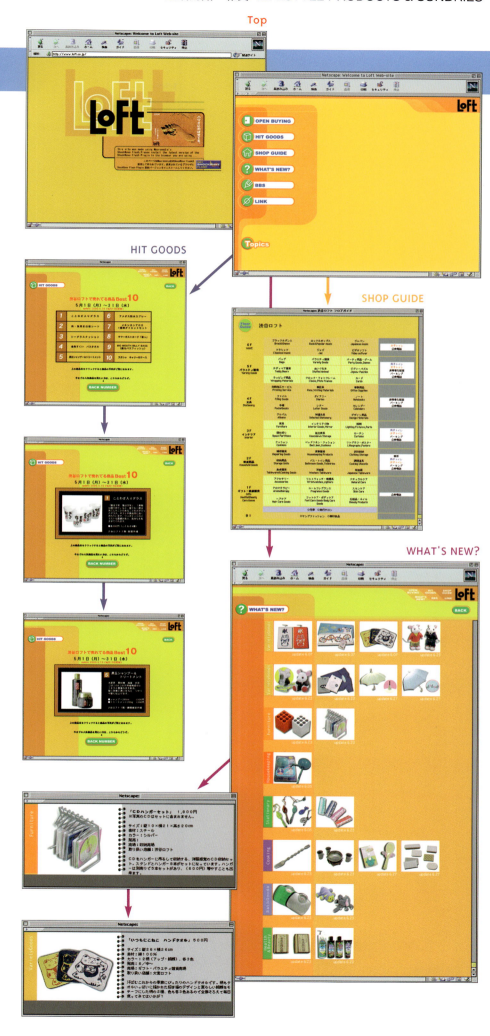

日用品、雑貨販売
LIFESTYLE PRODUCTS SALES　2000

CL: ロフト　LOFT
CD: 及川 晃　Akira Oikawa
AD, D: 小林範章　Noriaki Kobayashi
SB: ビーツー・エンジン　B2 ENGINE

※2000年7月11日現在のデータを使用　As of July 11, 2000

Catalog + Web

Sony Plaza

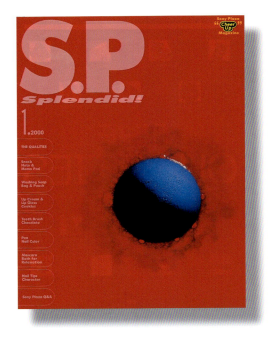

中綴 Stapled in the center／260×346mm

ソニープラザの店頭で無料で配布しているフリーマガジン。毎月のイチオシ商品やこれから先の新商品の情報を先取りできます。本当にこれで無料？と疑いたくなるような内容の濃さには定評あり。ぜひ店頭でゲットして下さい。

This is a free magazine distributed in Sony Plaza shops. Hot products are featured, as well as advance information about new items. The variety and detail of the popular magazine's contents are such that people often ask, "Is this really free?" Please get a copy at the store.

輸入雑貨専門店　IMPORT GOODS STORE 2000

CL, SB: ソニープラザ　Sony Plaza Co., Ltd.
CD: ソニーマガジンズ　Sony Magazines

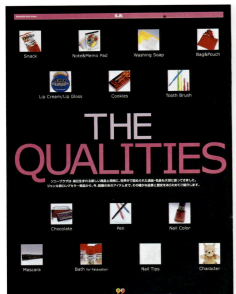

page 2, 3

page 6, 7

page 8, 9

HOME: 生活用品・雑貨　LIFESTYLE PRODUCTS & SUNDRIES

Catalog+Web

Sony Plaza

www.sonyplaza.co.jp/

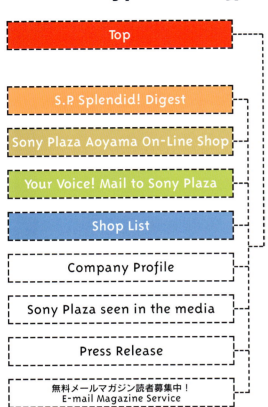

いつも話題と刺激でいっぱいの輸入雑貨専門店ソニープラザ。そのワクワク感をウェブでも楽しんでほしい!という願いをこめたのがこの『P's g@te(ピーズゲート=プラザへの入り口の意)』。情報誌『S.P.Splendid!』のダイジェスト版を始めとし、ショップの「今」がわかる情報欄や掲示板『Your Voice!』、マップ付きのショップリストなど、ソニープラザ情報満載です。品揃え1,000点以上のオンラインショップも大好評!2000年9月にはコスメ情報ページもスタート予定で、日々バージョンアップ中のサイトです。

Sony Plaza is a shop specializing in imported goods, and is always interesting and stimulating. "P's g@te" was created to allow people to enjoy this excitement on the Web. The site contains many kinds of information about Sony Plaza, such as a digest version of the "S.P. Splendid!" information magazine, an information corner that lists what's currently happening in the shops, the "Your Voice!" bulletin board, and a list of shop that includes maps. The online shop is very popular, offering more than 1,000 items. There are plans to launch a cosmetics information page in September 2000. The site is updated on a regular basis.

輸入雑貨専門店　IMPORT GOODS STORE 1998

CL, SB: ソニープラザ　Sony Plaza Co., Ltd.
D: ソニーコミュニケーションネットワーク　Sony Communication Network Co., Ltd.

※2000年7月4日現在のデータを使用　As of July 4, 2000

Shop List

Your Voice! Mail to Sony Plaza

HOME: 生活用品・雑貨 LIFESTYLE PRODUCTS & SUNDRIES

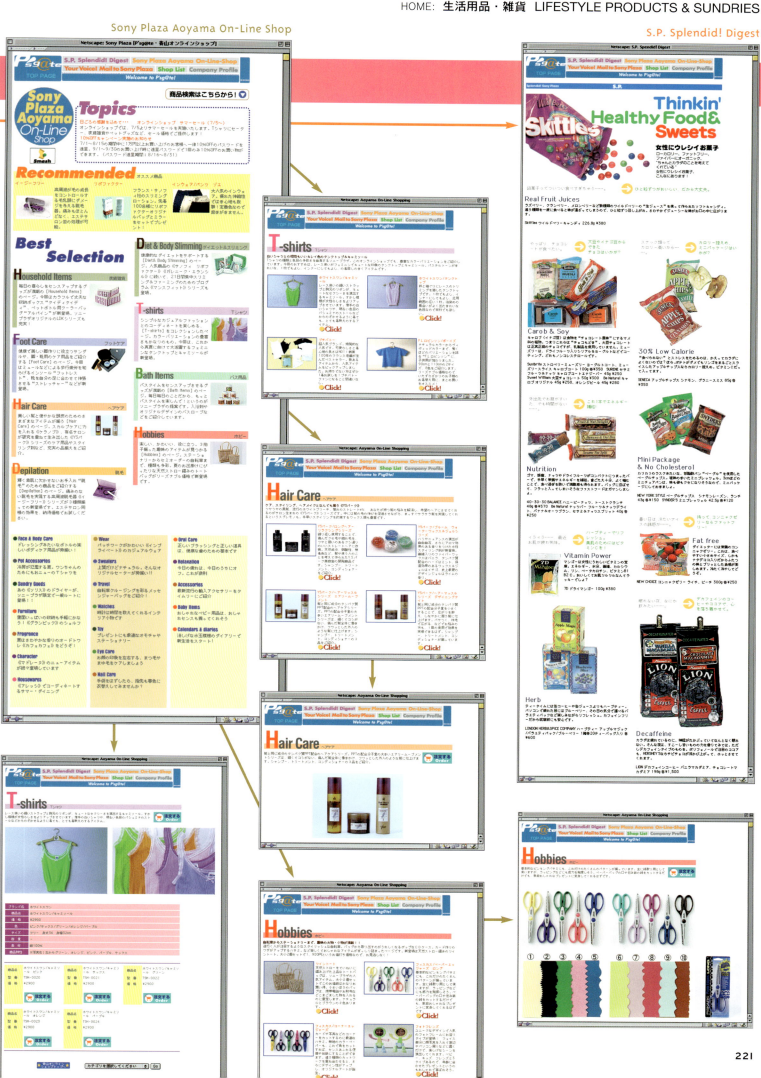

Catalog + Web

HEMING'S

ジャバラ Accordion fold／108×215 mm
(開いた状態 When fully unfolded：756×215mm)

HEMING'Sの「ハーネスファクトリーメイドシリーズ」は、10年を迎えました。デビュー当時のカタログは、全てイラストで、イメージを伝える事を優先された物でしたが、ある程度イメージを伝えられた時点で現在のカタログに変更しました。なぜなら今度は、イメージだけではなく、ストーリーや商品の各部分まで細かく理解して頂き、商品の購入までつなげていくツールとしたかったからです。特に気をつけた点は、商品の質感を出した写真と、ジャバラ式で全てのアイテムを表裏で全て見られる形状にしたことです。又、商品各部所の説明も入れ、ストーリー性も強調しました。

It has been 10 years since Heming's introduced the Harness Factory Made series. Early catalogs were full of illustrations, with priority given to communication of brand image. At the point when we felt that such communication had mostly succeeded, the catalog's style was changed to the current one. In this catalog, we wanted to not only convey images, but also give our customers detailed information about the various parts of the products and stories about the items, ultimately leading them to purchase the products. Careful attention was paid to the photographs as well as the format. We selected photographs that show the texture of the products; the accordion format was chosen so that all items could be shown on the front and back pages.

鞄、雑貨製作・販売
LUGGAGE・HANDBAG・SUNDRIES MANUFACTURE & SALES 1999

CL, SB: ヘミングス HEMING'S INC.
CD, AD: 神谷敬久 Takahisa Kamiya

HOME: 生活用品・雑貨　LIFESTYLE PRODUCTS & SUNDRIES

HARNESS FACTORY MADE SERIES

TRAVEL

GEAR KIT CASE
COTTON/SADDLE LEATHER
a. 321801　¥8,800　230m/m×160m/m×60m/m
b. 321901　¥7,800　230m/m×120m/m×60m/m
c. 322101　¥6,800　140m/m×100m/m×60m/m

カバンの中で散らばりがちな細々した物を収納するケース。目的に合わせてチョイス出来る様に3サイズで展開。

THREE DAYS FLIGHT BAG
COTTON/SADDLE LEATHER
320001　¥128,000　350m/m×560m/m×320m/m
3日以上の旅を目的とした多機能なバッグ。

バッグ本体のメインスペースにハンガーのまま収納出来るレザーストラップが付く。

バッグのメインフラップを開けると3つの収納ポケットの上に折りたたみ乗車券用のレザーホルダー付き。

TRAVELER'S WARDROBE CASE
COTTON/SADDLE LEATHER
320101　¥98,000　350m/m×500m/m×235m/m
出し入れのしやすいフルオープンタイプで多機能なデザイン。

裏にP.V.Cをひいたナイロン素材のしきりポケットはアンダーウエアーやタオル等の多少汚れた物も収納可。

このバッグにもハンガー用レザーストラップが付く。

両サイドに付いたキンチャク式ポケットには、細々とした物等収納可。

型崩れ防止の為にコの字型にアルミフレームが入っている。

TRAVELER'S EXPRESS BAG
COTTON/SADDLE LEATHER
320201　¥65,000　340m/m×500m/m×170m/m
列車での旅を想定し、網上の棚に乗せ降ろしをしやすい型にデザイン。やはりアウトサイドのフロントに乗車券用レザーホルダー付き。

EXPLORER'S BAG
COTTON/SADDLE LEATHER
320301　¥78,000　320m/m×430m/m×165m/m
サイズ的にデイリーユースからオーバーナイトの旅行までと幅広く対応出来るデザイン。

BUSINESS

TWO INCH BRIEF CASE
COTTON/SADDLE LEATHER
321101　¥39,000　290m/m×420m/m×60m/m
アウトサイドにファスナー式のニュースペーパーポケットが付くヌキ手式ブリーフケース、インサイドの仕様は、3インチブリーフケースと同様。

THREE INCH BRIEF CASE
COTTON/SADDLE LEATHER
321201　¥46,000　300m/m×420m/m×90m/m

ショルダーとハンドルの2ウェイタイプのブリーフケース。中にはマチ付きポケット、しばり型ペンケース、Wケフポケットと機能的なデザイン。又、2インチブリーフケース同様ニュースペーパーポケットがアウトサイドに付く。

COMMUTER'S CASE
COTTON/SADDLE LEATHER
321301　¥39,000　300m/m×420m/m×80m/m
ジップトップ式のショルダー付きブリーフケース。アウトサイドの両面にマガジンポケットが付き、比較的多くのものを収納出来るデザイン。

CORRESPONDENT'S CASE
COTTON/SADDLE LEATHER
321001　¥45,000　290m/m×420m/m×90m/m
ファスナーがサイド部分まで開く為、出し入れがしやすく、中に付いた3つのラフポケットがとても機能的で使いやすい。アウトサイドのバックにドットボタン式マガジンポケット付き。

CLUTCH BAG FOR VALUABLES
COTTON/SADDLE LEATHER
321401　¥15,000　170m/m×250m/m×85m/m
ベーシックなデザインのクラッチバッグ。幅のサイズが広く、クラッチバッグとしては以外と多くのものも出来る。

PRESS ATTACHE
COTTON/SADDLE LEATHER
321501　¥39,000　420m/m×290m/m×85m/m
B4ファイルが入るサイズのソフトブリーフケース。革製の丸型グリップを束ねる着脱式のショルダーベルト、ファスナーの開きが大きく荷物の出し入れがしやすい。内ポケットにファイル用が1つと3つのラフポケットがバッグの中身をシステマチックに収納。

SHAVER WITH CASE
321601　¥3,900

TOOTH BRUSH WITH CASE
321701　¥2,500

※カタログ掲載商品の色は印刷の為実品とは多少異なる場合がございます。

223

Catalog + Web

HEMING'S

www.heming's.co.jp

- Top
- 商品・ショッピング Products Information・Shopping
- ブランド紹介 Brand Information
- 取扱ショップ紹介 Shop Information
- アイディア募集 Call for Ideas
- 会員申込 Membership Registration
- メール Mail
- ラストチャンス LAST CHANCE

HEMING'Sの「ハーネスファクトリーメイドシリーズ」の鞄は、何十年にも渡り、欧米に馬具を送り続けてきた輸出馬具工場の職人達の技と、ヘミングスのトラディショナルなデザインがつくりあげた逸品です。ホームページ上ではブランドのイメージもさることながら鞄各部の革の厚みや、縫い糸の太さの違いなど、馬具職人ならではの仕様を理解して頂ける様にするのに苦労致しました。商品価格も3万円台から10万円台までと高価な為、ひとつひとつのパーツ等の説明も加え、ネット販売でも安心出来るよう、また、より物づくりの背景が伝わる様に注意をはかりました。

Heming's "Harness Factory-Made" series consists of premium luggage created by craftsmen in their harness factory, from which products have been exported to Western countries for decades, all featuring Heming's traditional design. On the Web site, in addition to presenting the brand image, we made an extra effort to include specific details about the luggage; the differences of leather and thread thickness depending on the part of the bag, for example, is something that only harness craftsmen can gauge. Because the products are rather expensive, ranging in price from ¥30,000 to ¥100,000, we included explanations of each component, taking special care to convey production backgrounds, so that customers will feel secure when shopping via the Internet.

鞄、雑貨製作・販売
LUGGAGE・HANDBAG・SUNDRIES MANUFACTURE & SALES 1999

CL, SB: ヘミングス HEMING'S INC.

※2000年7月5日現在のデータを使用 As of July 5, 2000

Top
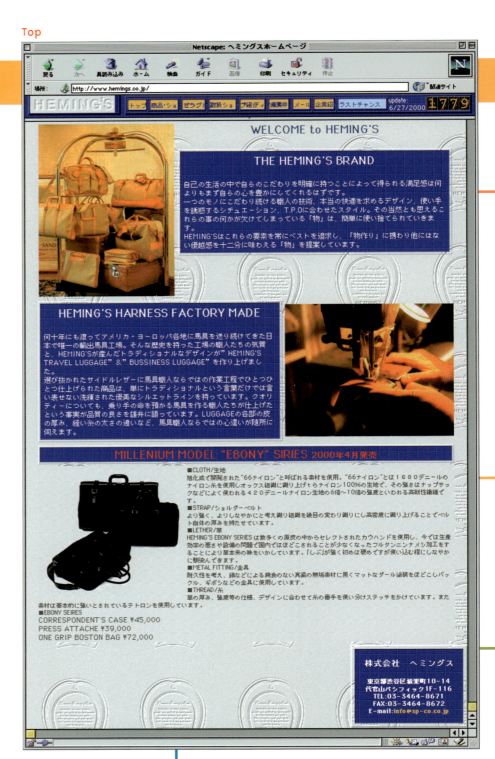

ラストチャンス LAST CHANCE ↓

HOME: 生活用品・雑貨　LIFESTYLE PRODUCTS & SUNDRIES

商品・ショッピング　Products Information・Shopping

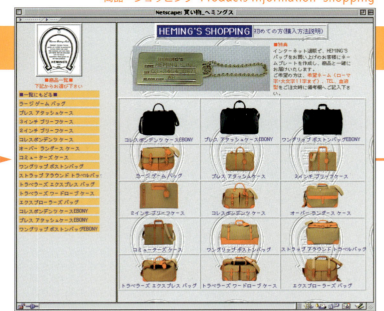

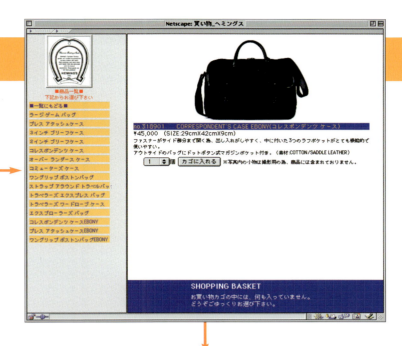

取扱ショップ紹介　Shop Information

アイディア募集　Call for Ideas

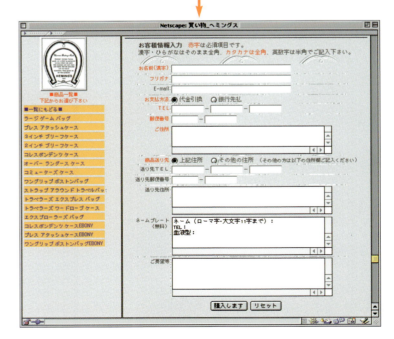

Catalog + Web

Mr. Friendly

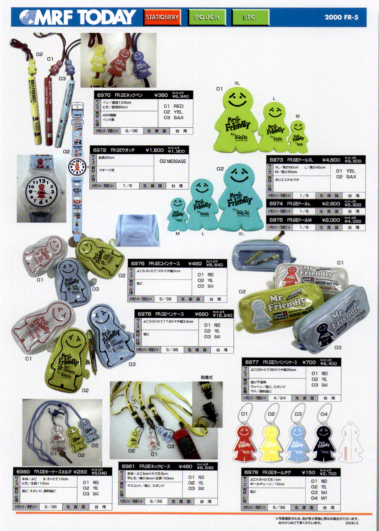

シート Sheet／210×297mm

Mr.Friendlyのコンセプトは LOVE & PEACE。明るい Happy なイメージをアメリカの新聞のヘッドラインになぞらえて、デザインをしました。横にはアイテムのカテゴリーも併記しています。商品説明はあくまでも日本語で、お客様にわかりやすく表記してあります。

Mr. Friendly's concept is Love & Peace. The catalog was designed with a bright, happy image, imitating a headline from an American newspaper. Item categories are included to the side. Product information is presented in Japanese, to make it easy for the customers.

雑貨製造・販売
SUNDRIES MANUFACTURE & SALES 2000

CL, SB: スーパープランニング Super Planning Co., Ltd.
CD, AD: 神谷敬久 Takahisa Kamiya
D: 高橋信子 Nobuko Takahashi

Catalog + Web

HOME: 生活用品・雑貨　LIFESTYLE PRODUCTS & SUNDRIES

www.MrFriendly.co.jp

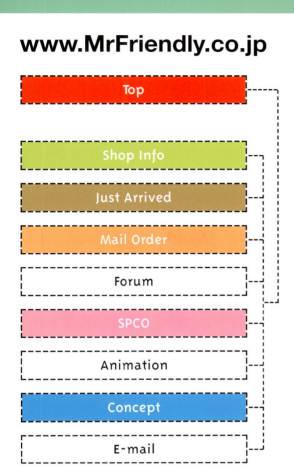

- Top
- Shop Info
- Just Arrived
- Mail Order
- Forum
- SPCO
- Animation
- Concept
- E-mail

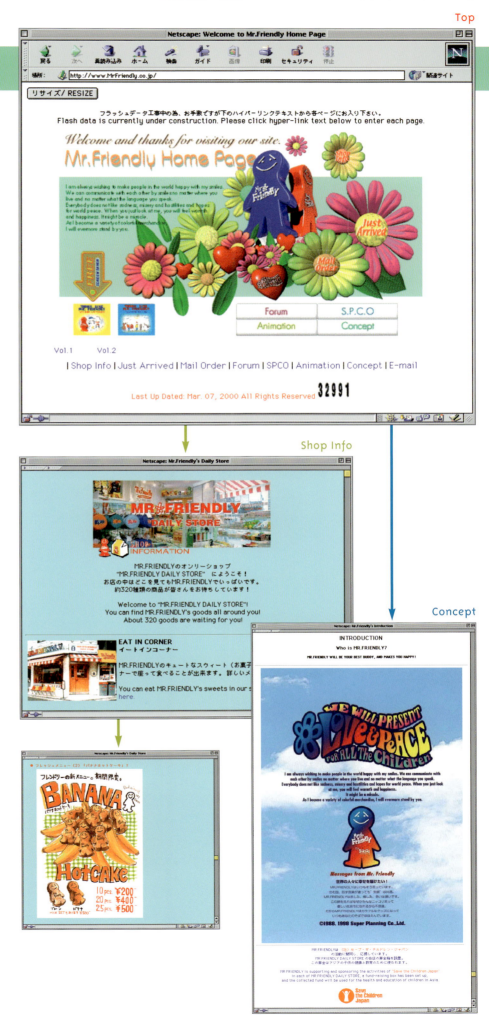

（株）スーパープランニングのオリジナルキャラクター「ミスターフレンドリー」の公式ホームページ。1996年7月にスタートしました。キャラクターのコンセプト・グッズの新商品や、直営店「Mr. Friendly Daily Store」の情報もご紹介しています。1998年の10周年を記念して作られた絵本「Think Like Mr. Friendly」のイラストのスクリーンセーバーが、無料でダウンロードできます。Mr. Friendlyのテーマは"LOVE & PEACE"。"笑顔"は住む国・話す言葉が違っても共通。この顔を見ればなぜかみんなニッコリ笑って優しい気持ちになれるから不思議です。

This is the official site of Mr. Friendly, an original character of Super Planning Co., Ltd. The site first went online in July 1996. It introduces new character concepts goods and presents information about the Mr. Friendly Daily Store, a chain of shops directly managed by the company. A screen saver of illustrations from the picture book "Think Like Mr. Friendly," which was created in commemoration of the company's 10-year anniversary in 1998, can be download with no charge. The theme of Mr. Friendly is "love and peace." The smiley face is common in many different countries, and does not require translation. It is wonderful that people can smile and be friendly when they look at this face.

雑貨製造・販売
SUNDRIES MANUFACTURE & SALES　1996

CL, SB: スーパープランニング　Super Planning Co., Ltd.
CD, AD: 神谷敬久　Takahisa Kamiya
※2000年7月5日現在のデータを使用　As of July 5, 2000

Catalog + Web

Mr. Friendly

Top

Mail Order

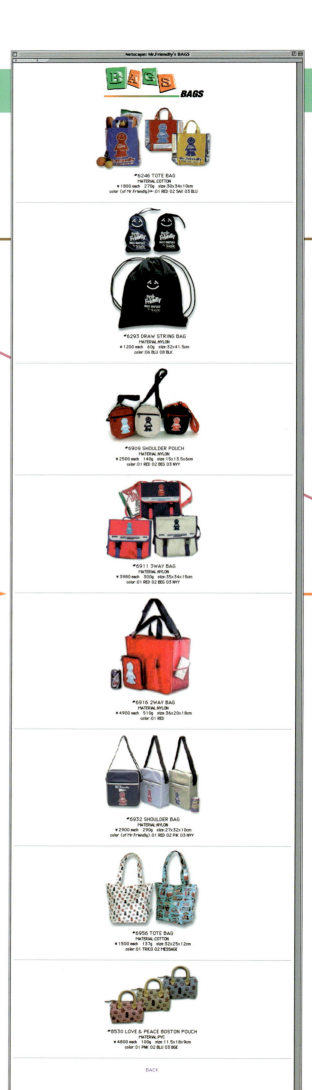

※2000年7月5日現在のデータを使用 As of July 5, 2000

HOME: 生活用品・雑貨　LIFESTYLE PRODUCTS & SUNDRIES

Just Arrived

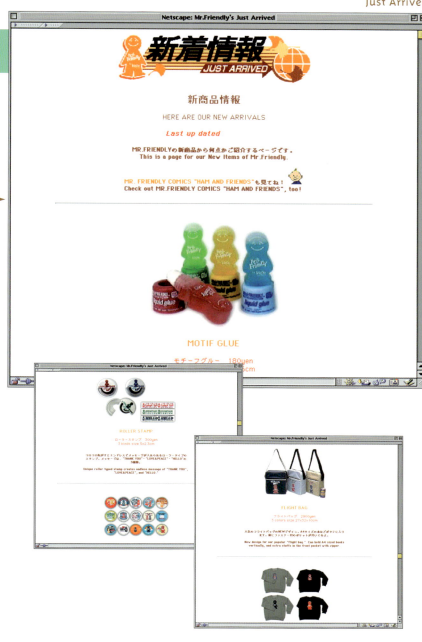

SPCO

Catalog + Web

GLADEE

シート Sheet／210×297mm

1991年11月に創業。陶器の取扱いから始める。現在、テーブルウェア・ぬいぐるみ・衣料など生活関連雑貨の企画、製造、販売や、オリジナル商品の企画、開発、また輸入商品の販売などを行っています。

Established in November, 1991; started by selling ceramics. Currently, Gladee's business has expanded to the planning, manufacture, and retail of lifestyle goods such as tableware, stuffed toys, clothing, and original shop goods, as well as retail of imported goods.

輸入雑貨販売 IMPORT GOODS SALES 2000

CL, SB: グラディー Gladee inc.
D: 佐沢一馬 Kazuma Sazawa

HOME: 生活用品・雑貨 LIFESTYLE PRODUCTS & SUNDRIES

Catalog + Web

GLADEE

www.gladee.co.jp

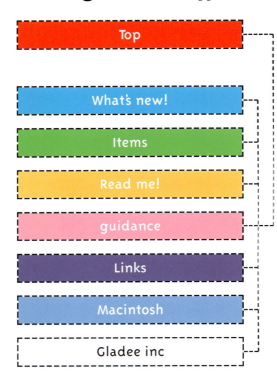

弊社ホームページは、ショッピングできるページではありますが、ウェブ上からのオーダーをおすすめしている訳ではありません。「弊社の品物をできるだけ広く皆様に知ってもらい、どこかで出会っていただけたら……。」と思って制作しています。「どこか出かけた先で、その様な物たちに出会えるときっと、楽しいだろう。」と考えています。ショッピングしなくても、見て・読んで・楽しいウェブサイトでありたいと思っています。

Although our web site is made for shopping, it doesn't mean that we recommend that customers buy from the site. The site is created so that more and more people can get to know our products and hopefully meet our products somewhere. We think that it is fun to find our goods when they go out. We are aiming at a site that is fun to look at and read, even if the visitors do not actually make purchases online.

輸入雑貨販売　IMPORT GOODS SALES　2000

CL, SB: グラディー　Gladee inc.
D, I: 佐沢一馬　Kazuma Sazawa
※2000年7月4日現在のデータを使用　As of July 4, 2000

HOME: 生活用品・雑貨　LIFESTYLE PRODUCTS & SUNDRIES

Items

Items

Read me!

Catalog + Web
GLADEE

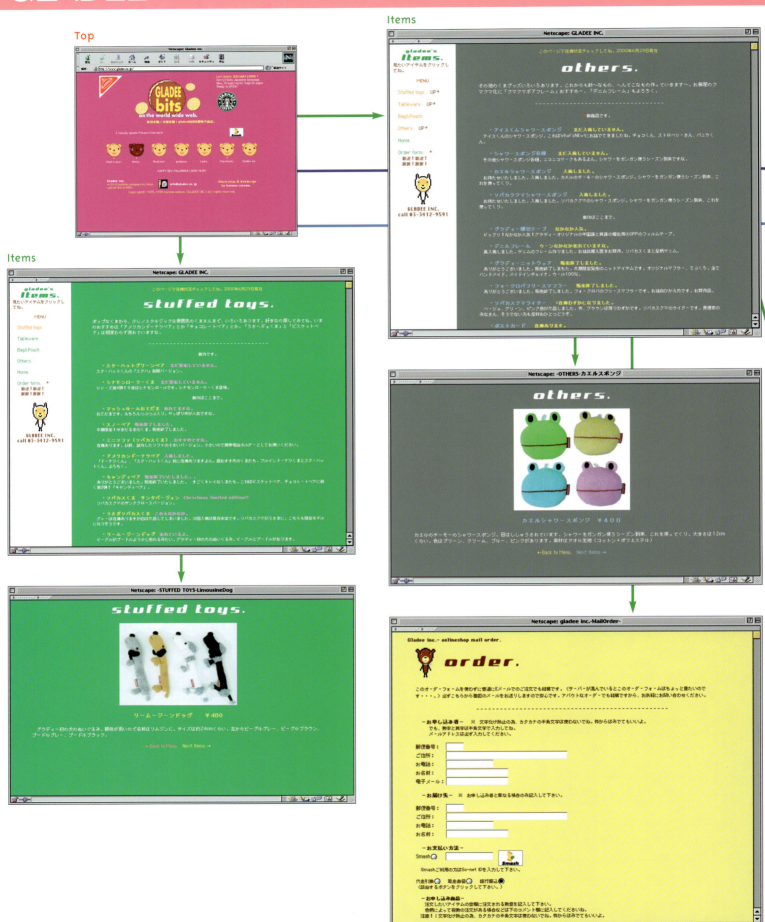

※2000年7月4日現在のデータを使用　As of July 4, 2000

HOME: 生活用品・雑貨　LIFESTYLE PRODUCTS & SUNDRIES

Links

Macintosh

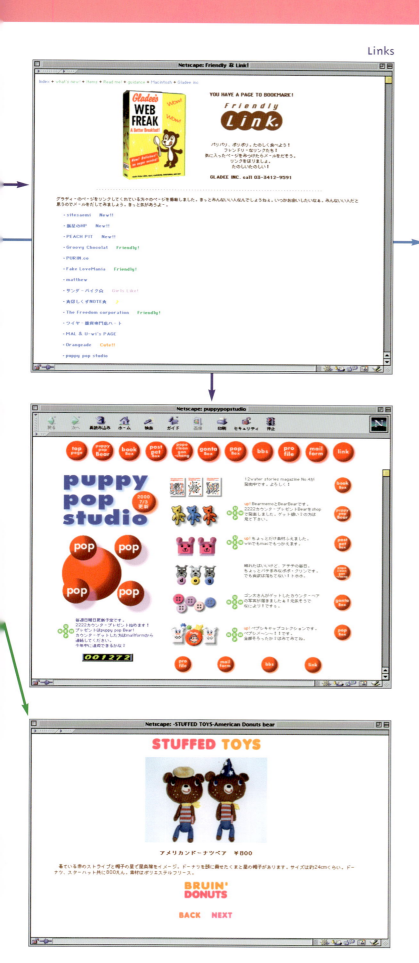

Catalog + Web

ARANZI ARONZO

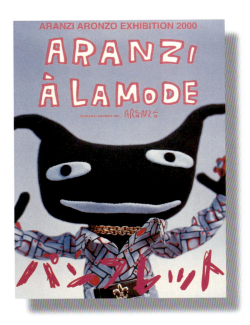

中綴じ Stapled in the center／210×285mm

アランジアロンゾは雑貨をつくっている会社の名前です。アランジアロンゾがつくったものを売っている店の名前です。その上、人の名前でもあります。人というより人達の名前です。音楽だったらバンド名。ユニット名。芸名。ペンネーム。とにかくアランジアロンゾです。1991年にとりあえず会社をつくりました。そして自分達のつくりたいものをつくって売る。という商売を始めました。雑貨をつくったり、お店をつくったり、本をつくったり、広告の仕事をやったり、通信販売をやったりしています。これはその通信販売ができるカタログです。

Aranzi Aronzo is a company that makes a wide range of products. Aranzi Aronzo is the name of a shop that sells items produced by Aranzi Aronzo. On top of that, Aranzi Aronzo is a person's name. To be exact, it is not a person, but a group of people. In music, it is a band name, group name or stage name. Anyway, it is Aranzi Aronzo. We created the firm in 1999, and started a business to create and sell what we wanted to create and sell. Aranzi Aronzo creates goods, shops, books and advertising, and has catalog shopping as well. This is the shopping catalog.

雑貨製造・販売
SUNDRIES MANUFACTURE & SALES 2000

CL, CD, AD, D, P, I, CW, DF, SB: アランジアロンゾ
ARANZI ARONZO INC.

236

HOME: 生活用品・雑貨 LIFESTYLE PRODUCTS & SUNDRIES

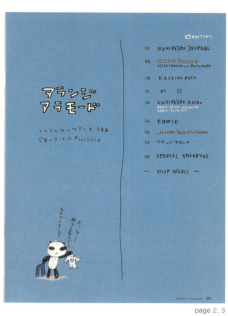

page 2, 3

page 48, 49

page 50, 51

Catalog + Web

ARANZI ARONZO

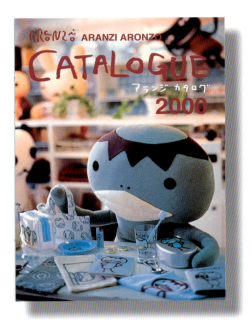

平綴 Bound／183×256mm

page 1

page 2, 3

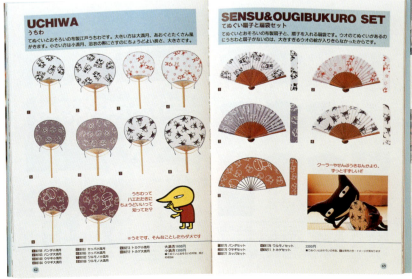

page 62, 63

雑貨製造・販売
SUNDRIES MANUFACTURE & SALES

CL, P, I, CW, SB: アランジアロンゾ ARANZI ARONZO INC.
D: 風間美紀 Miki Kazama
武沢朝子 Asako Takezawa (12 to 12)
P: 赤井賢一 Kenichi Akai／鈴木康久 (千代田スタジオ)
Yasuhisa Suzuki (Chiyoda Studio)／中里和人 Kazuto Nakasato
初谷恵美 Emi Hatsutani

HOME: 生活用品・雑貨　LIFESTYLE PRODUCTS & SUNDRIES

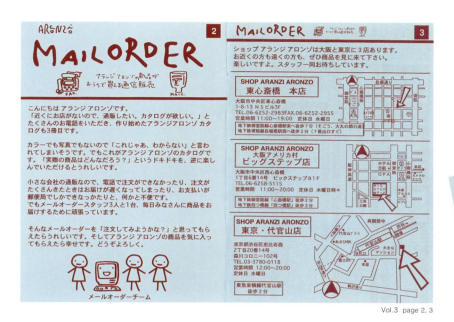

Vol.3 page 2, 3

Vol.3 page 8, 9

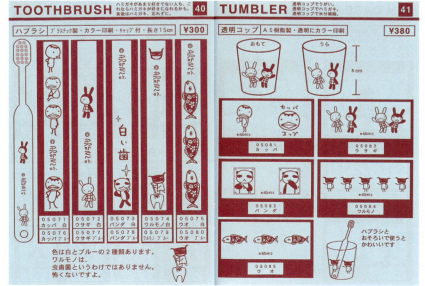

Vol.3 page 40, 41

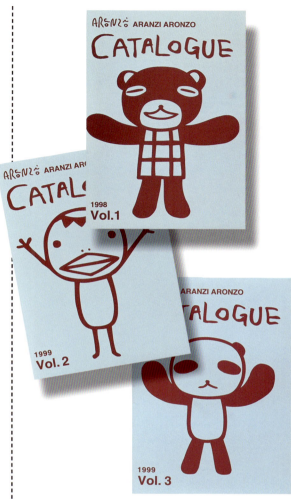

中綴 Stapled in the center／106×149mm

雑貨製造・販売
SUNDRIES MANUFACTURE & SALES 1998-99

CL, CD, AD, D, P, I, CW, DF, SB: アランジアロンゾ
ARANZI ARONZO INC.

Catalog + Web

ARANZI ARONZO

www.aranziaronzo.com/

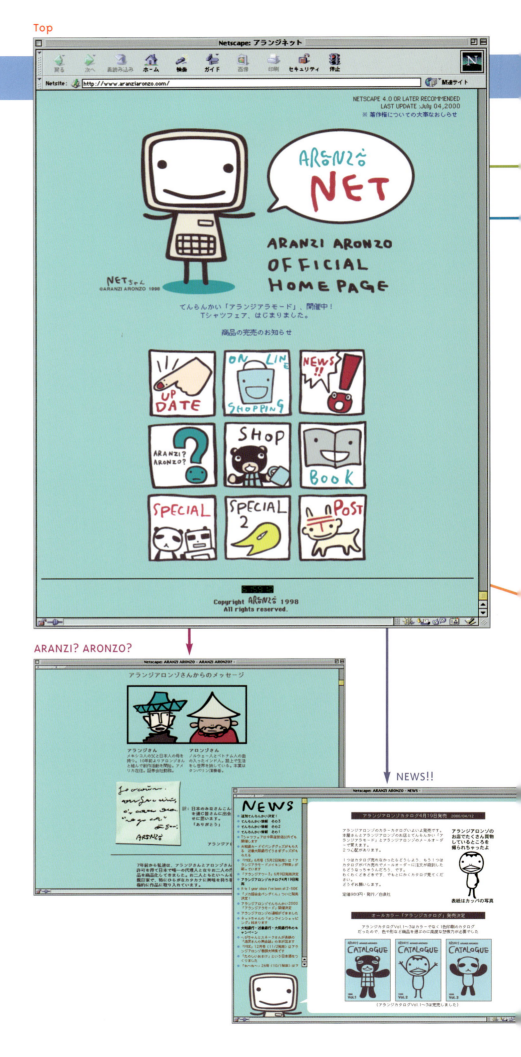

アランジアロンゾのホームページを第三者が作るということは、その世界観を崩すことなく、なおかつ、制作者がアランジアロンゾの"かわいくてへんてこで楽しい世界"を理解した上で初めて成立すると思っています。だから私は、アランジアロンゾが大好きだし、勝手にアランジアロンゾの一員であるかのようにアランジネットを楽しんで作っています。個人的に作り手でありながらインターネットヘビーユーザーでもあるので、「いかにわかりやすく伝えるか？簡単に操作できるか？楽しいか？おもしろいか？」そして最後に「いかに作っていて楽しいか」これに尽きます！

Creating the Aranzi Aronzo homepage as a third party can only be successful if the designer understands their "cute, strange, but enjoyable" world. I enjoy designing this site, because I like Aranzi Aronzo very much. I selfishly feel as if I am a part of the company. As I myself am a heavy Internet user, I design Web sites with the following in mind: "How well can the site communicate?" "Is the site easy to use?" "Is it fun to use?" And finally, "Am I enjoying designing this Web site?"

雑貨製造・販売
SUNDRIES MANUFACTURE & SALES 1998

CL, AD, P, I, CG: アランジアロンゾ ARANZI ARONZO INC.
CD, D, M, PR, DF: 梶原綾子 Ayako Kajiwara (Bitwave)
SB: Bitwave
※2000年7月4日現在のデータを使用 As of July 4, 2000

HOME: 生活用品・雑貨 LIFESTYLE PRODUCTS & SUNDRIES

ON LINE SHOPPING

SPECIAL

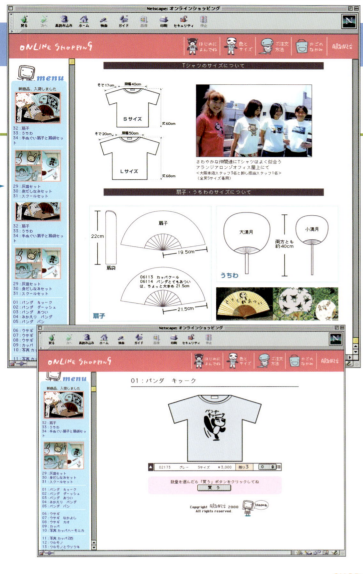

SHOP

Catalog + Web
ACE

page 1, 2

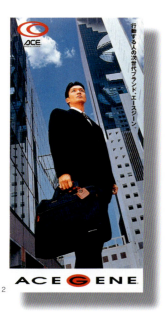

page 17, 18

わが社は、全国の百貨店、専門店、小売店のルートセールスを主とするバッグ・旅行用品の総合卸商社です。グループ企業との連携により、消費者ニーズにすみやかに対応できる独自の生産システムを持ち、現在、業界のトップ企業として評価をいただいています。さまざまな国々でエースブランドが愛用されているエースは、世界のバッグメーカーとしての道を着実に歩んでいます。

Ace Co., Ltd. is a general wholesaler of luggage and travel goods, selling primarily to department stores, specialty stores, and retailers nationwide. With an original production system, linked to group companies, that can quickly handle customer needs, Ace is currently considered to be the top company in the industry. With the Ace brand loved in many countries, Ace is steadily proceeding towards becoming the best luggage manufacturer in the world.

1、ジャバラ Accordion fold／102×220mm
（開いた状態 When fully unfolded：612×220mm）
2、中綴 Stapled in the center／103×220mm

鞄製造・販売
BAGS・LUGGAGE MANUFACUTURE & SALES 2000

CL, SB: エース ACE Co., Ltd.
CD, AD: 松田寿徳 Toshinori Matsuda (1)／青山一郎（エース）Ichiro Aoyama (ACE) (2)
垣田英信（電通）Hidenobu Kakida (Dentsu Inc.) (2)
D: マック MAQ Inc. (1)／森内一枝（ジョグ）Kazue Moriuchi (JOG) (2)
P: 和田正治（グリーンサム）Masaharu Wada (GREEN THUMB Co.,Ltd)
CW: 村上和也 Kazuya Murakami

HOME: 生活用品・雑貨 LIFESTYLE PRODUCTS & SUNDRIES

3、8ツ折 Eightfold：102×220mm
(開いた状態 When fully unfolded：408×440mm)

鞄製造・販売
BAGS・LUGGAGE MANUFACUTURE & SALES

CL, SB: エース ACE Co., Ltd.
CD, AD: 青山一郎 (エース) Ichiro Aoyama (ACE)
垣田英信 (電通) Hidenobu Kakida (Dentsu Inc.)
D: 森内一枝 (ジョグ) Kazue Moriuchi (JOG)
P: 和田正治 (グリーンサム)
Masaharu Wada (GREEN THUMB Co.,Ltd.)
CW: 村上和也 Kazuya Murakami

Catalog + Web

ACE

www.acebag.co.jp

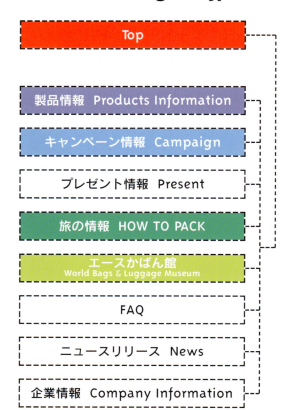

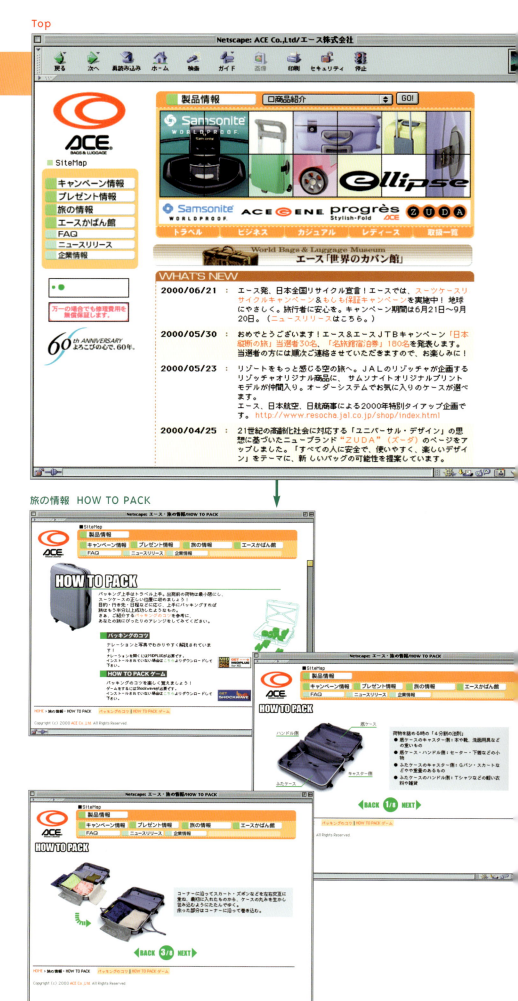

エース(株)が製品情報や旅行情報などをきめ細かに発信するビックサイズ・ホームページ。エース社が販売するスーツケース「サムソナイト」の最新シリーズや、オリジナルブランドの「エースジーン」などを詳しく紹介する便利なウェブカタログをめざしましたHOW TO PACKのコーナーではショックウェーブを駆使した楽しいゲームも採用。また、世界中の逸品や珍品など骨董的価値の高いバッグの数々を紹介する「世界のカバン館」は、バッグマニアならずとも見逃せない内容となっています。

The expansive and detailed Web site of Ace Co., Ltd., presenting product, travel, and other information. This well-organized site provides full introductions to the latest Samsonite suitcases, Ace's original "Ace Gene" brand, and more. In the "How To Pack" corner you will find an entertaining game created with Shockwave. Not just for luggage aficionados, nobody will want to miss the "World Bags & Luggage Museum," which showcases dozens of valuable antiques, including rare and high quality items.

鞄製造・販売
BAGS・LUGGAGE MANUFACUTURE & SALES 2000

CL: エース ACE Co., Ltd.
CD, CW: 柳 光洋 Mitsuhiro Yanagi
AD: 井上缶人 Takehito Inoue
D: 寺内 聡 Satoru Terauchi
P: ヒロ西川 Hiro Nishikawa
I: 軸屋亮太 Ryota Jikuya
PR: 杉本明香 Sayaka Sugimoto
PLANNER: 横山 久仁子 Kumiko Yokoyama
SB: ベイシス Basis Co., Ltd.

※2000年7月6日現在のデータを使用 As of July 6, 2000

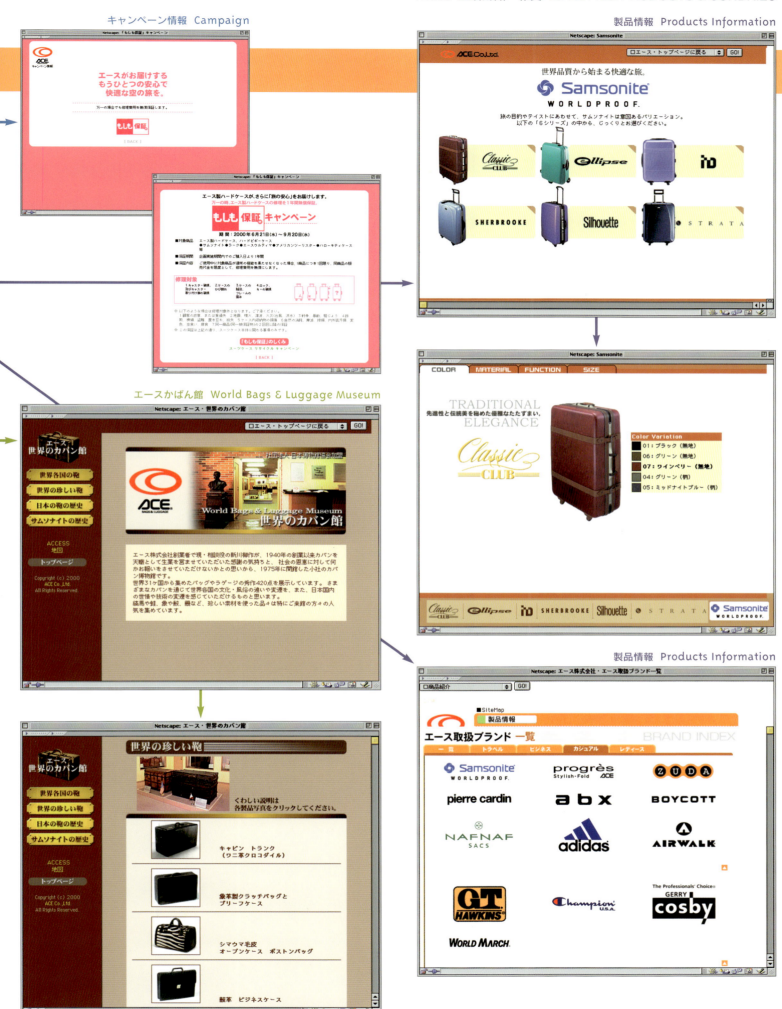

Catalog + Web

Sony pepz

www.sony.co.jp/pepz

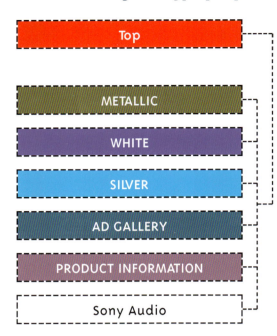

Top

PRODUCT INFORMATION

好みやインテリアに合わせて選べる上、MD・CD・TAPE・FM/AMの1つの音楽ソースが楽しめる4 BOXステレオ〈pepz〉の魅力をウェブで表現するためにFLASHを活用しました。それにより、pepzの特長のひとつである、本体と取り替えるスピーカーカバーとの組合せを、インターネット上で再現することができました。また、マス4媒体とは違ったアプローチでウェブオリジナルの広告表現もウェブCMとして用意し、映像と音でpepzの魅力を表現しました。

Shockwave Flash is used to illustrate the attractiveness of "pepz," Sony's 4-in-1 stereo system (MD, CD, cassette, and FM/AM radio). Available in a variety of styles to fit the customer's taste and interior, the site allows you to interchange speaker covers, which is one of pepz' special features. Different from the approaches offered to traditional advertising media, Web commercials have been designed just for the Web, using images and sound to fully show the beauty of pepz.

電子機器販売・マーケティング
ELECTRIC APPLIANCES SALES & MARKET RESEARCH 2000

CL, SB: ソニーマーケティング Sony Marketing (Japan) Inc.
PRODUCTION: め組 Megumi
PLANNING: インタービジョン INTERVISION inc.
※2000年7月6日現在のデータを使用 As of July 6, 2000

HOME: 電気製品 ELECTRICAL PRODUCTS

METALLIC

Catalog + Web
Sony pepz

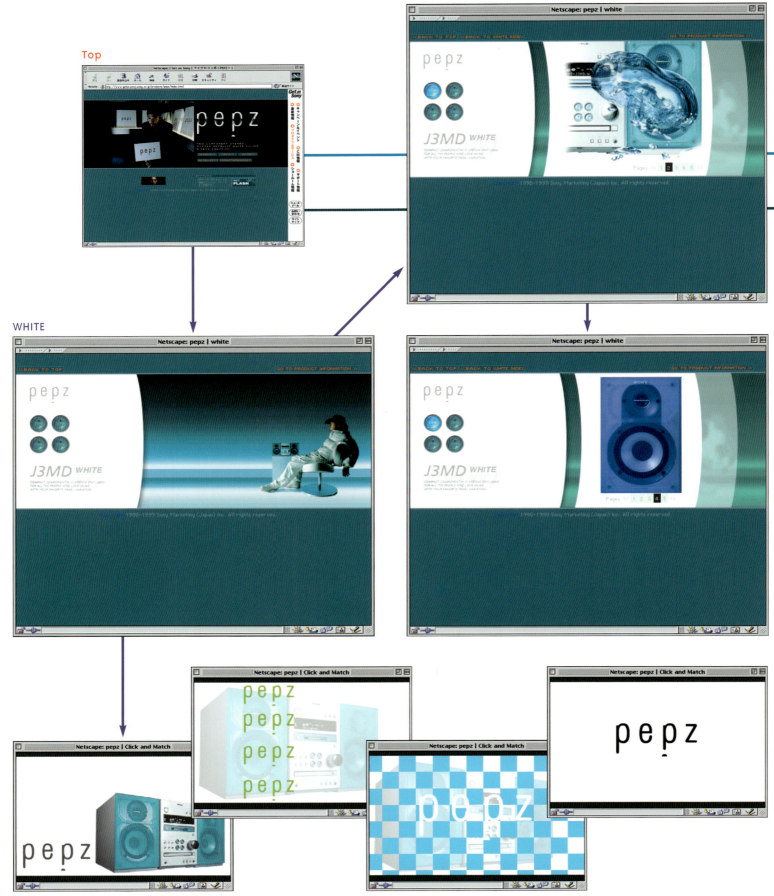

※2000年7月6日現在のデータを使用 As of July 6, 2000

HOME: 電気製品 ELECTRICAL PRODUCTS

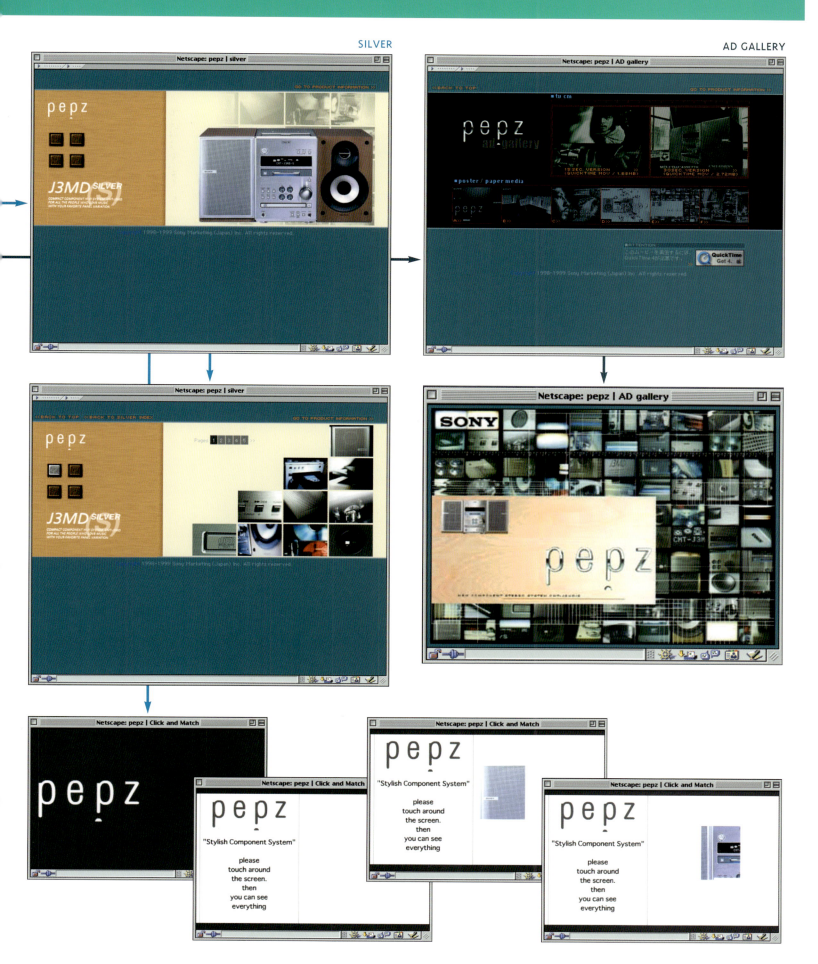

Catalog + Web

Sony VX 2000

www.sony.co.jp/sd/ProductsPark/Consumer/VD/VX2000/index.html

当ホームページは既存のカタログと同等の内容ですが、サンプル画像のダウンロードやGIFアニメによる画面の効果例など、ウェブならではのメリットを活かして、紙面で表現しきれなかったフィーチャーを訴求しています。また「各部名称」では、特長紹介の該当箇所へリンクを貼ったり、フラッシュを使用して細部を見せるなど、ディテールの詳説にもこだわっています。

Created with the same general contents as the printed catalog, the site utilizes characteristics of the Web, such as downloading of sample images, and on-screen effects using GIF animations, to introduce detailed features of products in ways not possible with printed materials. In the "Component Names" section, links are made to applicable sections of characteristic introductions, and part details are shown using Flash animation.

電子機器販売・マーケティング
ELECTRIC APPLIANCES SALES & MARKET RESEARCH 2000

CL, SB: ソニーマーケティング　Sony Marketing (Japan) Inc.

※2000年7月6日現在のデータを使用　As of July 6, 2000

HOME: 電気製品 ELECTRICAL PRODUCTS

主な特長 Important Special Features

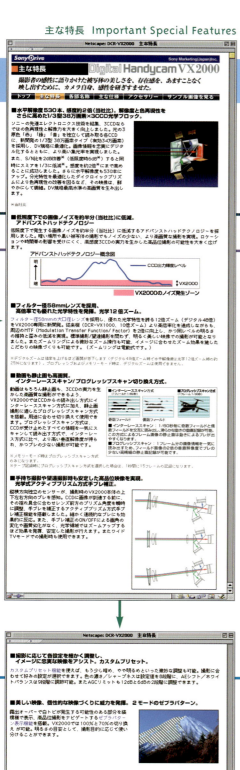

ハンディカムカスタマー登録のご案内 Customer registration

各部名称 Part Names

主な仕様 Features

Catalog + Web

PHILIPS

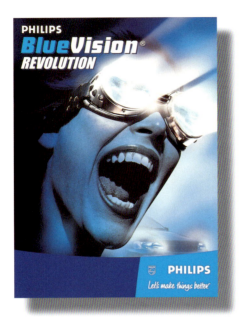

2ツ折 Single-fold・シート Sheet／210×297mm・中綴
Stapled in the center／297×210mm

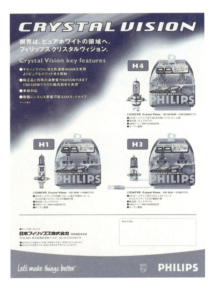

"クリスタルヴィジョン"・"ブルーヴィジョン" は、シェーバーやオーディオ機器で知られ、自動車ヘッドランプ分野で世界トップクラスのシェアをもつフィリップスの自動車用高効率ヘッドランプ・ブランドです。両製品ともに戦略としてインパクトのあるキャラクターを設定し、全ての販促物に適用しました。カタログはその中でもイメージ形成の中心的手段と位置づけ、イメージカラーを特色などを用いて一貫したイメージ伝達を心がけました。表面の要素はキャッチコピーと最低限の要素だけを残し、具体的な製品詳細は中面・裏面で詳細に紹介しています。

"Crystal Vision" and "Blue Vision" are highly efficient automobile headlamps made by Philips, a company known for shavers and audio equipment, and are among the best selling headlamps in the world. As the strategy for both products, impact-making image characters were developed, and are utilized in all promotional materials. The catalog was positioned as the main means of creating a brand image. We attempted to communicate a consistent image by using a special color as the image color. The cover has only catch copy and a minimum number of design elements, while details of products are introduced on the inner pages and back cover.

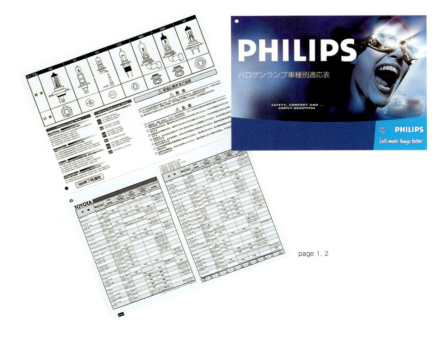

page 1, 2

エレクトロニクス機器製造・販売
ELECTRIC APPLIANCES MANUFACTURE & SALES 2000

CL, SB: 日本フィリップス　Philips Japan, Ltd.

Catalog+Web

HOME: 電気製品 ELECTRICAL PRODUCTS

www.philips.co.jp/lighting/auto/

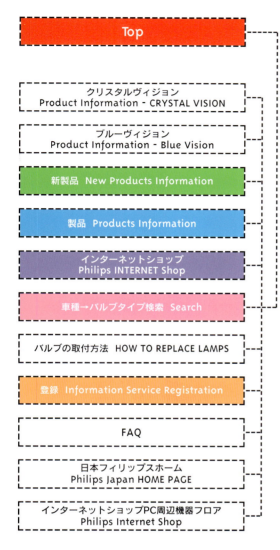

一般の車ユーザーには現段階ではあまり馴染みの無い「高効率ヘッドランプへの交換」に関する「認知から検討、検証、購買まで」をウェブ上で実施できるサイトとしての機能、ユーザーの利便性、イメージという3者のバランスを最大限に考慮しました。デザイン面ではフィリップス＝クール＆高性能というイメージを実現するために、ボタンや色使いなど細かい点に留意しながら、全体にヨーロッパ的な雰囲気をもたせ、高いデザイン性を保つことを重要視しました。フラッシュは"CM"と位置づけ、ユーザーの環境に応じてSKIPできるように工夫しました。

The average car owner is not yet familiar with the idea of converting to high-efficiency headlamps. The major consideration when planning this Web site was maintaining a balance of the following factors: Site function from education to examination, verification, and purchase, all on the Web; user convenience; and brand image. In order to realize the image of "Philips = Cool & High-Performance," the site was designed giving full attention to such details as navigation buttons and use of color. We wanted to give the site a European feel, and maintain high design standards. Flash animations were used to create "commercials," which can be skipped if the user so desires.

エレクトロニクス機器の製造・販売
ELECTRIC APPLIANCES MANUFACTURE & SALES 2000

CL, SB: 日本フィリップス Philips Japan, Ltd.
※2000年7月6日現在のデータを使用 As of July 6, 2000

Catalog + Web
PHILIPS

Top

新製品 New Products Information

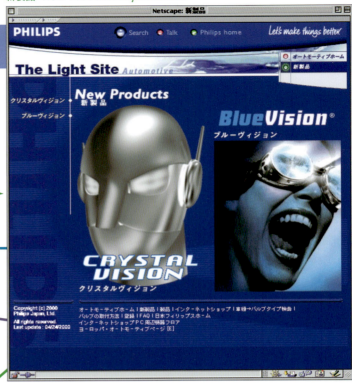

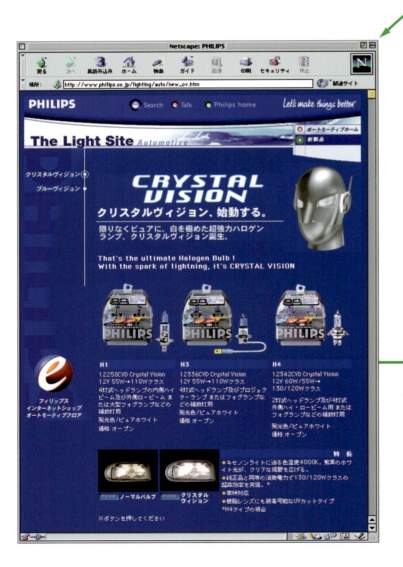

※2000年7月6日現在のデータを使用 As of July 6, 2000

HOME: 電気製品　ELECTRICAL PRODUCTS

製品　Products Information

インターネットショップ　Philips INTERNET Shop

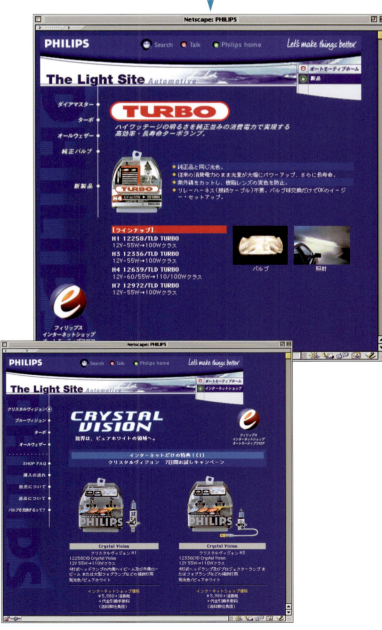

Catalog+Web

TOYOTA bB

カタログキット（紙パッケージ・中綴）
Catalog kit (Paper Package・Stapled in the center)

紙パッケージ Paper Package／312×312mm
中綴 Stapled in the center296×296mm

bBは「若者が望むクルマとは？」のテーマのもと、「トヨタの枠にとらわれない、スタイリッシュな外観と充実した機能性を併せ持つクルマ」として開発されました。そこでカタログも、商談ツールとしての機能だけでなく、ターゲットとする20代の男性に支持されるデザインとパッケージを目指し、bBの先進的でアナログなスタイルを表現できるアイテムとして、LP盤レコードをモチーフに制作しました。若者とbBの関わり、bBが傍らにあるシーン等、エッジの効いた表現、デザイン、レイアウトにこだわりながら、「bBらしさ」を演出しています。

"bB" was developed as a car with a stylish look and rich functions that go beyond Toyota's traditional framework, with a theme of "What is the type of car that young people want?" This catalog was created not only to be used as a sales tool, but also to be designed to interest the target consumers, men in the 20's. As a motif, an LP record was used to express bB's advanced analog style. The relationship that young people have with their bB, scenes with the bB, and other situations, were expressed using design and layout with an edge.

page 2, 3

page 6, 7

自動車製造・販売
AUTOMOBILE MANUFACTURE & SALES 2000

CL, SB: トヨタ自動車 TOYOTA MOTOR CORPORATION

page 10, 11

page 20, 21

page 22, 23

Catalog + Web

TOYOTA bB

www.toyota.co.jp/bB

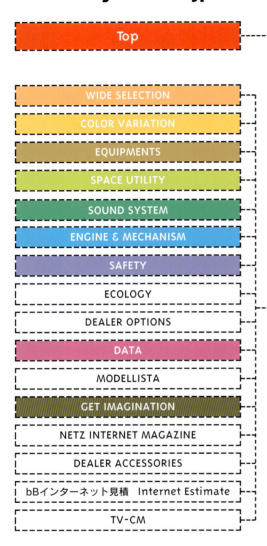
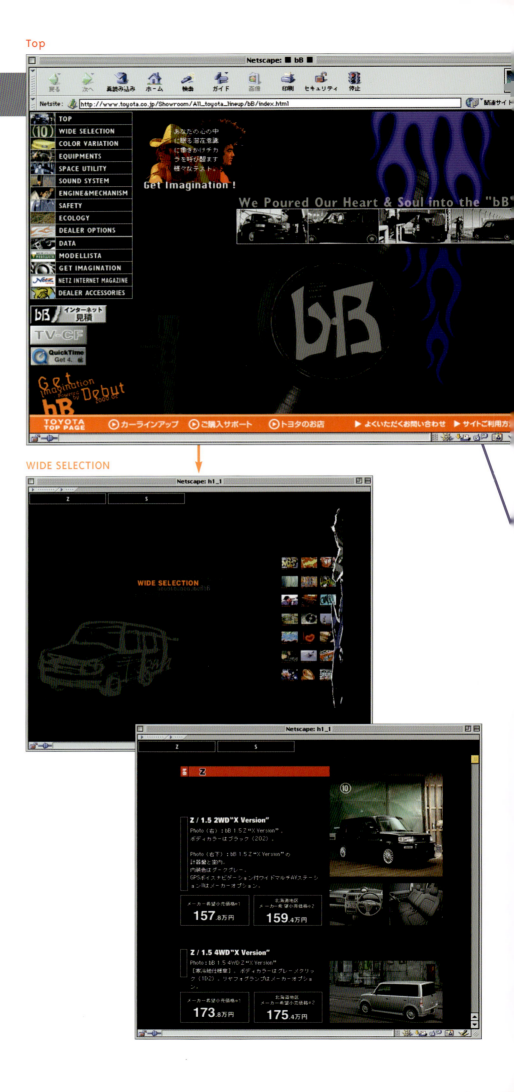

bBの商品情報を分り易く訴求、伝達するだけでなく、bBがターゲットとする20代の男性に支持されうるサイトを目指し、制作しました。商品情報の詳細よりも、商品のイメージやコンセプトを感じてもらい、興味を持ってもらうことを目的とし、若者とbBの関わり、bBが傍らにあるシーンなど、エッジの効いた表現、デザイン、レイアウトにしました。また、ターゲットの趣向に合わせ、CMの外伝・占い・ランキング登録付のゲーム・メールの配信など、高い娯楽性と内容の更新によるリアクセス率の高い、アミューズメントサイトにトライしています。

This site was created to present bB product information, but the site itself will be of interest to bB's target customers, men in their 20's. It aims at being a site where the viewer can get a feel for the product's image and concept and become interested, rather than simply reading detailed product information. The relationship between young people and the bB, scenes together with the bB, and other situations, were expressed using design and layout with an edge. To match with the tastes of the target visitor, the site tries to be entertaining. By keeping it fun and regularly updating such contents as behind-the-scenes stories about commercials, fortune telling, and game mail distribution, it maintains a high rate of repeat visitation.

HOME: 自動車・バイク・自転車　CARS, MOTORCYCLES & BICYCLES

COLOR VARIATION

EQUIPMENTS

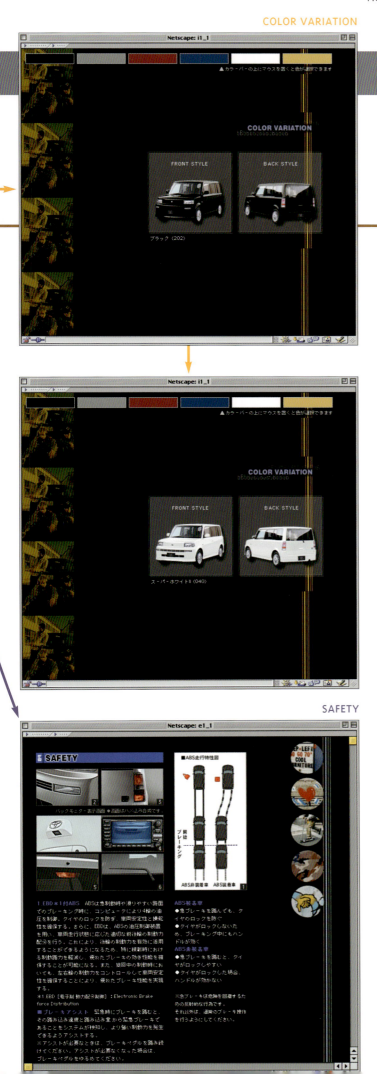

SAFETY

自動車製造・販売
AUTOMOBILE MANUFACTURE & SALES　2000

CL, SB: トヨタ自動車　TOYOTA MOTOR CORPORATION
※2000年7月11日現在のデータを使用　As of July 11, 2000

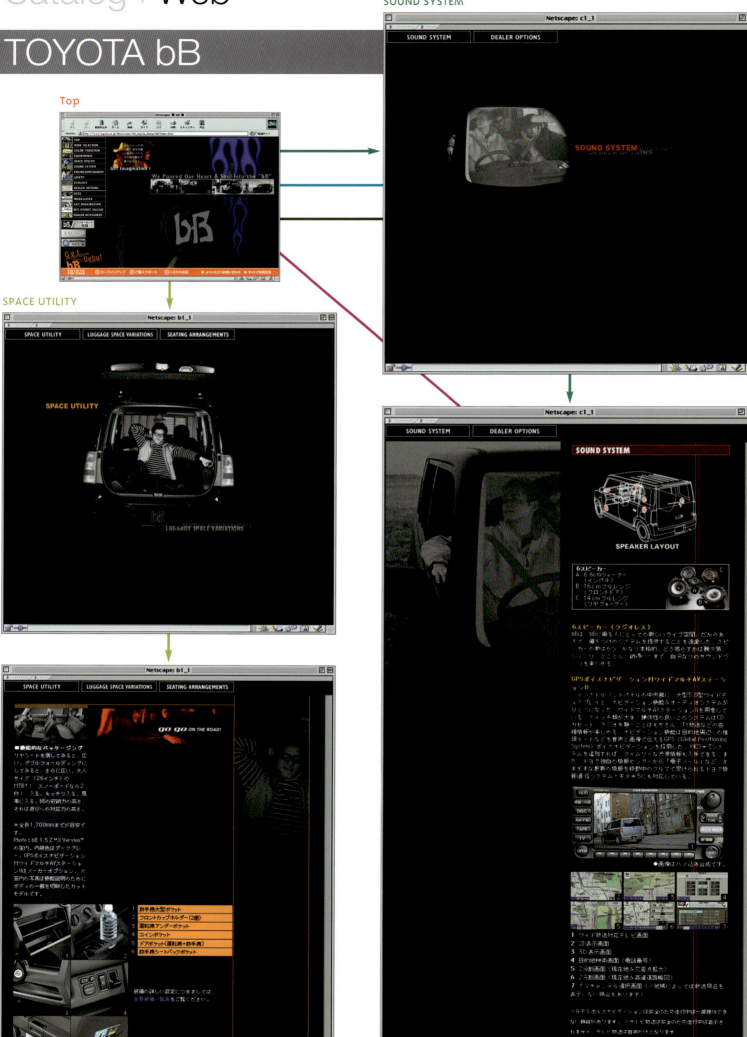

HOME: 自動車・バイク・自転車　CARS, MOTORCYCLES & BICYCLES

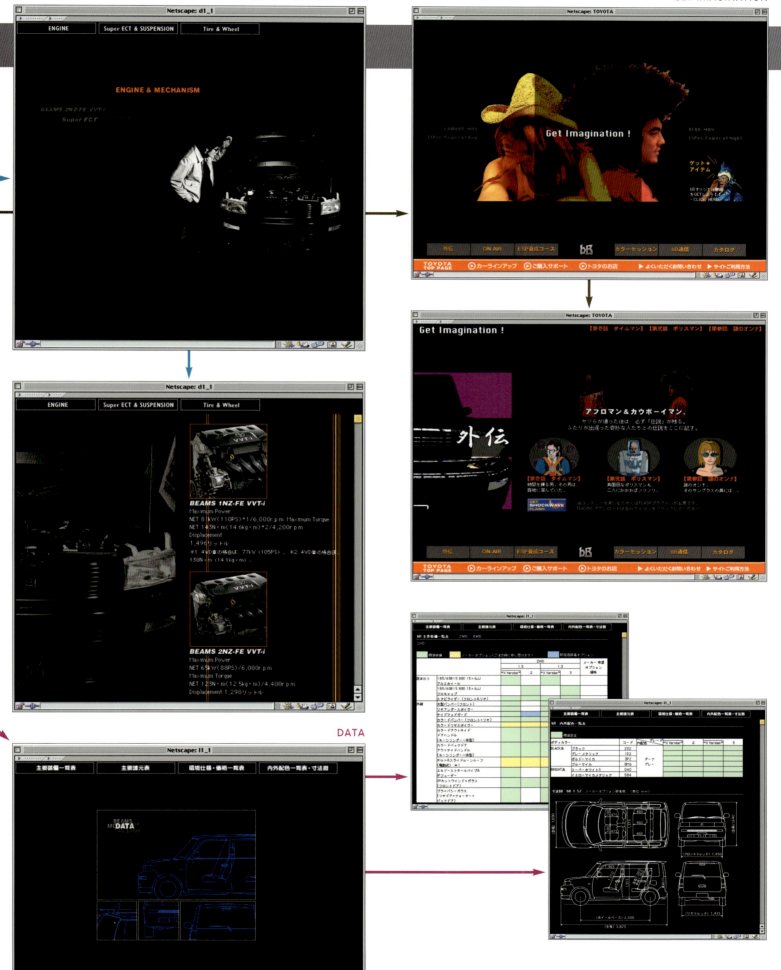

※2000年7月11日現在のデータを使用　As of July 11, 2000

Catalog + Web

HONDA HR-V

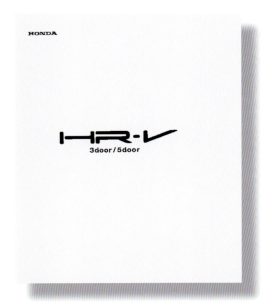

中綴 Stapled in the center／225×296mm

若者に向けた新ジャンルのクルマ"HR-V"は斬新なスタイルと優れた使い勝手、爽快な走りをコンパクトなボディに凝縮しつつ、世界最高水準の安全・環境性能を両立させており、カタログも上記を表現した構成となっています。既存のカテゴリーをこえたスタイリングのキーワードはアーバンクール。都会の香りとアウトドアの爽快さを同時に表現しつつ、若者にも分かりやすく環境や安全に対して説明しつつ、他との差別を図る為、ホンダ独自のデュアルポンプシステム等も分かりやすく説明しています。

The HR-V, a new genre of automobile targeting the younger generation, has everything in its compact body, from its original design to a superior driving style. It also incorporates internationally top class safety standards and an environmentally friendly performance. The catalog expresses these elements. The keyword for styling that goes beyond existing categories is "Urban Cool." With both an urban feel and an outdoor freshness, the catalog provides explanations of environmental and safety issues that are easy for young people to understand. To differentiate the car from others, Honda's original Dual Pump System and other features are clearly explained.

輸送機器製造　TRANSPORTS MANUFACTURER 1998

CL, SB: 本田技研工業　HONDA MOTOR CO., LTD.

HOME: 自動車・バイク・自転車　CARS, MOTORCYCLES & BICYCLES

デートしたい所に行きたい。スノボもキャンプもしたい。アタマの中は、いつもしたいこと、気持ちいいことでいっぱいだ。僕達の生活のパートナーであるクルマも、そんなヨクボーを満たしてくれるキャパシティがあるかどうかが選択のキーになる。ボードが何枚積めるか。遊び仲間がらくらく乗せられるか。最優先するのは、まずこのスペースユーティリティ。それから、都市にも大自然にもフィットするスタイリング。ワインディングを軽やかに駆け抜けるパフォーマンスも欲しい。数えあげればキリないけれど、ようするに一着のブレザーをドレスアップしたり、ドレスダウンしながら着こなすように、さまざまなシーンで使い分けられるクルマが僕達には必要だ。もちろん、自分のヨクボーだけでなく、環境や人への優しさも考えたクルマであればgood。それは地球という星に暮らしている僕達の義務でもあるのだから。そんな気持ちのいいクルマで、僕達は遊びたいと思う。

居住性や使い勝手を優先すると、クルマがみんな同じカタチになってしまうのはなぜだろう？そんな問いにホンダは、「JOYFUL＝楽しさ」を創造する「J・ムーバー」の最新作、ホンダHR-Vで答えました。コンパクトでシャープなボディに大径タイヤをプラスした、まったく新しいスタイル。都会からアウトドアまで、どんなシーンにもフィットします。遊び道具と友達を乗せて街やフィールドに飛び出せば、遊び方は無限大。便利なクルマに足りなかったデザインを追求しました。3ドアに5ドアが加わり、ラインアップが充実したアップ キャビン ワゴン、ホンダHR-V。今までのシーンが、そして自分が新しく見えてきます。

気持ちよく乗れる。楽しく遊べる。新しい走りのデザイン、ホンダHR-V。

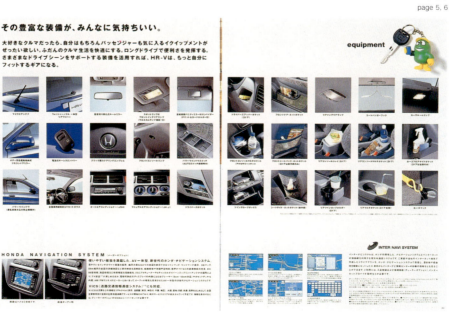

263

Catalog + Web

HONDA HR-V

www.honda.co.jp/HR-V/

まったく新しいスタイルで「楽しさ」を追求するHR-V自体のコンセプト「気持ちのいいクルマで遊びたい」を、またコンパクトでシャープな走りの感覚をモニター上で体感してもらうことをポイントとして構成しました。画面中央にスクリーンを配し、次々とスピーディーに画像を表示し、スクリーン上に新しいシーンが見えてくる期待感を演出しました。HR-V WORLDコーナーではHR-Vの特長をそれぞれ一画面で少ない操作で見られるように表現しました。スペックコーナーはカタログ情報をフルに網羅しました。また、HR-Vならではの全タイプ自由なバリエーション選択には見積シュミレーションを設置しました。

The Web site was created to experience the HR-V concept of "I want to have fun with a comfortable car!" on-screen, as well as convey the feel of its compact and sharp ride. Images appear quickly, one after another, in a screen in the middle of the page, generating viewer expectations to watch subsequent scenes. Features of the car can easily be seen in the HR-V World corner; the Spec corner includes all of the information that can be found in the printed catalogs. Additionally, the Estimate Simulation corner allows the user to freely choose their own options and calculate an approximate selling price, something possible only with the HR-V.

輸送機器製造　TRANSPORTS MANUFACTURER 2000

CL, SB: 本田技研工業　HONDA MOTOR CO., LTD.

※2000年7月5日現在のデータを使用　As of July 5, 2000

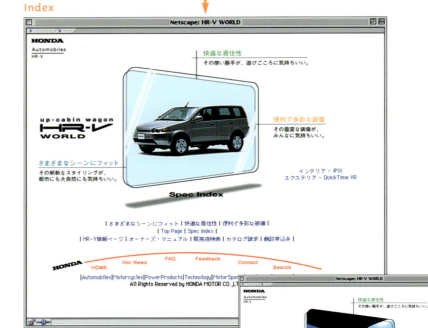

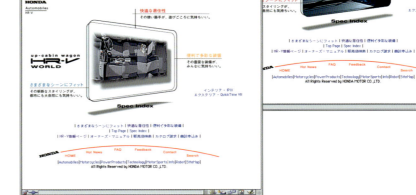

HOME: 自動車・バイク・自転車　CARS, MOTORCYCLES & BICYCLES

HR-V情報ページ　HR-V Information

Spec Index

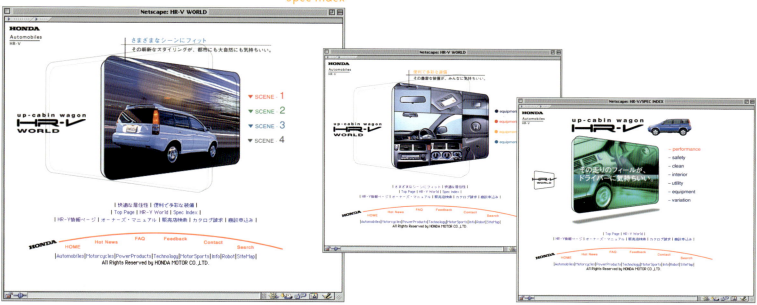

オーナーズマニュアル　Owner's Manual

Catalog+Web
PEUGEOT

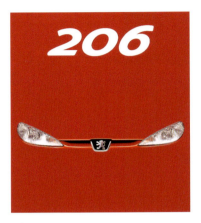

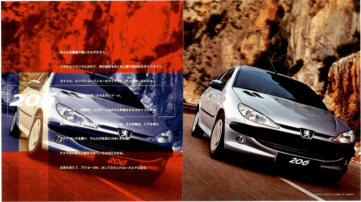

page 1, 2

 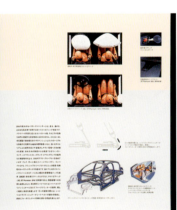

page 15, 16

中綴・3ツ折観音開き
Stapled in the center・French Threefold

中綴 Stapled in the center／257×296mm
3ツ折観音開き French Threefold／246×286mm

表紙デザインはプジョーの特徴である「ツリ目」（マイナーチェンジしたフロントグリル）をシンボリックに扱い、ブランドイメージをアピールしました。全体のデザインティストは、406のシンプルかつ堂々としたクラス感を訴求。写真を大きく扱い、そのスタイリッシュなフォルムとプジョーならではの技術力、そこから導きだされる卓越した走りを上品かつダイナミズムにあふれるトーンに仕上げました。コピーでは事実に基づいた特長をストレートに表現。406のステイタス感、スポーティ感などを実感できるように心がけました。

The cover emphasizes the brand image by a symbolization of Peugeot's slanted front grill, a feature that recently underwent a minor change. Overall, the catalog's design focuses on the appeal of the simple and dignified class of the 406. Large photographs incorporated into the layout emphasize the car's stylish form and superior handling ability, and Peugeot's original technology, expressed within a sophisticated and dynamic design. The copywriting details facts about the car's characteristics in a direct manner. It gives the reader a feel for the status and sporty feel of the 406.

HOME: 自動車・バイク・自転車　CARS, MOTORCYCLES & BICYCLES

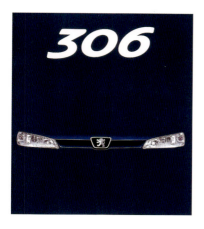

page 9, 10

page 1, 2

page 13, 14

自動車輸入・販売　AUTOMOBILE IMPORT & SALES
1999

CL: プジョー・ジャポン　Peugeot Japon Co., Ltd.
CD: 千葉 篤　Atsushi Chiba (4MD)
AD: 木原秀樹　Hideki Kihara (4MD)
D: 大森照明　Teruaki Omori
　　滝口勝敏　Katsutoshi Takiguchi (Hotline-Com)
CW: 後藤裕彦　Hirohiko Gotoh
SB: 博報堂：リンタス　HAKUHODO:LINTAS

267

Catalog + Web

PEUGEOT

www.peugeot.co.jp/

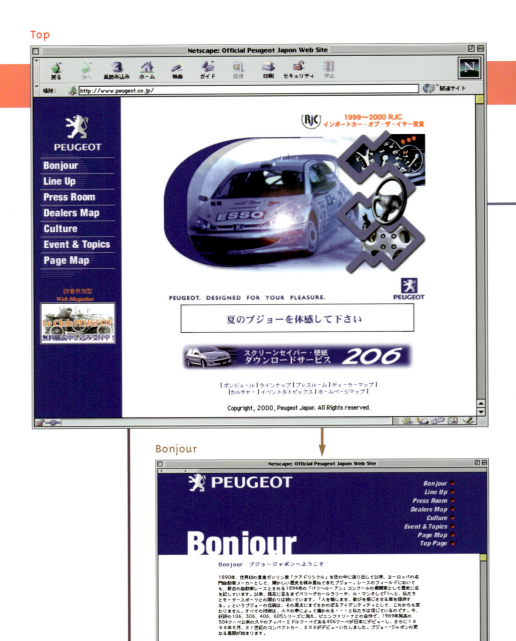

「現代生活との共存」を命題にプジョーならではの「スピード」「カジュアル」「コンパクト」といったテーマでデザインを展開しています。またネットワーク・インフラの現状を把握した上でユーザー（見る側）の立場からのレスポンスの良いサイト運用を心がけています。なお、プジョーでは次期リリース予定のフラッグショップモデルから、よりカジュアルになったコンパクトスポーツまで、フレンチカジュアルのフルラインアップメーカーとして、現在のサイトの衣替えに着手しています。より機能的、官能的なPEUGEOT JAPON ウェブサイトをお楽しみに！

With "Coexisting with Modern Life" as the concept, the Web site was designed with the themes of the "Speed," "Casualness," and "Compactness" that are possible with Peugeot. Also, by understanding current infrastructure of the Internet, we maintain the site in the most efficient manner possible, to ensure good user response. Peugeot has started to redesign the Web site, which will cover the full line of French casual automobiles, from the next-generation flagship model to more casual and sports-type models. Look forward to the more functional and sensual Peugeot Japon Web site!

自動車輸入・販売
AUTOMOBILE IMPORT & SALES 2000

CL: プジョー・ジャポン　Peugeot Japon Co., Ltd.
CD: 小泉章治　Shoji Koizumi
AD: 東條隆志　Takashi Tojo
D: 斉藤和佳　Kazuyoshi Saito
I: 荒尾啓太　Keita Arao
CG: 白川純一　Junichi Shirakawa
SB: テイルバック　tailback corp.

※2000年7月5日現在のデータを使用　As of July 5, 2000

HOME: 自動車・バイク・自転車　CARS, MOTORCYCLES & BICYCLES

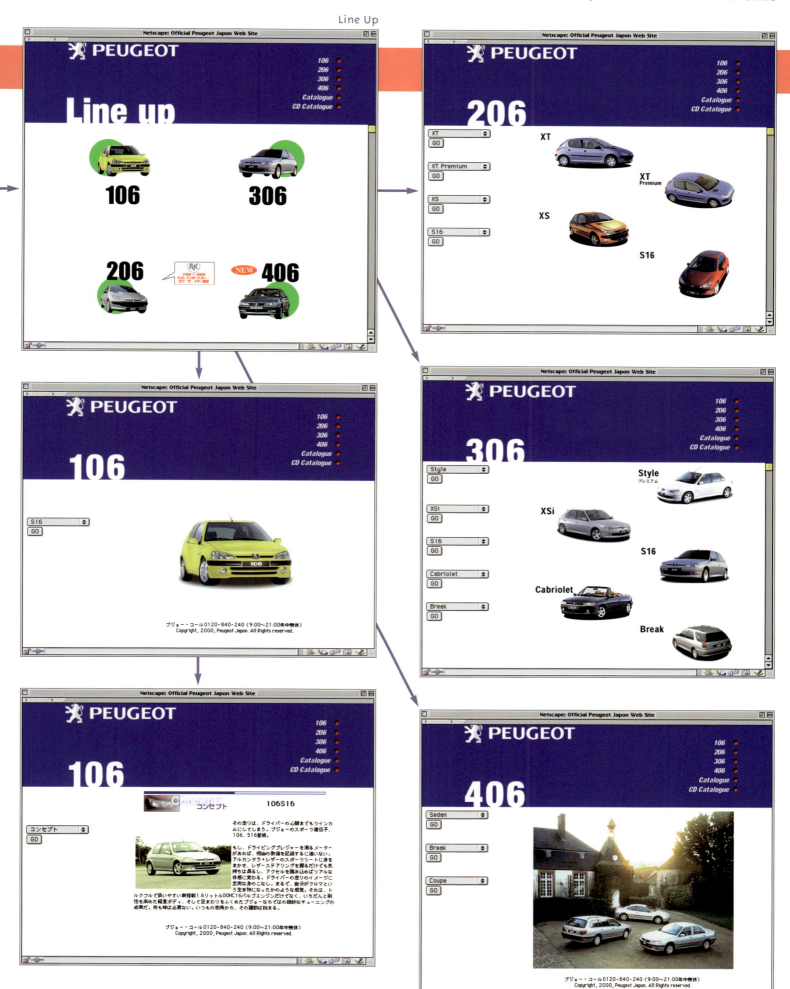

Catalog + Web

Mercedes - Benz

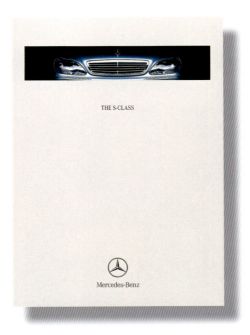

平綴 Bound／210×297mm

メルセデス ベンツの歴史は、そのまま、自動車の歴史と言えます。最初の自動車の「出生証明書」は、ベルリンにある帝国特許局が1886年1月29日に発行した、カール・ベンツの「ガス・エンジンを動力とする車両」への特許登録証でした。一方、カンスタットにおいて、ゴットリーブ・ダイムラーが「モーター・キャリッジ」の実験をおこなっており、推進力をもつ移動手段という、人類の長年の夢が、同じ年に2回も実現したことになります。時を同じくして別々に自動車を開発していたカール・ベンツとゴットリーブ・ダイムラーの2人が、新しい時代の基礎を築き、文字どおり世界を動かし始めました。世界初の2台の自動車、「ベンツ・パテント・モーターカー」と「ダイムラー・モーター・キャリッジ」から、初めて「メルセデス」と冠した車、レーシングカー、速度記録車、そしてハイテクを駆使した現代の自動車まで、世界最古の歴史をもつ自動車メーカーであるメルセデス・ベンツは、つねに時代の最先端で開発をつづけてきました。

The history of Mercedes Benz is the history of the automobile. The "Birth Certificate" of the very first automobile was issued by the Berlin Imperial Patent Office on January 29, 1886, as a patent registration certificate for Karl Benz's "mobiles of gasoline and engine power." Meanwhile, in Constat, Gottlieb Daimler was experimenting on his "motor carriage." Thus, the long-desired human dream of a means of transportation with motive power was realized twice in the same year. The two men, Karl Benz and Gottlieb Daimler, who developed automobiles separately at the same time, established the basis for a new era and literally started to move the world. From the world's first automobiles, the "Benz Patent Motor Car" and the "Daimler Motor Carriage," through the first Mercedes, racing cars, and speed record-breaking cars, to today's modern cars packed with high technology, Mercedes-Benz, with the longest history of any automobile company, continues development at the forefront of the era.

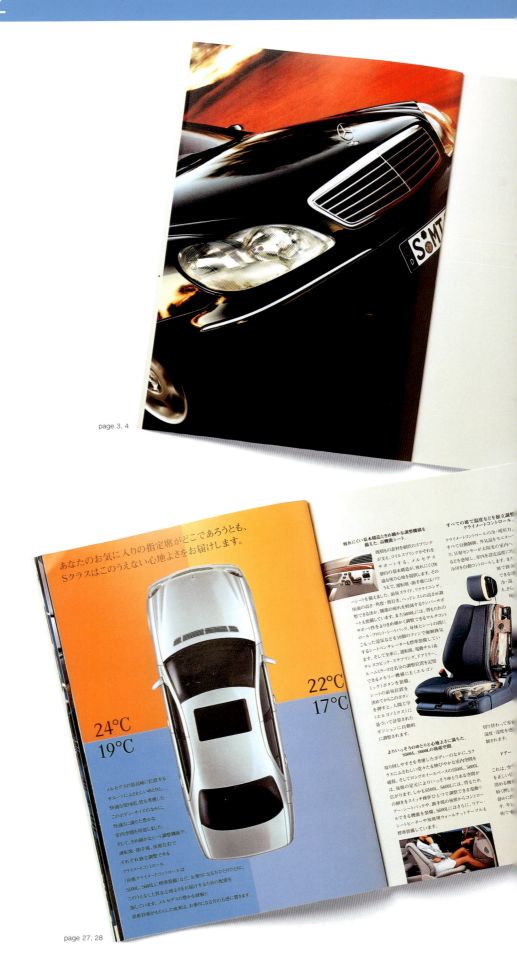

page 3, 4

page 27, 28

HOME: 自動車・バイク・自転車　CARS, MOTORCYCLES & BICYCLES

page 9, 10

page 31, 32

page 35, 36

自動車輸入・販売
AUTOMOBILE IMPORT & SALES 2000

CL, SB: ダイムラー・クライスラー 日本
Daimler Chrysler Japan Co., Ltd.

Catalog + Web

Mercedes - Benz

www.mercedes-benz.co.jp

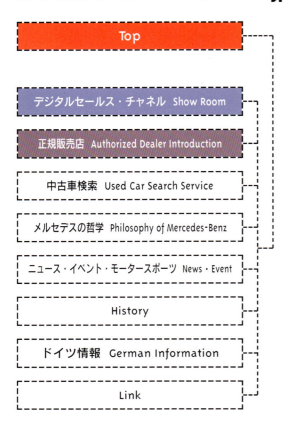

Top

正規販売店 Authorized Dealer Introduction

メルセデス ベンツ（日本）のサイトでは、ラインナップ紹介から見積、カタログの請求、中古車検索や商談予約といった幅広いサービスを提供しています。デザインは、世界共通のメルセデスのフォーマットに基づき、シンプルで機能的な作りになっています。全ページ共通のレイアウト、リンク方法のルール化等によって、使いやすいサイトになっています。

The Web site of Mercedes-Benz Japan has a wide range of offerings, including product line-up introductions, and a database for used car searches, as well as forms for requesting catalogs and estimates, and for making appointments. The design is based on Mercedes' international format, and is both simple and functional. By making layout common to all pages, and establishing standards regarding links, navigation within the site is effortless.

自動車輸入・販売
AUTOMOBILE IMPORT & SALES 2000

CL, SB: ダイムラー・クライスラー 日本
Daimler Chrysler Japan Co., Ltd.
※2000年7月11日現在のデータを使用 As of July 11, 2000

HOME: **自動車・バイク・自転車** CARS, MOTORCYCLES & BICYCLES

デジタルセールス・チャネル Show Room

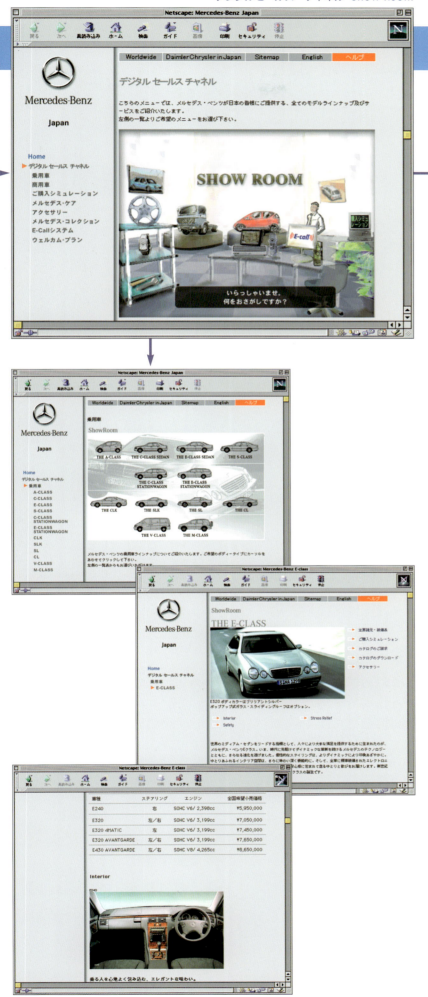
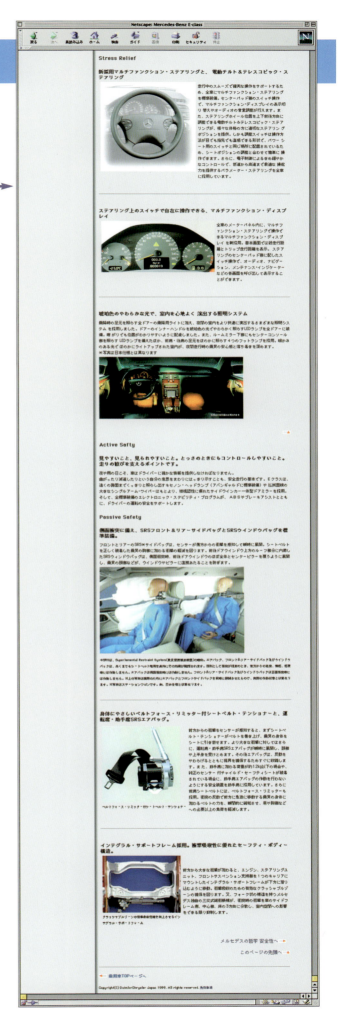

Catalog + Web

SATURN

front

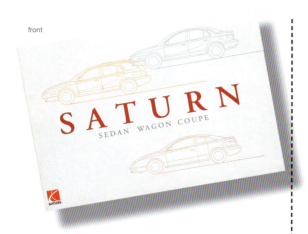

中綴じ：両面表紙
Stapled in the center :
Double cover／296×210mm

サターンは、1990年にアメリカでデビューして以来、10年間で200万台以上販売されているミリオンセラーカーです。そんなアメリカで愛されているサターンを紹介するために、カタログの約半分をロードムービー風写真集のページにしました。アメリカのごく普通の風景の中をドライブするサターンを多く見せることで、サターンに乗る喜びや楽しさといったイメージを大きくふくらませてもらえば、と思いました。この写真集のページと、クルマの性能や安全性といった情報をきっちりと分けるために、このカタログは両面表紙という構成にしました。

More than 2 million of Saturn's popular automobiles have been sold in the 10 years since its 1990 U.S. debut. In order to introduce America's beloved Saturn to Japan, almost half of the catalog was designed as a photo collection reminiscent of a road movie. By depicting the Saturn driving through typical American landscapes, people can imagine by extension the pleasures of driving a Saturn. To completely separate the photo essay from the pages containing information about performance, safety, and other aspects of the car, both front and back covers serve as main covers.

page 9, 10

page 17, 18

page 21, 22

HOME: 自動車・バイク・自転車　CARS, MOTORCYCLES & BICYCLES

page 3, 4

page 13, 14

back

自動車製造・販売
AUTOMOBILE MANUFACTURE & SALES 2000

CL: 日本ゼネラルモーターズ　General Motors Japan Ltd.
CD: 上野泰明　Yasuaki Ueno／安井 仁　Hitoshi Yasui
AD: 阿字地 睦　Mutsumi Ajichi／片山 裕　Yutaka Katayama
D: 渡部 淳　Atsushi Watanabe／高木 綾　Aya Takagi
　　福岡 南央子　Naoko Fukuoka
P: 羽金和恭　Kazuyasu Hagane／高木松寿　Matsutoshi Takagi
　　位田明生　Akio Inden
CW: 石橋充行　Mitsuyuki Ishibashi
SB: アサツー ディ・ケイ　ASATSU-DK INC.

Catalog + Web

SATURN

www.saturn.co.jp

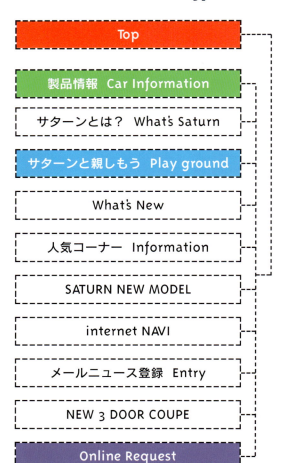

Top

Online Request

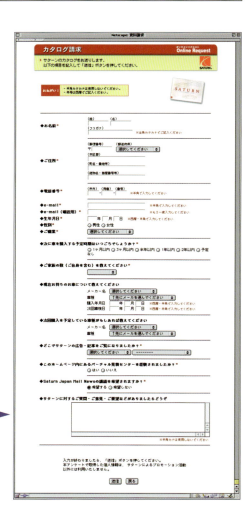

ウェブページにアクセスしてくれたユーザーにサターンを知ってもらい、乗りたいと思ってもらえるようなページを目指しています。写真と詳細なスペックや、情報誌「NAVI」による試乗記を掲載し、さらに、ペーパークラフトや性格判断などのお楽しみコンテンツも盛り込んでいます。新車発表の時期には、こまめにコンテンツを更新し、このページでしか得られない情報を少しずつ公開して、興味喚起を促しました。そして、ウェブページ上で興味を持ったユーザーには、オンラインで資料請求や試乗予約ができるコーナーを用意しています。

This Web page is designed to provide information about the Saturn to users who access the site, and to entice the viewer to go for a drive themselves. Photos, detailed specifications, and road test reports from "NAVI" magazine are included, as are such fun features as paper craft projects and personality tests. When new models are introduced, the site's contents are changed frequently, providing information that can't be found elsewhere, to maintain viewer interest in the site. Users intrigued by what they find may order catalogs online, or make an appointment to take a test drive.

自動車製造・販売
AUTOMOBILE MANUFACTURE & SALES 2000

CL: 日本ゼネラルモーターズ General Motors Japan Ltd.
AD: 佐藤 晶 Akira Sato
D: 薄井智子 Tomoko Usui／鈴木忠人 Tadato Suzuki
SB: アサツー ディ・ケイ ASATSU-DK INC.

※2000年7月11日現在のデータを使用 As of July 11, 2000

HOME: 自動車・バイク・自転車　CARS, MOTORCYCLES & BICYCLES

製品情報　Car Information

サターンと親しもう　Play ground

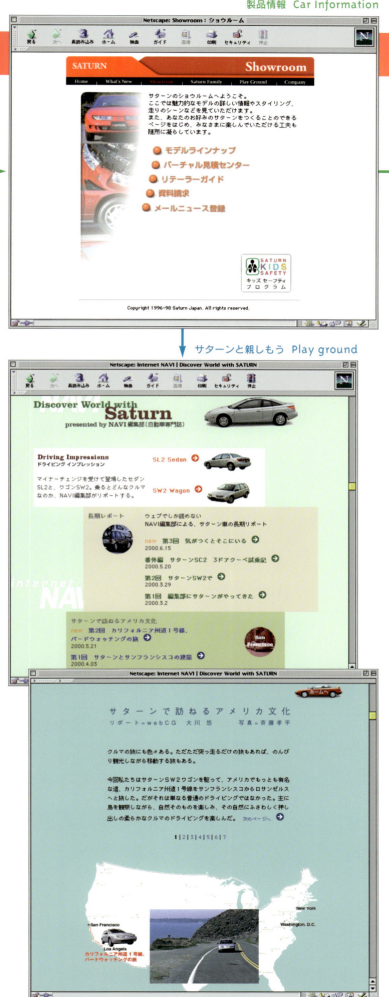

Catalog + Web

BMW

www.bmw.co.jp

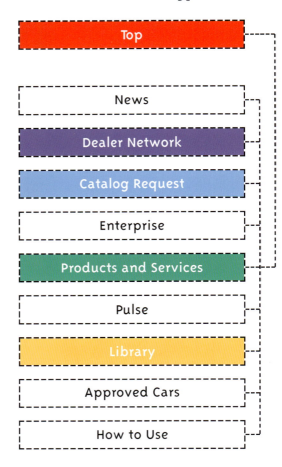

BMWのインターナショナルCIに従い、BMWの魅力をダイナミックに表現するよう努めています。また、ウェブサイトを重要なマーケティングツールの一つとして位置づけ、BMWのブランド強化、プローモーションの情報発信および見込み客の開発を常に行っています。

We have tried to express BMW's attractiveness in a dynamic way, according to BMW's international CI policy. The web site is as an important marketing tool, where enforcing brand image, providing information, and development of potential customers are always undertaken.

自動車製造・販売
AUTOMOBILE MANUFACTURE & SALES 1997

CL: ビー・エム・ダブリュー BMW Japan Corp.
SB: コーブ・イトウ広告社 COVE-ITO ADVERTISING LTD.
※2000年7月6日現在のデータを使用 As of July 6, 2000

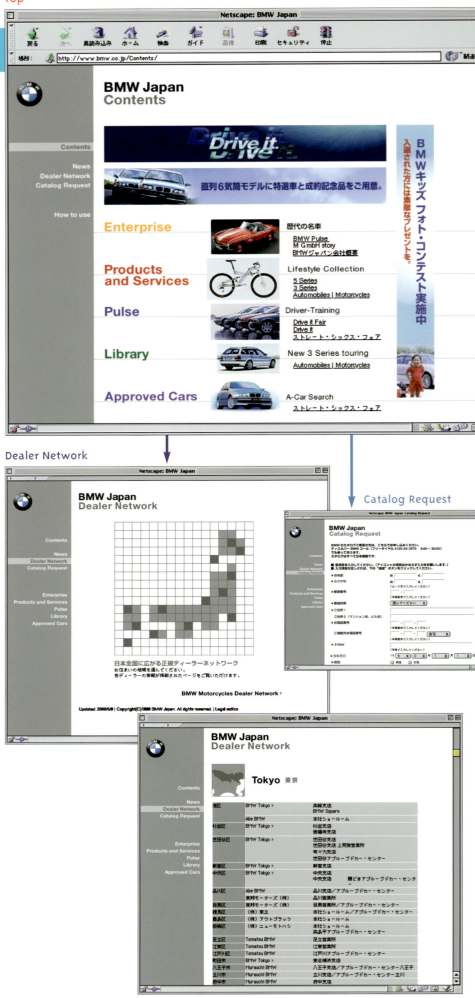

HOME: 自動車・バイク・自転車　CARS, MOTORCYCLES & BICYCLES

Products and Services

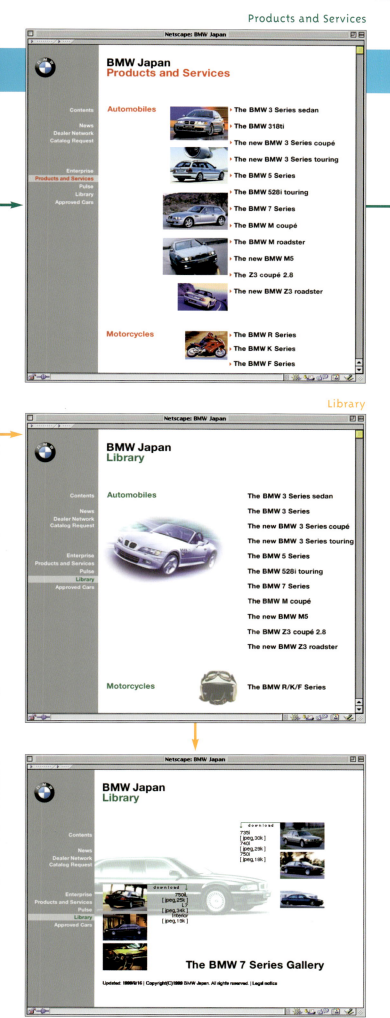

Library

Catalog + Web

Harley-Davidson

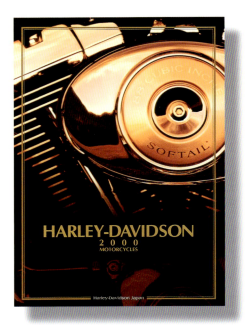

中綴 Stapled in the center／210×297mm

ハーレーダビッドソンは、1903年、ビル・ハーレーとアーサー＆ウォルター・ダビッドソン兄弟という3人の若者の手によりミルウォーキーで産声をあげました。97年間という歴史のなかで培われてきた有形無形の偉大な財産を活かしながら、真に必要とされる進化だけを、慎重かつ大胆に積み重ねるという哲学を、今も守り続けています。

Harley-Davidson was started in 1903 in Milwaukee by three young men: Bill Harley, and brothers Arthur and Walter Davidson. Utilizing the great wealth, both material and immaterial, that has been cultivated through the company's 97 years, we continue to follow our philosophy of deliberate and bold evolution.

オートバイ、部品輸入・販売
MOTORCYCLES IMPORT & SALES 2000

CL, SB: ハーレーダビッドソン ジャパン
Harley-Davidson Japan K.K.

HOME: 自動車・バイク・自転車　CARS, MOTORCYCLES & BICYCLES

page 1, 2

page 3, 4

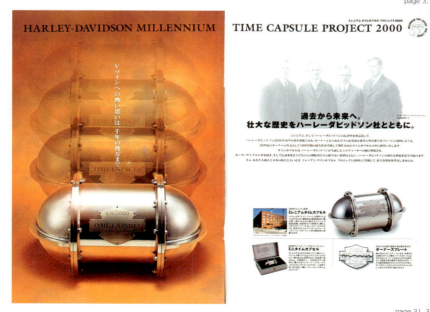

page 31, 32

Catalog + Web

Harley-Davidson

www.harley-davidson.co.jp/

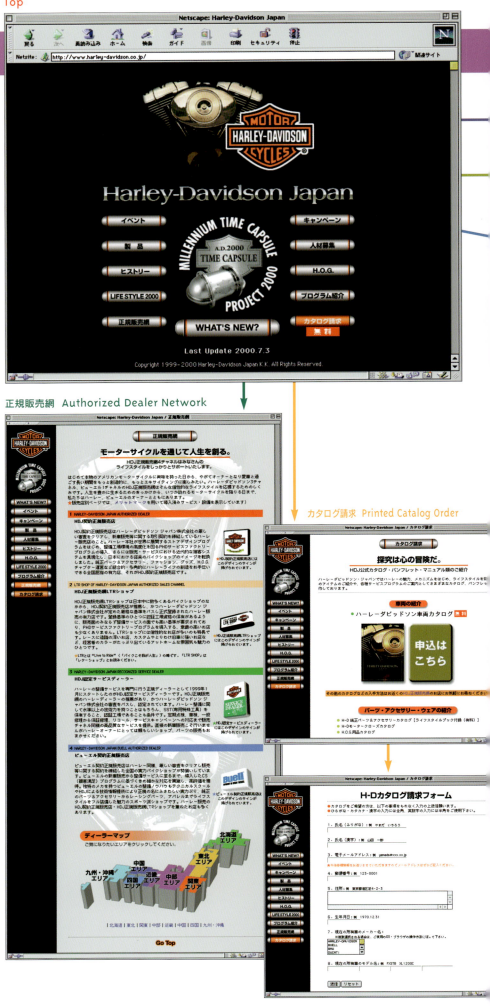

単なる製品紹介ではなく、ブランドの歴史やハーレーのあるライフスタイルを訴求できるホームページを目指しました。アメリカ文化を代表するブランドとして、自由な雰囲気と製品の持つ魅力をいかにシンプルにPRできるか、という点が最も苦労した部分です。イベント情報や販売店情報についても、タイムリーな更新はもちろんのこと、分かりやすさを主眼において編集しています。今後はiモード対応や全国の正規販売網ホームページとのリンクなどを予定しています。

Our goal was to create a Web site that would provide not only product information and a history of the brand, but promote a Harley lifestyle as well. Most challenging for us was to come up with a way to promote the free feeling and attractiveness of the products of a brand that is one of the representatives of American culture. Event and shop information is updated on a regular basis, and the site is edited with priority given to easy navigability. We are planning to develop links with NTT Communication's i-mode system, as well as establish a network with our authorized sales outlets nationwide.

オートバイ、部品輸入・販売
MOTORCYCLES IMPORT & SALES 2000

CL, SB: ハーレーダビッドソン ジャパン
Harley-Davidson Japan K.K.
※2000年7月11日現在のデータを使用 As of July 11, 2000

Catalog + Web

Buell

中綴 Stapled in the center／297×210mm

Buellは、エリック・ビューエルを創始者とするモーターサイクルメーカーです。彼のモーターサイクルへの理想である「自分が楽しめるモーターサイクルを創ること。」それは豊かな感性を持ち、ライディングの本来の楽しみを発見できるすべてのライダーに贈る、まったく新しいモーターサイクルの提案です。

Buell is a motorcycle manufacturer founded by Eric Buell, whose aspiration is "to make motorcycles that I can enjoy myself." It is a totally new proposition regarding motorcycles, for all of the riders with rich sensibilities who can really enjoy riding motorcycles.

page 13, 14

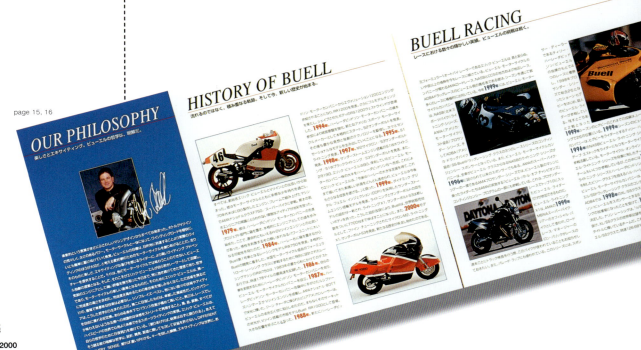

page 15, 16

オートバイ、部品輸入・販売
MOTORCYCLES IMPORT & SALES 2000

CL, SB: ハーレーダビッドソン ジャパン
Harley-Davidson Japan K.K.

284

HOME: 自動車・バイク・自転車　CARS, MOTORCYCLES & BICYCLES

page 1, 2

page 7, 8

page 9, 10

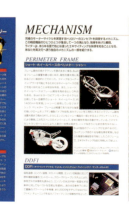
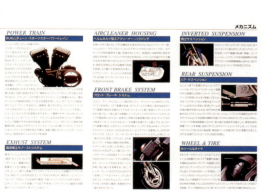

page 17, 18

285

Catalog + Web

Buell

www.harley-davidson.co.jp/buell/

Splash Page
↓
Top
- THE BIKES
- CONCEPT
- APPAREL & PARTS
- ABOUT BUELL
- DEALERS
- CATALOG ORDER
- New Information

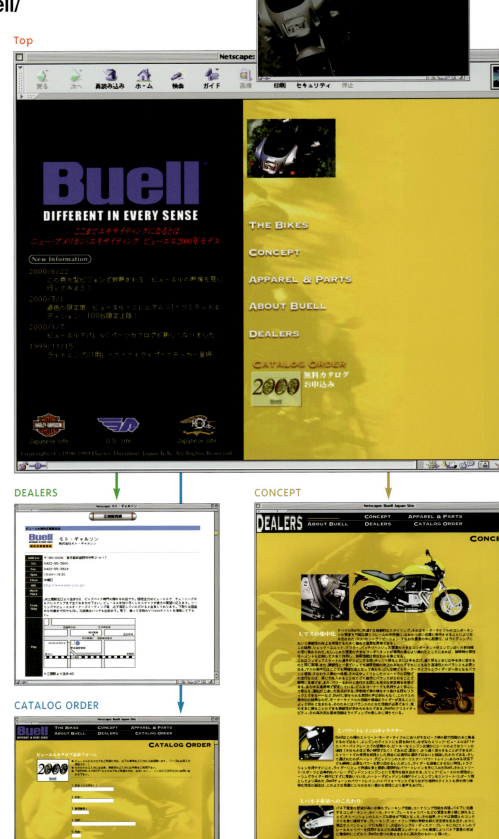

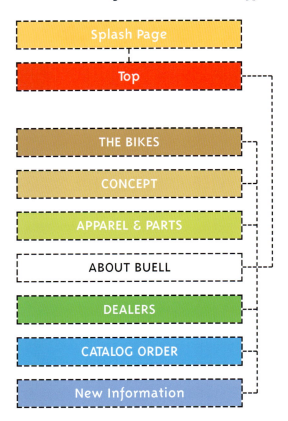

知名度および販売において、今まさに急成長を遂げているブランドとして、ハーレーのホームページよりもデザインに力を入れています。ビューエルというオートバイの魅力、コンセプトを理解していただくために、製品を詳細に至るまで徹底的に解説することを目指しました。このホームページを見た方が少しでもビューエルに興味を持っていただきたいと考えています。カタログ請求もホームページから出来ますので、ぜひお気軽にお申込み下さい。

The Buell Web site. Because name recognition and sales of this Harley-Davidson brand are both growing rapidly, we are putting even more effort into designing this site than we did with the Harley site. Our goal is to describe the products in detail, so that people will better understand the attractiveness and concept behind Buell. We hope that people who view the site develop even a small interest in Buell. Please feel free to request catalogs from our Web site.

オートバイ、部品輸入・販売

MOTORCYCLES IMPORT & SALES 2000

CL, SB: ハーレーダビッドソン ジャパン
Harley-Davidson Japan K.K.

※2000年7月11日現在のデータを使用 As of July 11, 2000

HOME: 自動車・バイク・自転車　CARS, MOTORCYCLES & BICYCLES

THE BIKES

New Information

APPAREL & PARTS

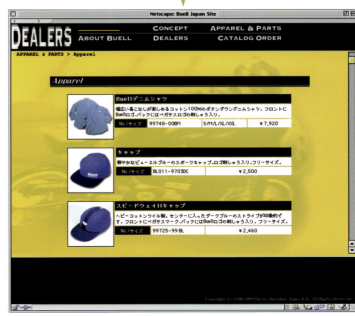

Catalog + Web

Kawasaki

www.khi.co.jp/mcycle

総合輸送機器メーカー、川崎重工業のオートバイ、ジェットスキー®に関するサイトです。現在販売されている製品の紹介や、名車と言われるモデルの開発物語や壁紙コーナーをはじめ、運営しているレーシングチームの情報や契約ライダーの公式サイトもあります。またユーザークラブである「KAZE」を紹介するページでは全国で開催されるイベント情報や提携施設の案内などが掲載されています。

The site introduces motorcycles and jet skis made by Kawasaki Heavy Industries, Ltd., a manufacturer of general transportation vehicles and equipment. The site introduces currently available products, and includes stories concerning development of prominent models, a wallpaper corner, information on the company's racing team, and links to the official Web sites of contracted riders. In addition, the KAZE introduction page includes information about owners' club, nationwide events, and related companies.

総合輸送機器製造　TRANSPORTS MANUFACTURER
1997

CL, SB: 川崎重工業 汎用機事業本部
Kawasaki Heavy Industries, Ltd.
※2000年7月5日現在のデータを使用　As of July 5, 2000

HOME: **自動車・バイク・自転車** CARS, MOTORCYCLES & BICYCLES

製品紹介 Products Information　　　　　　　　　　　　　**写真館** PHOTO STUDIO

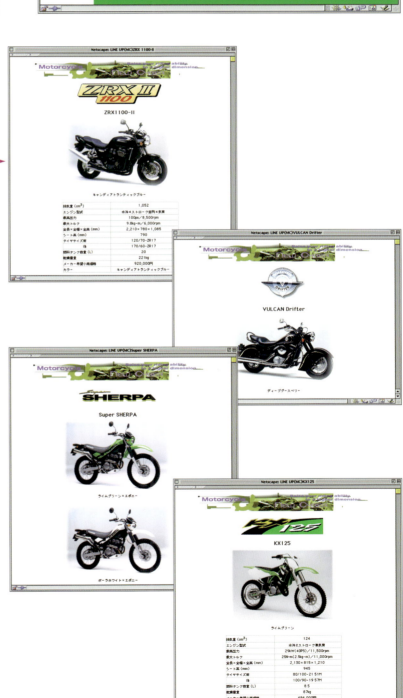

Special Site

Catalog + Web

SPECIALIZED

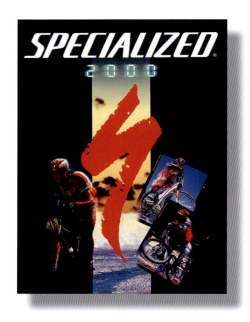

2ツ折・中綴
Single-fold・Stapled in the center

2ツ折 Single-fold／210×297mm
中綴 Stapled in the center／211×282mm

スペシャライズドブランドの特徴の一つに、スペシャライズドがバイカーズカンパニーと呼ばれるほど、社員の多くが本格的に自転車に乗り込んでいるということがあげられます。また、"INNOVATE OR DIE（新機軸か死か）"というスローガンを掲げ、常にオリジナリティー溢れる商品を創りだしています。弊社カタログでは、ただ単に商品の露出や説明にとどまらず、会社が持つバックグランドやポリシーについてを大きくアピールし、ブランド自体が持つ高い付加価値と、製品が確固たるポリシーのもとに作られていることを強調する内容にしています。

One of the characteristics of the Specialized brand is that many company employees ride bikes seriously. They are even called a bikers' company. With their slogan "Innovate or Die," the company always creates products with originality. This catalog contains not only product descriptions, but also fully explains the company's background and policies, emphasizing the brand's high value and products manufactured with set policies.

スポーツレジャー用品製造・販売
SPORT GOODS MANUFACTURE & SALES 1999

CL, SB: ダイワ精工 Daiwa Seiko

Catalog + Web

SPECIALIZED

www.daiwaseiko.co.jp/

スペシャライズド社は「バイカーズカンパニー」と呼ばれるほど、社員の多くが自転車に乗ります。彼らは自転車が好きだからこそ、世界中の人々に自転車の素晴らしさを知ってもらいたく、日夜、より良い製品創りに励んでいます。弊社のホームページでは、製品の紹介にとどまらず、スペシャライズドのマシンを馳せて各地のレースやイベントに参加するワークスライダーによるエッセイのページを設け、自転車ライフの楽しみ方を提案しています。自転車のハードとソフトの両面に関し、多くの情報を網羅したページになっています。

Specialized Inc. is called a "bikers' company" because the majority of their employees ride bicycles. They love bicycles. This is the reason why they work so hard, day and night, to improve their products, to make people around the world know the charm of bicycles. Our Web site not only presents product information, but also includes essays from the company's team riders, who participate in local races and events with Specialized bicycles, giving ideas for better enjoying a cycling life. The site covers both hardware and software aspects of bicycles, and is chock filled with information.

HOME: 自動車・バイク・自転車　CARS, MOTORCYCLES & BICYCLES

2000 MTB models　　　　　　　　　　　　　　　　2000 Others models

スポーツレジャー用品製造・販売
SPORT GOODS MANUFACTURE & SALES 1999

CL, SB: ダイワ精工　Daiwa Seiko

※2000年7月13日現在のデータを使用　As of July 13, 2000

Catalog + Web

HONDA New RACOON

中綴じ Stapled in the center／210×297mm

新型ラクーンを表現するにあたり、当該製品の開発キーワードである「軽い・安心・便利」を念頭に、軽快な走行感を幅広いお客様に向けた訴求を制作コンセプトとしています。また、世界初の自転車用タフアップチューブや、流麗なデザインのフレームなど、他社には無い利点を、どなたにでもわかりやすいよう図版や写真を多く用いながら解説しています。

The catalog for the New Raccoon was produced to appeal the smooth and comfortable ride to a wide range of customers, always keeping the development keywords "light, safe, and convenient" in mind. Descriptions of original features, such as the world's first "tough up" tube and a flowing frame design, are supplemented with many graphics and photographs, making it easy for anyone to understand.

輸送用機器製造
TRANSPORTS MANUFACTURER 1999

CL, SB: 本田技研工業　HONDA MOTOR CO., LTD.

Catalog+Web

HOME: 自動車・バイク・自転車　CARS, MOTORCYCLES & BICYCLES

www.honda.co.jp/RACOON/

- Top
- 電動アシストサイクルって？　What's RACOON?
- 機能紹介　Functions
- アクセサリー　Accessory Information
- 展示・販売店リスト　Shop Information
- スペックページ　Specifications

輸送用機器製造
TRANSPORTS MANUFACTURER 2000

CL, SB: 本田技研工業　HONDA MOTOR CO., LTD.
※2000年7月6日現在のデータを使用　As of July 6, 2000

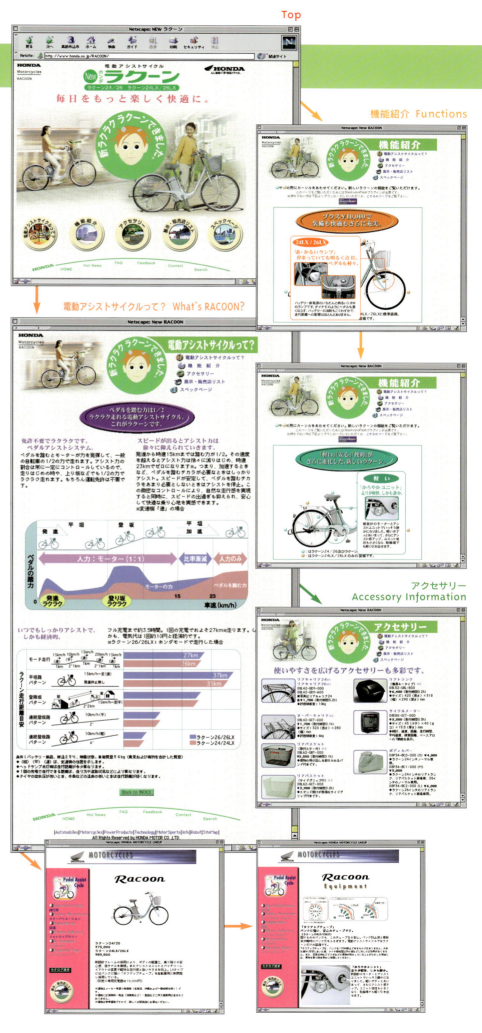

295

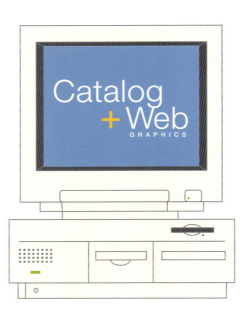

INDEX

クライアント CLIENTS

出品者 SUBMITTORS

日本語／英　語 Japanese／English

Index of Clients

Japanese

あ	アクス	78, 79, 80, 81
	アクタス	186, 187, 188, 189
	あぶち・アップルハウス	56, 57
	アボード 協和木工	182, 183, 184, 185
	アランジアロンゾ	236, 237, 238, 239, 240, 241
	アンリ・シャルパンティエ	138, 139, 140, 141
い	イースト バイ ウエスト	24, 25, 26, 27
	イオンフォレスト	104, 105, 106, 107
	伊藤ハム	164, 165
う	WiLL委員会	212, 213, 214, 215
え	エース	242, 243, 244, 245
	エテュセ	82, 83, 84, 85, 86, 87
	エフ・ディ・シィ・プロダクツ	70, 71, 72, 73
お	おかめ堂	160, 161
	オンワード樫山	30, 31, 32, 33
か	鐘紡 カネボウ化粧品本部	108, 109, 110, 111
	叶匠寿庵	148, 149, 150, 151
	亀屋万年堂	152, 153, 154, 155
	川崎重工業 汎用機事業本部	288, 289
く	グラディー	230, 231, 232, 233, 234, 235
	クラブハリエ	144, 145
こ	コラボレーション	20, 21, 22, 23
さ	ザ・コンランショップ	180, 181
	サザビー	88, 89, 90, 91
	三栄コーポレーション	190, 191, 192, 193
し	シップス	28, 29
	シュウ ウエムラ化粧品	92, 93, 94, 95, 96, 97
	ジュン ロペ	40, 41, 42, 43, 44, 45
す	スーパープランニング	226, 227, 228, 229
	スキャンデックス	198, 199, 200, 201
そ	ソニープラザ	218, 219, 220, 221
	ソニーマーケティング	246, 247, 248, 249, 250, 251
た	ダイムラー・クライスラー日本	270, 271, 272, 273
	ダイワ精工	290, 291, 292, 293
	たねや	146, 147
て	ティー・ファクトリー	202, 203
と	東京三都屋	172, 173, 174, 175
	都倉インターナショナル	194, 195, 196, 197
	トヨタ自動車	256, 257, 258, 259, 260, 261
な	ナイキジャパン	58, 59, 60, 61
に	日本ゼネラルモーターズ	274, 275, 276, 277
	日本フィリップス	252, 253, 254, 255
	日本ロレアル	98, 99, 100, 101, 102, 103
は	パーソンズ	36, 37, 38, 39
	バーニーズ ニューヨーク	116, 117, 118, 119
	ハーレーダビッドソン ジャパン	280, 281, 282, 283, 284, 285, 286, 287
ひ	ビー・エム・ダブリュー	278, 279
	ビームス	46, 47, 48, 49
	ビームスレコード	50, 51
	ビューティ ビースト	52, 53, 54, 55
ふ	フィン	74, 75, 76, 77
	フーセンウサギ	34, 35
	不二家	128, 129, 130, 131, 132, 133
	プジョー・ジャポン	266, 267, 268, 269
	フランス菓子・喫茶コーリンベール	142, 143
	文明堂 新宿店	156, 157, 158, 159

へ	ベイクルーズ	10, 11, 12, 13, 14, 15
	ヘミングス	222, 223, 224, 225
ほ	本田技研工業	262, 263, 264, 265, 294, 295
ま	マックス ファクター	112, 113, 114, 115
み	三起商行 (ミキハウス)	66, 67, 68, 69
	ミレニアム・ジャパン	16, 17, 18, 19
む	村田合同	166, 167, 168, 169, 170, 171
も	モロゾフ	134, 135, 136, 137
や	山本海苔店	162, 163
ら	ラップネット	122, 123
	ラフォーレ原宿	120, 121, 122, 123
	ランドウェル	62, 63, 64, 65
り	良品計画	204, 205, 206, 207, 208, 209, 210, 211
ろ	ロフト	216, 217
わ	ワイズフォーリビング	176, 177, 178, 179
	ワコールアートセンター	124, 125, 126, 127

English

A	abode - Kyowa Mokko	182, 183, 184, 185
	ABUCHI INC APPLE HOUSE	56, 57
	ACE Co., Ltd.	242, 243, 244, 245
	ACTUS CORPORATION	186, 187, 188, 189
	AEON FOREST CO., LTD	104, 105, 106, 107
	ARANZI ARONZO INC.	236, 237, 238, 239, 240, 241
	AXE CO., LTD.	78, 79, 80, 81
B	BARNEYS NEW YORK	116, 117, 118, 119
	BAYCREW*S Co., Ltd.	10, 11, 12, 13, 14, 15
	BEAMS Co., Ltd.	46, 47, 48, 49
	BEAMS RECORDS	50, 51

	beauty:beast LTD	52, 53, 54, 55
	BMW Japan Corp.	278, 279
	Bunmeido Shinjuku-Ten Co., Ltd.	156, 157, 158, 159
C	CLUB HARIE Co., Ltd.	144, 145
	Collaboration Co., Ltd.	20, 21, 22, 23
D	Daimler Chrysler Japan Co., Ltd.	270, 271, 272, 273
	Daiwa Seiko	290, 291, 292, 293
E	EAST by WEST Co., Ltd.	24, 25, 26, 27
	Ettusais Co., Ltd.	82, 83, 84, 85, 86, 87
F	F.D.C. PRODUCTS INC.	70, 71, 72, 73
	Fin inc.	74, 75, 76, 77
	Fransukashi Kissa Kolin Berl	142, 143
	FUJIYA Co., Ltd.	128, 129, 130, 131, 132, 133
	FUSEN-USAGI Corporation	34, 35
G	General Motors Japan Ltd.	274, 275, 276, 277
	Gladee inc.	230, 231, 232, 233, 234, 235
H	Harley-Davidson Japan K.K.	280, 281, 282, 283, 284, 285, 286, 287
	HEMING'S INC.	222, 223, 224, 225
	HENRI CHARPENTIER CO., LTD.	138, 139, 140, 141
	HONDA MOTOR CO., LTD.	262, 263, 264, 265, 294, 295
I	ITOHAM FOODS INC.	164, 165
J	Jun Co., Ltd. ROPÉ	40, 41, 42, 43, 44, 45
K	KAMEYA-MANNENDO. COMPANY	152, 153, 154, 155
	Kanebo.LTD. COSMETICS DIVISION	108, 109, 110, 111
	Kanou syoujuan	148, 149, 150, 151
	Kawasaki Heavy Industries, Ltd.	288, 289
L	LAFORET HARAJUKU CO., LTD	120, 121, 122, 123

	LanDwell Inc.	62, 63, 64, 65
	LAPNET	122, 123
	LOFT	216, 217
M	MAX FACTOR	112, 113, 114, 115
	MIKI SHOKO CO., LTD (MIKI HOUSE)	66, 67, 68, 69
	MILLENNIUM JAPAN LTD.	16, 17, 18, 19
	Morozoff Ltd.	134, 135, 136, 137
	Murata Interior Design Inc.	166, 167, 168, 169, 170, 171
N	NIHON L'ORÉAL K.K	98, 99, 100, 101, 102, 103
	NIKE JAPAN CORP.	58, 59, 60, 61
O	Okamedo	160, 161
	Onward Kashiyama Co., Ltd.	30, 31, 32, 33
P	PERSON'S CO., LTD	36, 37, 38, 39
	Peugeot Japon Co., Ltd.	266, 267, 268, 269
	Philips Japon, Ltd.	252, 253, 254, 255
R	RYOHIN KEIKAKU CO., LTD.	204, 205, 206, 207 208, 209, 210, 211
S	SANYEI CORPORATION	190, 191, 192, 193
	SAZABY Inc.	88, 89, 90, 91
	SCANDEX CO., LTD.	198, 199, 200, 201
	SHIPS, LTD.	28, 29
	Shu uemura cosmetics inc.	92, 93, 94, 95, 96, 97
	Sony Marketing (Japan) Inc.	246, 247, 248, 249, 250, 251
	Sony Plaza Co., Ltd.	218, 219, 220, 221
	Spiral / Wacoal Art Center	124, 125, 126, 127
	Super Planning Co., Ltd.	226, 227, 228, 229
T	T・FACTORY	202, 203
	TANEYA Co., Ltd.	146, 147
	THE CONRAN SHOP	180, 181
	TOKURA INTERNATIONAL CO., LTD.	194, 195, 196, 197
	Tokyo Mitoya Co., Ltd.	172, 173, 174, 175
	TOYOTA MOTOR CORPORATION	256, 257, 258, 259, 260, 261
W	WiLL PROJECT	212, 213, 214, 215
Y	Y's for living	176, 177, 178, 179
	YAMAMOTO NORITEN Co., Ltd.	162, 163

Index of Submittors

Japanese

あ	アクス	78, 79, 80, 81
	アクタス	186, 187, 188, 189
	アサツー ディ・ケイ	274, 275, 276, 277
	朝日広告社	162
	あぶち・アップルハウス	56, 57
	阿部博デザイン事務所	128, 129
	アボード 協和木工	182, 183, 184, 185
	アランジアロンゾ	236, 237, 238, 239
	アンリ・シャルパンティエ	138, 139, 140, 141
い	イースト バイ ウエスト	24, 25, 26, 27
	イオンフォレスト	104, 105, 106, 107
	伊藤ハム	164
え	エース	242, 243
	エテュセ	82, 83, 84, 85, 86, 87
	エフ・ディ・シィ・プロダクツ	70, 71
お	おかめ堂	160, 161
	オンワード樫山	30, 31, 32, 33
か	鐘紡 カネボウ化粧品本部	108, 109, 110, 111
	叶匠寿庵	148, 149, 150, 151
	亀屋万年堂	152, 153, 154, 155
	川崎重工業 汎用機事業本部	288, 289
く	グラディー	230, 231, 232, 233, 234, 235
	クラブハリエ	144, 145
こ	コープ・イトウ広告社	278, 279
	コラボレーション	20, 21, 22, 23
	コロン	28, 29
	コンテンツ	16, 17, 18, 19
さ	ザ・コンランショップ	180, 181
	サザビー	88, 89, 90, 91
	三栄コーポレーション	190, 191, 192, 193
し	ジャーナル スタンダード	11
	シュウ ウエムラ化粧品	92, 93, 94, 95, 96, 97
	ジュン	40, 41, 42, 43, 44, 45
す	スーパープランニング	226, 227, 228, 229
	スキャンデックス	198, 199, 200, 201
	スコープ	216
そ	ソニープラザ	218, 219, 220, 221
	ソニーマーケティング	246, 247, 248, 249, 250, 251
た	ダイムラー・クライスラー日本	270, 271, 272, 273
	ダイワ精工	290, 291, 292, 293
	たねや	146, 147
て	ディー・エヌ・ピー・デジタルコム	165
	ティー・ファクトリー	202, 203
	テイルバック	268, 269
と	ドゥーズィエムクラス	11
	東京三都屋	172, 173, 174, 175
	都倉インターナショナル	194, 195, 196, 197
	トヨタ自動車	256, 257, 258, 259, 260, 261
な	ナイキジャパン	58, 59, 60, 61
に	日本フィリップス	252, 253, 254, 255
	日本ロレアル	98, 99, 100, 101
は	パーソンズ	36, 37, 38, 39
	バーニーズ ジャパン	116, 117, 118, 119
	ハーレーダビッドソン ジャパン	280, 281, 282, 283, 284, 285, 286, 287
	博報堂	212, 213, 214, 215
	博報堂：リンタス	266, 267

ひ	ビーツー・エンジン	217
	ビームスクリエイティブ	46, 47, 48, 49, 50, 51
	ビギン	163
	ビットウェイブ	240, 241
	ビューティ ビースト	52, 53, 54, 55
ふ	フィン	74, 75, 76, 77
	フーセンウサギ	34, 35
	不二家	130, 131, 132, 133
	フランス菓子・喫茶コーリンベール	142, 143
	文明堂 新宿店	156, 157, 158, 159
へ	ベイクルーズ	10, 13, 14, 15
	ベイクルーズ IÉNA事業部	12
	ベイシス	244, 245
	ヘミングス	222, 223, 224, 225
ほ	本田技研工業	262, 263, 264, 265, 294, 295
ま	マックス ファクター	112, 113, 114, 115
み	ミームデザイン	72, 73
	三起商行(ミキハウス)	66, 67, 68, 69
む	村田合同	166, 167, 168, 169, 170, 171
も	モロゾフ	134, 135, 136, 137
ら	ラフォーレ原宿	120, 121, 122, 123
	ランドウェル	62, 63, 64, 65
り	良品計画	204, 205, 206, 207, 208, 209, 210, 211
ろ	ロレアル パリ	102, 103
わ	ワイズフォーリビング	176, 177, 178, 179
	ワコールアートセンター	124, 125, 126, 127

English

A	abode - Kyowa Mokko	182, 183, 184, 185
	ABUCHI INC APPLE HOUSE	56, 57
	ACE Co., Ltd.	242, 243
	ACTUS CORPORATION	186, 187, 188, 189
	AEON FOREST CO., LTD	104, 105, 106, 107
	ARANZI ARONZO INC.	236, 237, 238, 239
	ASAHI ADVERTISING INC.	162
	ASATSU-DK INC.	274, 275, 276, 277
	AXE CO., LTD.	78, 79, 80, 81
B	B2 ENGINE	217
	BARNEYS JAPAN CO.LTD	116, 117, 118, 119
	Basis Co., Ltd.	244, 245
	BAYCREW*S Co., Ltd.	10, 13, 14, 15
	BAYCREW*S Co., Ltd. IÉNA div	12
	BEAMS CREATIVE INC.	46, 47, 48, 49, 50, 51
	beauty:beast LTD	52, 53, 54, 55
	BEGIN CO., LTD.	163
	Bitwave	240, 241
	Bunmeido Shinjuku-Ten Co., Ltd.	156, 157, 158, 159
C	CLUB HARIE Co., Ltd.	144, 145
	Collaboration Co., Ltd.	20, 21, 22, 23
	:Colon inc.	28, 29
	Contents Co., Ltd.	16, 17, 18, 19
	COVE-ITO ADVERTISING LTD.	278, 279
D	Daimler Chrysler Japan Co., Ltd.	270, 271, 272, 273
	Daiwa Seiko	290, 291, 292, 293
	DEUXIÈME CLASSE	11

	DNP DIGITALCOM CO., LTD.	165
E	EAST by WEST Co., Ltd.	24, 25, 26, 27
	Ettusais Co., Ltd.	82, 83, 84, 85, 86, 87
F	F.D.C. PRODUCTS INC.	70, 71
	Fin inc.	74, 75, 76, 77
	Fransukashi Kissa Kolin Berl	142, 143
	FUJIYA Co., Ltd.	130, 131, 132, 133
	FUSEN-USAGI Corporation	34, 35
G	Gladee inc.	230, 231, 232, 233, 234, 235
H	HAKUHODO Inc.	212, 213, 214, 215
	HAKUHODO:LINTAS	266, 267
	Harley-Davidson Japan K.K.	280, 281, 282, 283, 284, 285, 286, 287
	HEMING'S INC.	222, 223, 224, 225
	HENRI CHARPENTIER CO., LTD.	138, 139, 140, 141
	Hiroshi Abe Design Office	128, 129
	HONDA MOTOR CO., LTD.	262, 263, 264, 265, 294, 295
I	ITOHAM FOODS INC.	164
J	JOURNAL STANDARD	11
	Jun Co., Ltd.	40, 41, 42, 43, 44, 45
K	KAMEYA-MANNENDO. COMPANY	152, 153, 154, 155
	Kanebo.LTD. COSMETICS DIVISION	108, 109, 110, 111
	Kanou syoujuan	148, 149, 150, 151
	Kawasaki Heavy Industries, Ltd.	288, 289
L	L'ORÉAL PARIS	102, 103
	LAFORET HARAJUKU CO., LTD	120, 121, 122, 123
	LanDwell Inc.	62, 63, 64, 65
M	MAX FACTOR	112, 113, 114, 115
	Meme Design Ltd.	72, 73
	MIKI SHOKO CO., LTD (MIKI HOUSE)	66, 67, 68, 69
	Morozoff Ltd.	134, 135, 136, 137
	Murata Interior Design Inc.	166, 167, 168, 169, 170, 171
N	NIHON L'ORÉAL K.K	98, 99, 100, 101
	NIKE JAPAN CORP.	58, 59, 60, 61
O	Okamedo	160, 161
	Onward Kashiyama Co., Ltd.	30, 31, 32, 33
P	PERSON'S CO., LTD	36, 37, 38, 39
	Philips Japan, Ltd.	252, 253, 254, 255
R	RYOHIN KEIKAKU CO., LTD.	204, 205, 206, 207, 208, 209, 210, 211
S	SANYEI CORPORATION	190, 191, 192, 193
	SAZABY Inc.	88, 89, 90, 91
	SCANDEX CO., LTD.	198, 199, 200, 201
	SCOPE INC.CO.	216
	Shu uemura cosmetics inc.	92, 93, 94, 95, 96, 97
	Sony Marketing (Japan) Inc.	246, 247, 248, 249, 250, 251
	Sony Plaza Co., Ltd.	218, 219, 220, 221
	Spiral / Wacoal Art Center	124, 125, 126, 127
	Super Planning Co., Ltd.	226, 227, 228, 229
T	tailback corp.	268, 269
	TANEYA Co., Ltd.	146, 147
	T · FACTORY	202, 203
	THE CONRAN SHOP	180, 181
	TOKURA INTERNATIONAL CO., LTD.	194, 195, 196, 197
	Tokyo Mitoya Co., Ltd.	172, 173, 174, 175
	TOYOTA MOTOR CORPORATION	256, 257, 258, 259, 260, 261
Y	Y's for living	176, 177, 178, 179

Catalog+Web GRAPHICS

カタログ+Web グラフィックス

Designer

Yutaka Ichimura
Junji Iijima

Jacket design

Yutaka Ichimura

Editor

Jun Yonami

Photography

SOOK STUDIO

Translator

Douglas Allsopp
Setsuko Noguchi

Typesetter

Yoshimi Takamatsu

Publisher

Shingo Miyoshi

2000年10月18日初版第1刷発行
2001年4月25日初版第2刷発行

発行所　ピエ・ブックス
〒170-0003 東京都豊島区駒込4-14-6 #301
編集 TEL: 03-3949-5010　FAX: 03-3949-5650
営業 TEL: 03-3940-8302　FAX: 03-3576-7361
e-mail:editor@piebooks.com
　　　sales@piebooks.com
http://www.piebooks.com

印刷・製本　㈱サンニチ印刷

©2000 by P・I・E BOOKS

ISBN4-89444-144-6 C3070

Printed in Japan

本書の収録内容の無断転載、複写、引用等を禁じます。
落丁、乱丁はお取り替え致します。